DESIGNED TO THRIVE

A HUMAN DESIGN GUIDE FOR PARENTS

CHETAN PARKYN

PIPPA WILFORD

Published 2026

ISBN: 979-8-89591-328-4

Cover Design: Sally Taylor – represented by Luis Ramos

Editor: Nataša Smirnov

Interior Design: Madeline Kosten

Before working with this book, please visit the following website with your own and your child's birth information: (Date, Place and ideally Time of Birth), to receive your Free Human Design Charts and Reports sent by email.

www.EvolutionaryHumanDesign.com

or

www.EvolutionaryHumanDesign.com/app/

to download the Free App for Android and iOS to create Human Design Charts

Free Report

Free App

Personal Human Design Readings

Understanding your own design and that of your child can bring remarkable clarity to family life.

While this book introduces the principles of Human Design, many parents find it especially helpful to explore their own and their child's chart in more depth through a personal reading.

Pippa Wilford offers individual Human Design readings and mentoring for parents who want to apply these insights thoughtfully in everyday life.

To enquire about a reading:
psw@dagaz.me
www.dagaz.me/humandesign

Readers of *Designed to Thrive* are welcome to mention the code **THRIVE** when making an enquiry.

*This book is dedicated to parents doing the best they can in a rapidly changing world,
and to children who arrive with wisdom of their own.*

CONTENTS

PREFACE

"The moment a child is born, the mother is also born. She never existed before. The woman existed, but the mother, never. A mother is something absolutely new."

—OSHO

PARENTS AND CHILDREN THROUGH TIME – A BRIEF RECENT HISTORY

Within the past few hundred years, most of society has moved from a pastoral, farming scene to an urbanized, industrial one. It has moved from a tribal, community-based model to collective, rules-based systems.

In pastoral times, parents raised their children to be involved with the land, crops, and livestock in a close-knit community. Children learned directly from parents, relatives, and community members. They were rarely involved beyond neighboring villages. With the advent of the Industrial Revolution and the migration of whole populations to cities, responsibilities associated with tending a family farm gave way to providing for a collective society engaged in supply and demand, justice, health, education, and other systems. Political systems replaced tribal, community, or feudal ones; issues once handled by elders and landowners, who were mostly guided by common sense and what served a community or family, were now regulated by rules, policymaking, and governmental oversight.

Children who had spent their whole lives in family surroundings, engaging with nature, seasons, crops, and livestock, were now sent to school to learn basic ways of functioning in a collective society. These schools, in large part, evolved from the British Empire's need for clerks in colonies who obtained enough training to run their businesses. Thus, reading, writing, and arithmetic were considered the essential tools for a collective system and became the norm for school attendance and completion. Once children had completed their schooling from teachers who were most likely complete strangers, teaching mandatory subjects that may or may not be relevant to leading a well-informed life, they were placed in various jobs to support themselves and their future families by being valuable members of society.

So long as collective systems work, society keeps pace with them as best it can. However, it must be acknowledged that many of the systems involving government, religion, education, politics, finance, energy, transport, world climate, and health – including physical, mental, emotional, and spiritual – are crumbling around us. The arrival and rapid growth of the internet, smart devices, artificial intelligence, and robotic serving mechanisms are changing our circumstances every day. Although schools offer a wide range of subjects, many children feel that their individual needs and interests are not being acknowledged. This sense of not being represented at school can lead to a lack of engagement and fulfilment during the time they are required to spend there. What's more, students often struggle to identify a clear and personally relevant direction for their lives beyond school.

In this time of rapid transformation for the whole planet, it is essential that children are given the best opportunity to succeed in living a fulfilling lifetime. It is also essential that parents have the best possible means to engage with and guide their offspring in ways that bring profound satisfaction to everyone involved.

Children are likely to spend less and less time in the family environment when they are placed in childcare, so their parents can go to work. Then come kindergarten, primary, secondary, and high school, perhaps college, and then university, before finding a job and, hopefully, the means to support themselves independently. Alternatively, if a child doesn't succeed in school or with finding worthwhile employment, they might end up living with their parents and "failing to launch" successfully.

If a strong and meaningful connection between parent and child is not established, and clear and loving communication is not honored during each interaction, then the whole question of being involved in raising a family arises. From the child's point of view, if they do not feel recognized, supported, and encouraged to live their own life by their parents and family, they can find it difficult to spend time around them. As traditional roles between parents and children change, it becomes increasingly important to develop new understandings and roles and to implement a conscious approach to interacting in the simplest ways possible.

We are all living in tumultuous times, the results of which will cause society to remake itself and all the systems that contribute to it. For many young people, beyond dealing with all the comparisons and influence of social media, their outlook for life can seem extremely bleak. All parents want to give their children what they need to thrive, and so the question arises: What are the essential means for children to rely on in order to be resilient in gaining and maintaining their balance and clarity in these times?

This book is not about psychology, quick fixes, or therapy; it concerns our ability to outline some essential keys for identifying distinctive and specific traits in both children and parents.

Everyone is unique.

There are no duplicates.

The world prospers through diversity.

In this book, we offer the means through Human Design to assist parents and children in recognizing and accepting their uniqueness.

We will point out how each family member finds and uses their particular keys to thrive from a place of inner certainty, in whatever confronts them in their lives. We recognize that being confident in oneself is the greatest gift we can give ourselves, and the means to embrace this gift fully is what we put forward here. It has been said that the two most important days in your life are the day you are born and the day you find out *why*.

CHAPTER I

FAMILY DYNAMICS

"You don't choose your family. They are God's gift to you, as you are to them."

— DESMOND TUTU

The mother's body opens to reveal a new child, a new presence, a new being to the world. It is an extraordinary sequence of events, full of energy, ecstasy, pain, passion, fear, worry, anxiety, and all kinds of emotions, leading to an easy or complicated arrival. Life is never going to be the same again.

We are witnesses to an inexplicable and glorious event that touches the extremes between our physical and mystical worlds.

No one can tell exactly what this child will encounter in life, just as no one can really tell the parents what to expect, but in this moment of birth, the die is cast.

In formative years, every child is completely dependent on parents and care-givers, all of whom have their own ideas – often borrowed – of what is appropriate to do with an infant. But very soon, the child becomes aware of their environment and naturally seeks to act out their own nature. This is unlikely to accord with what their parents and caregivers believe they "should" do. As they explore, we worry about their safety. They test us and find us all too human and imperfect. And as they find that their will is not the same as ours, they learn we are stronger, at least for now. Thus, the stage is set for the joys, triumphs, and challenges of childhood.

Maybe we know, or have been told of, a child that doesn't seem to "belong" in a family. The one who must be forced out of their bedroom to be sociable when the wider family and friends arrive for a party. Or the one that is seemingly never at home, always out with their own friends, engaged in some sport ... or experiment ... or club. Or that member of the "awkward squad" who responds to every suggestion with some variation of *no*. Then there's the bookworm lost in a family of sports enthusiasts; the jock whose family would rather go to the theatre than watch him or her play; the daydreamer who forgets the family plans, causing infuriating havoc, albeit unwittingly. What's going on? Surely, you'd expect that your children would share at least some of your characteristics.

We project our own ideas of who a person is almost the minute they are born, as a way of signaling "ownership" or belonging. You hear this in comments like, "oh, he looks just like his daddy," "she's got her mother's eyes," "just like Uncle Alfie," and so on. Memorably, during a heated argument, a father was overheard shouting at his wife, "... and why did you have to go and recreate your mother?" whilst gesticulating at their attention-seeking young daughter. These expectations can form subtle assumptions about behaviors and ways of being. Dad is a football fanatic, so of course you will be, too. If you are lucky, someone standing just outside the nuclear family will not only spot that you have great hand-eye coordination but will also advocate that you be encouraged to try a sport that capitalizes on that talent instead. Or maybe not, and there's either a missed opportunity or frequent family friction as you try to assert yourself.

Family matters can be further complicated by the decisions we make as children about what it is to be in the world. Some of these decisions are made before we have the words to express ourselves, which can confuse even our own understanding. Maybe you decided that the world wasn't safe, so you are ultra-cautious … or that you weren't much loved, so you always try to fit in … or that you mustn't grow up, so you maintain a child-like or childish approach to everything. These sorts of interpretations of the world are made by all of us, and sometimes, we manage to unpick them as adults. These decisions can be highly influenced by our place in the family, too. Stereotypically, the eldest child is often (but not always!) the responsible one; the next child chooses a different role to ensure their individuality – maybe the jester in contrast to the seriousness of number one, and so on as each new child joins the family. But who are we really when we strip away the camouflage we've given ourselves?

Human Design gives us an unparalleled view of the blueprint we have for this lifetime. It shows us how our energy flows, how to make authentically aligned decisions, the people we're most likely to resonate with on first meeting, and our chief concerns. Unlike any other system, it gives insight into our unconscious activations, which we seem to run on "autopilot" until someone points them out, as well as the ways of being of which we are perhaps more conscious and aware. Discovering this as an adult is life-changing and life-enhancing as we discover previously unknown navigation tools and can relax into being who we are, rather than trying to fit into familial or societal norms. How much more exciting to raise our children to be who they are, authentically and energetically, so they are free to offer their unique gifts to the world, "without let or hindrance"?

Clearly, there's much personal understanding to be had from knowing your own Human Design chart, and there's an art to sitting with it for a while and seeing how it all hangs together for you. It's enormously beneficial for any relationship to know each other's too – who has lots of energy, who is good at multitasking, who needs to take time over decision-making, who benefits most from soothing sounds, who especially needs creative outlets, and so on. Imagine knowing all this and more about your own precious newborn? Before they get pushed into any societal straitjackets, you are there encouraging them to be themselves. You know that your firstborn has pressure to power and needs lots of physical exercise if he is to sleep or be able to concentrate on book-learning; that your second child is easily overwhelmed by the fears of others; and that your third child will respond better to invitation than instruction. We can avoid the pitfall of assuming that to be fair, everything must be the same and instead look for the best fit. As above, the eldest is best suited to run the groceries over to granny; the next can lay the table for dinner; and the youngest can be invited to collect the laundry from the basement. They are each doing chores and contributing to the family, but in ways that honor who they each are.

Take energy, for example, where most people have an internally generated supply so long as it is in the pursuit of something they enjoy. If this is you, or your child, how critically important is it to find out what it is that you really enjoy? It's not that we don't all want to spend time in enjoyment, but rather that if you are blessed with a battery pack of your own, you want to make the most of it. Maybe we look at how we each communicate – perhaps your child is a natural storyteller and, knowing this, you can ensure they have opportunities to hone this skill. After all, we'll make the greatest contribution and have the most fun in life if we build our careers on our strengths.

So, these pages have been written by two who share a capacity to direct and guide the energies of others – no surprise perhaps! We're each driven by a desire to encourage the world to look at the gifts every individual brings, rather than assuming we all need to be filled with the same information and corralled into rote learning. This book arose from many conversations about family dynamics between the two of us, unpicking the potential for understanding (or not!) between the generations, how siblings can respond so differently to the same outer experience, and where friendship can be stronger than blood. The catalyst was an invitation from a parent in the publishing industry who asked Chetan to write a book for parents. Knowing something of Pippa's own parenting joys and struggles, and that she was writing *The Nurtured Nest* at the time, Chetan asked her to join the endeavor.

Born into a post-war English family with a birth mother who often mentioned she preferred animals to humans, a present, genius stepfather, an older brother, two younger sisters, a foster sister, foster cousin and a household of several staff, countless horses, dogs, cats, cows, birds, sheep, goats and other members of a menagerie, Chetan can now say he had a very interesting upbringing. It all seemed very normal until boys' boarding schools interrupted the fun. Travels hitchhiking across France for grape harvests, and then America at the time of the Vietnam War, changed many perspectives, meeting kids joining or dodging that war. Returning to the U.K., Chetan completed a university degree and an apprenticeship in mechanical engineering, travelled the world fixing mechanical things, and then "hit a wall" after a six-month safari across Africa.

An inner calling took him to Osho's ashram in Poona, India, where he was reintroduced to meditation. While there, he was guided to have a reading with a savant "Shadow Reader" in Mumbai. [1]The Shadow Reader told Chetan all about his past, present, and future, concluding with an invitation for Chetan to work with him "because you know how to do this work...." After great hesitation, Chetan turned the Shadow Reader down. When this man had finished laughing, he advised Chetan to start reading for people and rekindle that ability "because a new system is going to come, and you are going to write books about it and introduce it to the whole world, and it's going to change people's lives forever." This was in 1979.

In 1987, Human Design came into being, and in 1993, into Chetan's life. Now, 10,000 readings for families, businesspeople, healers, teachers, and students, three Human Design books, and countless trainings worldwide later, here is the

---

1. In India, there exist systems that defy modern-day explanations. The *Chhayashastri,* or Shadow Reader, can measure the length of a person's shadow at a particular place before midday, and from that measurement — along with astrological and numerological calculations — select a single page from hundreds of books that exactly describes that person's multiple lifetimes and their complete destiny for the current lifetime.

guide for parents and children, offered with as much insight, love, and laughter as possible.

Pippa was brought up by two energetic souls who couldn't understand why she didn't rush out into the garden to play after school, preferring instead to curl up on the sofa with a good book or even just the cat. Learning that this was "lazy" behavior, she pushed herself at school, college, and then work with long hours and crazy schedules until she literally fell over in her early forties, badly breaking her ankle, which enforced rest – much to the dismay of her own neuro-diverse family who relied heavily on her capacity to organize, thankfully only temporarily off-line! Learning Human Design gave Pippa permission to be herself and work accordingly, away from the nine-to-five, and rather in bursts of activity, getting lots done in a short amount of time and multitasking as she went, before resting again.

Her own children were teenagers when Pippa "discovered" Human Design and realized that her admonishment of her youngsters to "use their words" when she got an "ah-ha," or a "nuh-uh," wasn't necessarily helpful to them. For them, it was an expression of whether their energy was rising or falling, a "yes" or a "no/not now" – a mechanism absent from Pippa's own Design but so helpful for them to each be able to tune into their own sense of what was right for them in that moment. The desire to share all this was crystallized by a young mom who listened to her baby son's reading with awe. As the penny dropped and mom understood that her son was an entirely different being with different needs and wants from her own; giving him the childhood she wished she had wouldn't be what he needed. An understanding of Human Design really does take us a step closer to enabling our children to be the people they were born to be.

So, as you read these pages, look first to your own Design as this is where you'll develop a felt sense of what we are describing. For example, do you have the capacity to sense your own energy rising or falling? If so, is it something you already know and rely on, or is it a practice that you'd benefit from honing?

If you are reading this with a newborn in your life, congratulate yourself on having the most phenomenal head start in knowing who they are! With their Human Design chart or blueprint in hand, you will know how best to bring out their inborn talents. Maybe they are very tactile or respond best to soothing sounds. Perhaps they have an inbuilt sense of timing, so rather than fighting it, you may as well roll with it.

Maybe you have toddlers in your life. Do they need as much freedom for themselves as you can safely allow? Or are they unusually sensitive to their environment? Perhaps you have a child who needs to finish one thing before they can start another? Or someone who is changing their mind constantly, no sooner having taken a bite out of an apple than they want an orange? Or a little one who simply observes what's going on around them until they are invited to join in? Chapter 9 explores the foundation for these characteristics in detail.

By the time your child is in school, you are likely to see some consistent themes in how they move through life (see Chapter 12) and can encourage them to harness their natural talents. Maybe they are very logical, and math comes easily to them. Perhaps they have a gift for storytelling, and they love literature. Maybe they can turn their hand to anything and become proficient, given enough practice. Self-esteem builds confidence and resilience, so how wonderful to have a guide to help you encourage your child's innate gifts.

The teenage years can be challenging as your child naturally starts to separate from their family of origin and forge their own path. What might be their biggest challenges, and how can you best support them? We're not suggesting you borrow trouble; rather, recognize where you can offer the most value to your child from their perspective. Maybe they need to speak out their ideas before committing them to paper. A youngster with particularly strong and irrational emotions is well served by being shown that emotions are okay, can be expressed safely at home, and can be processed with breath-work, music, creative projects, and connection to the natural world. As your child matures toward adulthood, you may wish to share their Design so they can live it, consciously, and without necessarily getting caught up in the fashionable exploits of the moment. Of course, you may have an experimenter on your hands, in which case you know that you will simply need to provide a safe harbor for those moments when it's all gone horribly wrong.

Young adults can have a tough time flying the nest and fledging, going out into the world and finding a source of income, a partner, and a home of their own. Understanding their own Human Design can short-circuit a lot of the trial and error – at least for those who aren't wired to test everything out for themselves. You will know how best they can receive this information (visually, orally, kinesthetically), and it's often best taken in from a third party.

Maybe you've picked up this book once your own children are well-established and you have the joy of meeting grandchildren. What fun to look across the generations and see how each member of your family fits with or challenges the others. Now you know, maybe it's time to share your insights (or this book!) with the new parents.

As you've no doubt realized, Human Design is a very rich source of knowledge and understanding. Chapters 2 and 3 will give you an overview of the main elements, and subsequent chapters offer a more detailed look with real-life examples to give you a sense of how these manifest in different people. The latter half of the book is dedicated to making practical sense of Human Design elements so you can ground your newfound insight in day-to-day family living, without forgetting our furry friends, who are oftentimes an important part of the family.

Welcome to a world of insight and understanding!

CHAPTER 2

THE CENTERS - STRUCTURE

"All that you touch you change. All that you change changes you. The only lasting truth is change."

— OCTAVIA E. BUTLER

Looking at a Human Design chart is a little like looking at a treasure map — where are the gifts, the potential challenges, the most reliable ways of being? The cornerstone of understanding this map is to know the Centers, which we'll explore in this chapter, and the Keys, which we look at in the next. If you are already well-versed in Human Design, you may wish to skip on to Chapter 4. Otherwise, welcome to the practical building blocks of Human Design understanding.

To give you some background and context, Human Design brought many revelations, including that we humans have evolved from a seven-Centered Being to a nine-Centered Being. The previous understanding of the seven Centers comes from the Chakra System, a profound and ancient Indian knowledge that posits that the body contains energy vortices. These swirls of energy at specific places within the body determine how well-balanced a person is in particular aspects and at any time in their life. Coinciding with the discovery of the planet Uranus by the astronomer Herschel in 1781, the understanding of the human body began to shift toward the idea of nine energy Centers, or vortices within it. The apparent changes were the splitting of the Root and Spleen Centers, and the Self or G Center with the Willpower/Heart, or Ego Center. We can say, particularly in the Western world, that from 1781, the commencement of the modern scientific age, and a deep inquiry into establishing knowledge about life beyond superstitions and religious belief systems took place. We also started to have the potential to expand our quality of life and life expectancy.

The Nine Centers are laid out in a particular grid or chart, and are linked by thirty-six *Channels*, or branches, that connect them in a specific framework akin to the Tree of Life in Kabbalah wisdom. On either end of each Channel are one of sixty-four *Gates* which correlate with the sixty-four Hexagrams of the IChing[1]. Every Center has several Gates within it, providing certain aspects or flavors of our access to, and participation in life.

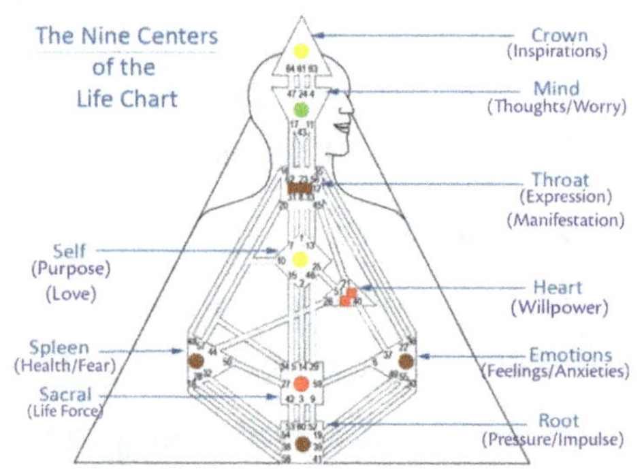

Every human has these nine Centers in their makeup, and in 99 percent of the population, at least two of these Centers are *defined* or *colored.*

It must be clearly stated that there is no such thing as a "good" chart, or a "bad" chart. There is no point in making comparisons because no two people are born to live the same life, even if they are born seconds apart from the same womb or in the

---

1. The IChing is at least a 5000-year-old wisdom system. Birthed in China, it is, in simple terms, called "The Book of Changes" and describes all changing patterns and activities in human life. Traditionally, it is used for predictions. However, in Human Design, it has been updated to reflect behavior patterns that exist in our genetic coding. *The Book of Lines, A 21*[st] *Century View of the IChing* has been specifically written for Human Design and these times.

next bed. There is no great advantage in having more or fewer Centers colored. What is important is to recognize how each Center works, and how it works for each individual.

DEFINED, UNDEFINED, AND OPEN CENTERS

There are three ways in which each Center operates, according to potential connections within a chart:

- A Center can be *defined*, colored in, indicating it has one or more Channels connecting to (an)other Center(s). The coloring of the Center indicates that this Center is "turned on," running, consistently and reliably, 24/7, throughout the lifetime, in a way directly relating to the nature of the Channel of Channels connecting into it.
- A Center can be *undefined*, colored white, and with one or more latent, or "hanging" Gates marked on the Center, but no complete Channel connecting it to another Center. Such a Center gathers wisdom of the multiple ways it operates through interactions with people who have that Center defined in their charts.
- A Center can be *open*, also colored white, when it has no latent Gates and no complete connection to another Center. Such a Center is a pure mirror to other people who have that Center defined and activated in their chart. It can also gather wisdom in how the Center operates, but this is not where great attention must be placed in the person's life.

Gathered wisdom from undefined or open Centers can best be offered "on demand," and in situations where it is called forth, rather than supplied at all times. It is possible for those with white, undefined, or open Centers to take in and live their lives according to the defined connections in other people's charts, becoming conditioned to live in a way that does not accord with their own chart ...

and their own life. We have recognized the harm that societal conditioning has done to generations of men with "real men don't cry" and to women with "a woman's place is in the home," both of which are behavioral straitjackets. Each family is apt to create its own with assumptions from our own design – Pippa's desire for logic; Chetan's preference for agreements based on trust – and those around us can be taught or learn that these ways of being are the "right" behaviors when the truth is ... they really don't fit everybody. This is much like the family jokes that persist from the days when Pippa's children were little: She was apt to say, "I'm cold, you need to put on a coat," completely disregarding the actual temperature of the child in question – or indeed the weather!

In the newer and more rapidly changing world of social media, peer pressures and uncertainties, all of us tend to succumb to conditioning at one time or another. This is particularly true of children who, like sponges, absorb the cultural norms and expectations of those around them, particularly from significant caregivers. If they can be guided to live through their own unique Design and encouraged to live as close to it as possible, much upset and therapy in later life can be avoided.

At the same time, adults might seek to decondition themselves through awareness; self-awareness itself is part of the gift of being human. In understanding your own Human Design and that of your partner and children, you have an opportunity to "short-circuit" the process of deconditioning and maybe limit the conditioning your children experience. That said, perfect conditions do not serve your child in preparing them for adulthood – it is the grit in the oyster that causes it to create a pearl.

So, let's go through the nine Centers and put some meaning to their presence in our lives.

The Crown Center

This Center provides a pressure to want to know about life. It is almost like an antenna, tuning into whatever is going on around us and giving it meaning. It is the Center of inspiration and the means to formulate life in three different ways through the three Gates within it. It can inspire us to connect to expand our consciousness toward something greater than ourselves. The Crown is unique in that it only connects to one other Center.

If this is colored in on a chart, it is always active, meaning that the quest for inspiration and insight runs continuously. You might be described as having a "busy mind," full of ideas, and with a pressure to calibrate and refine them. If this is your child, you may often be fielding apparently random questions like: "Wait, what if we moved the sofa here and then the dog would have more room, and also – why do people blink?"

If the Crown Center is not always active and therefore white on the chart, the ideas that come to you might well serve others more than you. Or if this is your child, they might come home from school, suddenly worried about volcanoes – not because they care about volcanoes, but because a classmate mentioned one.

Physiologically, the Crown Center relates to the pineal gland, which is shaped like a pinecone, and in many spiritual cultures it is seen as the connector between physical and mystical realms.

The Mind Center

Sometimes referred to as the *Ajna*, this Center is an extraordinary biocomputer that processes multiple inputs in manifest ways according to the environments, life experiences, and teachings it encounters. Most school systems base their training and evaluations on a mental instruction level rather than on an actual "educational" level. An educational environment is one in which a child's natural abilities are recognized and "drawn out" (as the origin of the word education means). Some children, by Design, excel at mental strategies; others do not, to the point that "regular" schooling does not work for them at all.

The Mind Center works through logic that looks toward a future, abstract thought that references the past, knowing that engages with the present, and often with a combination of these three differing processes. If it is colored in and therefore always active, the "busy mind" is seeking mental clarity – depending on which connections it has with the Crown or Throat Center – is this logical? Or does this accord with my lived experience to date? Or is this relevant to the present circumstance? It is constantly checking its environment. Alternatively, if it's white, you are likely to be genuinely open-minded. There's a standing joke that the most experimental children will try to put their fingers in an electric outlet twice – the second time to check! To the parent with a defined Mind Center, this is incomprehensible (and usually judged as naughty) because it is neither logical nor likely to be any different from their first experience.

Physiologically, the Mind Center relates to the pituitary gland, which, among other things, is said to regulate the body's glandular system, secreting hormones that affect our metabolism.

The Throat Center

The Throat Center has two major parts to play in our lives: one is obviously through language and communications, and the other is through our ability to manifest. All energy in any chart is seeking to find its way to be expressed at the Throat Center, and so it plays a pivotal role in all our lives. There are eleven Gates offering eleven differing ways of saying things, and eight of doing things.

The Throat Center influences not only what is said but also how it is said. It governs pitch, tone, and modulation of the voice, giving everyone a unique vocal autograph. It is the Center of all creative expression, including writing, singing, painting, and acting. The Throat also facilitates the aura's ability to transmit intentions, emotions, and even telepathic communications.

If the Throat is defined, you have a set way of communicating and making things happen. We will explore this in more detail in Chapter 6, but for now, we all know people who are gifted raconteurs, those who bark orders, and those who explain everything step by step, each of which is an expression of different Throat activations. If you match your voice to your audience, you likely have an undefined or open Throat, i.e., it is white on your chart. Great mimics often have white Throat Centers, and children practicing this gift can find that it gets them into trouble if they are thought to be mocking.

Physiologically, the Throat Center relates to the thyroid gland, which controls our metabolism, growth, and several other bodily functions, and the parathyroid gland, which regulates blood calcium levels, particularly affecting the bones, kidneys, and small intestine.

The Self Center

The Self Center, also known as the *G Center*, with its relationship to the Nautilus spiral, the Fibonacci sequence, and our connection to everything in the Universe through perfect geometry, is the Center of identity. It gives us clues about our life purpose, direction, connectedness, and love. The Self Center offers guidance on living authentically and being fulfilled. It has a magnetic quality, drawing people and experiences to us through love and their alignment with our lives. It can offer us a sense of validation that we are on the "right" track. In a rapidly changing world, it can give us an impression of identity through our accomplishments and the people and encounters we have in our lives. It has a profound influence on all our relationships and the opportunities and openings we draw to us throughout our lives.

The phrase "they know who they are" best describes those with a Self Center that is always active. Met in the boardroom or out jogging, they seem to carry themselves the same way. Those without a colored Self Center are much more chameleon-like and simply "fit in" wherever they are. On a motorbike or in church, they seem to belong everywhere and nowhere. The child with a defined Self Center might wonder how to express who they are, while the child without such definition might wonder who they are at all.

Physiologically, the Self Center relates to the liver, and among other things, the filtration of blood, the storage of vitamins, and the production of bile to assist digestion.

The Willpower, Heart Center

Willpower is applied to what is perceived to have value, particularly on the material level, but also potentially on the spiritual level. Willpower can produce results very quickly and thoroughly, simply by pushing through any obstacles. However, since willpower is so powerful, it must be used correctly to avoid straining the heart and other organs.

Recognizing what has personal value in life is essential, and then applying oneself to achieve it according to one's own Design is crucial. Willpower, as a can-do quality, is a much sought-after attribute, and in Human Design, only 30 percent of the world's population have defined Willpower Centers, and thus consistent access to the determination and drive available there.

For a parent to recognize whether they or their child has consistent willpower matters greatly, especially when deciding whether something is worth pursuing. Saying "I want," or "I will," does not automatically imply that it's correct for an individual to then follow through to achieve those objects. What might be hugely important and considered valuable to one might be totally uninteresting to another.

As you might guess, physiologically, the Heart Center does indeed relate to the heart muscle.

The Spleen Center

The Spleen Center plays an essential role in our physical well-being, through intuition and survival awareness. It acts as an instantaneous warning system for what is healthy and what is not, giving us the means to change course if the need arises. In addition to being closely related to our immune system, the Spleen Center provides a deep connection to nature and the primal wisdom that exists in all living things.

It can give us the means to distinguish between FEAR (False Evidence Appearing Real) and intuition and instinct that guide us perfectly through constantly changing life circumstances. When the Spleen Center is always active, it is influencing the environment. For example, the worrier feels better having shared their anxiety with others, leaving their collocutors at best puzzled and at worst worried themselves. Those for whom it's open or undefined will be reading the environment – is that route safe, is that person well – and have an internal knowing for the answer. These are the people who can be overwhelmed by another's worry and fear if they forget to check in with themselves first. For example, a sibling with defined Spleen might express their nervousness about an upcoming school test and immediately feel relieved. Their open-Spleen sibling, however, could become more anxious, suddenly fearful about a test they weren't worried about before. If a child with an open Spleen is not encumbered by others' fears and worries, they can be literally *fear-less*, and it is highly likely that they have psychic abilities that can be developed in their reading of the people and motivations in the world around them.

Since it guards our immune system, the Spleen Center is involved in keeping us fresh, healthy, and engaged with life from a place of clarity and overall well-being. When active, it is forever clearing the body's lymph system of uninvited viruses and bacteria.

Being attentive to healthy environments and interactions is an essential function of the Spleen Center.

The Sacral, Generator Center

The Sacral Center generates life-force energy that provides great endurance in all activities from a seemingly endless reservoir. This life-force energy is guided by what is often referred to as a *gut response*. This shows up as a rising of energy within the body ("Yes!") or a sinking of energy ("Not now!") when confronted by someone or something attracting attention. Once energy is committed fully, it is almost impossible to quit, because great momentum builds up immediately after its release. Habitual repetition and drudgery are the bane of the Sacral Center.

Most of the world's population (nearly 70 percent) has an active Sacral Center and is, thus, responsible for the construction and sustainability of great projects and achievements. It is extremely important for those who do not have an active Sacral Center to realize they do not have this sustainable life-force energy available to them. There is an *on-off* quality to this center. So if you have a child who goes, goes, goes and then drops, they are showing you this is action. Alternatively, if you have to "wind up" your child to get them going and they then choose to wind down gently at the end of the day, they are probably among the 30 percent who do not have this Center always available.

Relating closely to the Second Chakra in Eastern philosophy, the Sacral Center is directly connected to the reproductive system, fertility, and hormonal balances. The inherent nature of the Sacral Center is cross-pollination and, therefore, sexual in nature. Just as pollen triggers the formation of fruits and seeds, so it is in human nature to form connections that are fruitful and life-affirming. Of the nine Gates (activations) in the Sacral Center, only Gate 34 exhibits pure personal Sacral Power and is asexual.

The Root Center

The Root Center connects us, grounds us to Mother Earth, and, at the same time, pressures us to get involved in life, to grow, to evolve, and to be instruments of creativity. It highlights our ability to handle pressures and stress and find stability in changing scenarios and environments. Finding a balance between engaging in exciting activities and also holding to a full and wholesome lifestyle, dealing with potentially stressful situations, and finding an inner present tranquility, is a key cornerstone to living well.

Think of Freddie Mercury singing: "I want it all, and I want it *now!*" And the credits go to ... well, Brian May and Queen, but these familiar lyrics encapsulate the Root Center so well. There's a pressure to do ... make ... experience ... *now*, not tomorrow, not next week or someday. You'll see this in impatient children and parents alike – come *on!*

Closely related to the adrenal glands, the Root Center can easily succumb to fatigue, insomnia, and digestive problems if the life environment is continually stressful, potentially disturbing deep connections and longer-term commitments. Thus, in these increasingly stressful times, learning self-care, stress management, meditation, and relaxation techniques is essential.

The Emotions Center

The Emotions Center harbors pleasure and ecstasy, but also pain and agony, indicating that what goes up also goes down. Everything moves through waves in a roller-coaster ride that brings potential richness and depth to life. Finding emotional clarity requires great self-awareness and the need to be non-judgmental while learning to accept that emotions are an integral part of the human experience. Witnessing your own emotional waves and recognizing those around you requires patience and compassion.

The solar plexus, and the area below and behind our belly button, contains an amazing source of emotional energy and potential awareness. There are so many ways to describe and live emotions, and yet, recognizing that all emotions are transient, fluid, and constantly changing is essential to finding emotional clarity. All parents come to know that too much excitement and hilarity are followed by a downside that can include anger, tears, and tantrums, so identifying ways to find clarity and calm situations when they go over the top is worthwhile.

What might appear exciting and wonderful in one moment can look the opposite as the emotional wave and mood change. Through all highs and lows, there is a consistency, a stillness within, that is not attached to the waves. This stillness in the belly, uninvolved in the turbulence, indicates clarity. Breathwork, high-level physical activity, laughter, and meditation can all contribute to being able to find the detached still-point and inner clarity.

If Centers give us the basic building blocks of a Human Design, how they work together starts to give us a sense of an individual's unique perspective and likely outlook on life. Simply knowing the building blocks isn't enough to understand how you and your child move through the world. It's a bit like knowing all the ingredients in a recipe, but you still need to know whether to bake, boil, or simmer to create the finished dish. That's where Strategy and Authority come in – they're the keys that help your child unlock their Design.

CHAPTER 3

THE KEYS: STRATEGY, AUTHORITY, AND PERSONAL EXPRESSION

"He who lives in harmony with himself lives in harmony with the universe."

— MARCUS AURELIUS

While every person's Human Design is unique, there are groups of characteristics that can provide a shorthand for understanding some of the major distinctions in how different people operate. Again, if you're new to Human Design, it's worth getting to know the Human Design Keys before getting into the intricacies of understanding individual charts.

THE FIRST KEY: THE FIVE TYPES IN HUMAN DESIGN.

Knowing the Type of Design that you and your children have is often a gamechanger in terms of recognizing who has sustainable, self-generating energy and who doesn't, and how to use it for the best results. In a hypothetical family where all types are represented, you might find Dad methodically finishing one thing before starting another, while Mom somehow manages to do six things at once but drives everyone mad changing her mind every two minutes. The first-born, let's call him Leo, might do his own thing, exploring and experimenting to an alarming degree until given boundaries. The second child, Flora, might watch the chaos until invited to share her thoughts and then surprise everyone with a suggestion that creates calm, at least for a while. Meanwhile, the youngest, Ginny, seemingly reflects the calm or the chaos and then retreats to her bedroom, thankful for her own space.

Generators and Manifesting-Generators (MGs)

We talk a lot about the Sacral Center because it is the place where we source life-force energy, and nearly 70 percent of the world's population has this Center active in their Design. We know them as Generators, who account for about 33 percent, and Manifesting-Generators (MGs), the other 37 percent. In the example above, Dad is a Generator, and Mom is a Manifesting Generator.

Generators have the ability to keep on going when many others are flagging or looking for alternative pursuits. The very important thing for all Generators and MGs is to pay attention to their gut response before moving on anything. Generators and MGs are both in response mode 24 hours a day. Everything, and potentially everyone, is trying to get their attention (and participation), and their simple gut response tells them, energetically, in their lower belly, whether something is interesting or not, instantly.

Children who are born as Generators or MGs are very easy to read. Ask them a yes-no question and watch what happens. They will come back instantly with an obvious *yes*, whether that is in words, body movements, or just an energetic "lightening up." Or they will respond with a *no*, a sagging body posture, or a face of dismay. If you are getting a yes, then press on. If you are getting a no, what is being relayed is a "not now!" They are expressing something intrinsic and quite natural for them. "Not now!" means exactly that: "Not now, maybe later, who knows?" If you insist, there will be issues that can exhaust everyone involved. Of course, there are many situations where things must move anyway, but noticing and honoring the child's response is very important. You can honor the response later by offering something that appeals to the child and is easy for you to provide. It is worth appreciating that an absolute *no* can interrupt all activity until something else brings about a fresh gut response.

When Generators get a clear, gut-response *yes*, they are ready to go and commit their considerable energy toward someone or something that resonates with them, like Dad finishing what he started in the example above. However, with a little awareness, a Generator can remain open to new affirmative or negative gut responses that might give them course corrections, rather than being completely lost in what they are doing, whether it's fulfilling them or not.

For MGs, it's a different story. The gut response that indicates a yes reveals that something interesting has come to their attention. It's really a "yes, maybe." It doesn't mean they are ready to commit to it, but it does mean that they have now started a process of due diligence. They start finding out what it was that caught their attention. The more they explore whatever got their response, the clearer they can be when their "moment of truth" arrives, and they are either going to go for it or drop it altogether. In the example above, this showed up as Mom appearing to change her mind so frequently. It is very important for the MG to realize their involvement has nothing to do with a mental decision, but rather it is continuously attuning to their gut response that will ultimately either indicate a final yes – in which case, they will disappear in a cloud of manifesting energy, fully committed and unstoppable – or, a final no, indicating an immediate cessation of interest, almost as though nothing happened, while they prepare for the next response.

Anyone expecting an MG to proceed with something automatically is often in for a surprise; it looked like the MG was going to be fully involved, and instead, there is a sudden and complete loss of interest. The MG is not being flaky; they are just being clear in following through with commitments that involve personal fulfillment and avoiding those that don't. If you're raising an MG, they will appreciate not having to explain constantly why, in certain situations, they suddenly lose interest in someone or something that looked like a sure thing.

We'll look again at the Sacral Center in Chapter 4 and Generators and MGs in Chapter 9.

Manifestors

Around 10 percent of the world's population has a Manifestor Design, with which they literally catalyze activity wherever they go – remember Leo, the exploring firstborn? Manifestors have an undefined or open Sacral Center. As babies, the moment they learn to crawl, they have places to go and things to see. From day one, they don't understand the words *no* and *don't*. Yikes, right? As a parent, you must try to find a way to deal with this phenomenon ... and still have a life.

Manifestors are upset and often enraged by roadblocks and holdups that disrupt what they perceive as a natural flow of things. Give them a sense of being honored and recognized by opening up and showing that all things are possible. Here are some examples of how to guide your Manifestor responsibly: "Run as far down the street as you like, but not past the blue house," "Stay up as late as you like, but not past 8 p.m.," "Play your video games as much as you like, after you've fed the dog, taken out the trash and done your homework." Manifestors work through an inner urge to engage with life according to the particular nature that is inscribed in their Design. They are self-catalyzing and can often catalyze everyone else, too!

It is essential that Manifestors inform people what they are about to do, and for Manifestor parents, just because you are ready to move on something does not necessarily mean that everyone else is.

Projectors

Around 20 percent of the world's population has Projector Designs, and as such, they are natural-born guides for the world around them – Flora in our example above. They have undefined or open Sacral Centers and have the means to reflect and offer wisdom on how Generators, MGs, and even Manifestors can use their energy to the best advantage. However, does anyone stop and ask for directions?

Projectors, being surrounded by the energy Types, often feel compelled to jump into activities, groups, clubs, teams ... only to find out they are outsiders. They must be outsiders. They have to stand on the perimeter to be able to offer the guidance that wells within them. If they are as involved as everyone else, they lose their clear perspective and ability to give good guidance.

Projectors are not here to be anti-social, and yet they can't consider that they have automatic entry to everything. Of all the five Types, Projectors must know their Design better than anyone. They must know their defined Centers and Channels, and the significance of what they are "projecting" out to the world through their aura. Recognition for a Projector is very important. Otherwise, they can often feel left out, ignored, or unloved, which leads them to make themselves unavailable

Whether the energy Types are aware of it or not, they pick up Projectors' abilities, and either engage with them or not. It is so important for Projectors to realize their unique gifts and abilities; to know they do not have the sustained energy that the Generators and MGs have; and to be very comfortable in their own company until they are recognized and included in ways that they can offer what is natural to them: their guidance. Recognition and invitation are the watchwords if you have a Projector in the family – a simple "thank you, that was lovely" will go a long way for a Projector to feel seen. If you see them hanging back, invite them to join in; they won't naturally assume that they are welcome just because everyone else is. Over time, you will probably come to realize that your Projector child has been quietly guiding the family in their own particular way from the moment they first appeared.

Reflectors

Making up less than 1 percent of the world's population, Reflectors find themselves living a completely different life on a chaotic planet. Their Human Design charts are instantly recognizable because all nine Centers are undefined and uncolored. This implies that there is nothing fixed or consistent in their Design, and they live in the environments of everyone else's energies, needs, wants, desires, activities, and moods. They are perhaps the most sensitive people alive because they pick up on everything going on around them, near and far, hence Ginny's need to retire to her bedroom periodically in our example above.

To find their own place within all the turbulence of life, Reflectors crave their own space, a sanctuary, where they can let off steam and digest whatever they've been exposed to. They have a need to know how to de-stress and relax. For parents or children with a Reflector Design, it is an enormous help to introduce them to meditation, to exercise they enjoy, to pets, to nature, and to other activities and environments where they can relax and reset.

As the name implies, Reflectors literally reflect the world and the people in it back to themselves. Their reflections are loving and very likely to be without any guile or trickiness. Reflectors can accurately perceive and recognize underlying dynamics in any circumstance or interaction, giving them the means to offer insights that clarify. With this depth of perception, the Reflector child can be caught up in situations way beyond their years and may need support to calibrate their insights.

Frequently confused in trying to find a consistent identity, Reflectors can become lost trying one thing after another, often feeling overwhelmed and disconnected while others seem so assured in their lives and pursuits. It is important for Reflectors to create boundaries, drop any kinds of comparisons, embrace quiet time, and engage in creative activities and self-reflection.

Reflectors are constantly living in the flow of life, sometimes the wild ride of life, responding to the apparent whims of life, finding acceptance in whatever life sends their way. When decisions are needed, Reflectors are advised to check anything and everything that might be relevant to their situation. They need to research and, most importantly, to take time, up to a month, to settle into knowing what is right for them. During this time, the Moon cycles through all sixty-four Gates, activating each one for ten hours at a time, and neutrally and naturally fills out a whole arena of possibilities. By the end of the Moon's cycle, the whole picture becomes clear, and further involvement (or not) can be determined. With this practice, Reflectors naturally become some of the wisest people on earth.

If you are lucky enough to have a Reflector in your family, give them space. They are processing far more than the other 99 percent of the population and need peace and quiet within which to let it all percolate. Their own corner is an absolute must, allowing for retreat and reflection. Then observe – they will show you your family dynamics, giving you an opportunity to refine them if you don't like what you see!

THE SECOND KEY: AUTHORITY AND MAKING CORRECT DECISIONS

Making good decisions is perhaps the most important thing we can do for ourselves, our families, friends, and co-workers throughout our lives. One of the gifts of knowing our Human Design is the ability to recognize our unique way of making the right decisions according to whatever confronts us at any moment in time.

Children are born in a natural state, with their inherent Authority intact and working exactly in accordance with their Design. However, the conditioning of a fast-moving world can quickly suppress and override their natural decision-making process. In the early years, if a child is encouraged to continue using their own natural Authority, they will be more self-assured throughout their own life. They will bypass so many issues involved in making poor, bad, or disastrous decisions that lead to regret and take them on unconstructive detours.

In Human Design, there are seven different Authorities, one of which we each carry with us throughout our lifetime to use whenever we make a personal decision. When we are involved in partnerships or close relationships, our Authority might need to meld with that of another person or a group of people. So it is good to know who has which personal Authority, and what is the overriding Authority involved in making combined decisions.

Of course, parents must take responsibility for their children's well-being, especially in the early years, making multiple decisions for them. However, recognizing how you and your child make decisions for yourselves is going to serve everyone enormously as time goes on. This is an extensive and important subject which we'll cover in more detail in Chapter 10.

THE THIRD KEY: PROFILES AND OUR CONNECTIONS IN THE WORLD

In Human Design, Profiles describe a way in which the world sees you, and to whom and what you are naturally drawn, with what and whom you attune, and who and what requires a bit more effort.

There are twelve Profiles in Human Design, and we each have one for our lifetime. Our Human Design Profile is derived from the Line numbers associated with our Conscious and Unconscious Sun. Profile is therefore expressed as two numbers, each between one and six, in one of twelve different combinations. The

Profile provides another layer of understanding into how an individual interacts with the world and how the world sees them.

Of the twelve, seven are what are called *Personal* Profiles. This is to say that the lifetime is largely a personal search that might involve many other people, but it is founded in living personal experience to act through and on one's own behalf.

The Personal Profiles are:

1/3, 1/4*, 2/4, 2/5*, 3/5, 3/6*, 4/6.

There are four *Interpersonal* or *Transpersonal* Profiles through which life is lived by interacting with and on behalf of others, often taking responsibility for guiding or overseeing other people's lives as a way of life.

The Inter- or Transpersonal Profiles are:

5/1, 5/2*, 6/2, 6/3*.

The rarer *Fixed Fate* Profile's Design involves upholding one very specific aspect of human life and participation. Such a Profile has a fixed trajectory throughout the lifetime and does not know, nor wants to know, how to handle "alternative" suggestions and instructions from others:

4/1*.

The Profiles marked with the asterisk are rarer.

In meetings with others, there is an almost instant recognition between two people with the same Profile. There can be an easy flow of conversation and compatibility, regardless of other features in their respective Designs. There can be instances with the rarer Profiles, in which there are fewer opportunities for Harmonic interactions. This is not to say that the rarer Profiles make less meaningful connections, but it does imply they might have more singular ways of going through life.

We will explore Profiles in greater detail in Chapter 11.

THE FOURTH KEY: THE LIFE THEME (OR INCARNATION CROSS)

In Human Design, there are 192 different Life Themes, and we each have one for our whole lifetime. It is like the storyline of a book, or the theme music to a movie, and it highlights so much in an unfolding story in all the chapters of our life. This important subject, including a page on each of the 192 Life Themes, has been covered in great detail by Chetan in *The Book of Destinies: Discover the Life You Were Born to Live,* which is available from all good booksellers.

For now, notice that there are two calculations in Human Design, one from the moment of birth, the Conscious or Personality calculation (shown in black), and one from a point in time 88 degrees of Solar Arc (shown in red), or about three months before the birth. The Conscious calculation involves what is to be lived out in this lifetime on one's own behalf. The Unconscious calculation represents potential past-life influences and everything inherited genetically from the family tree, going all the way back through time. Each of the 192 Life Themes indicates clear patterns of a personal balance between past and present and includes inherited behaviors and aptitudes that come naturally to us. Once these are recognized and accepted, they give great reassurance on our way through life. Each Life Theme is associated with each Profile, some Life Themes are very personally oriented, some more interpersonally, and some fixed in how they play out. We all have a unique story to be lived in life, and knowing yours and your child's individual Life Themes holds open natural pathways to greater appreciation, understanding and fulfilment.

We've now identified the four major keys that shape a child's place in the world – their Type, their Authority, their Profile, and the overarching Life Theme that scores their entire lifetime like background music. These keys help us understand *who* we are and *why* we're here. The next question naturally becomes: How does all this energy move through us, day by day?

To answer that, we step into the engine room of Human Design, the Sacral Center. Whether it hums steadily, responding to life with reliability and vitality, or remains undefined and changeable, influenced by those around us, the Sacral shapes how we work, create, and engage with the world.

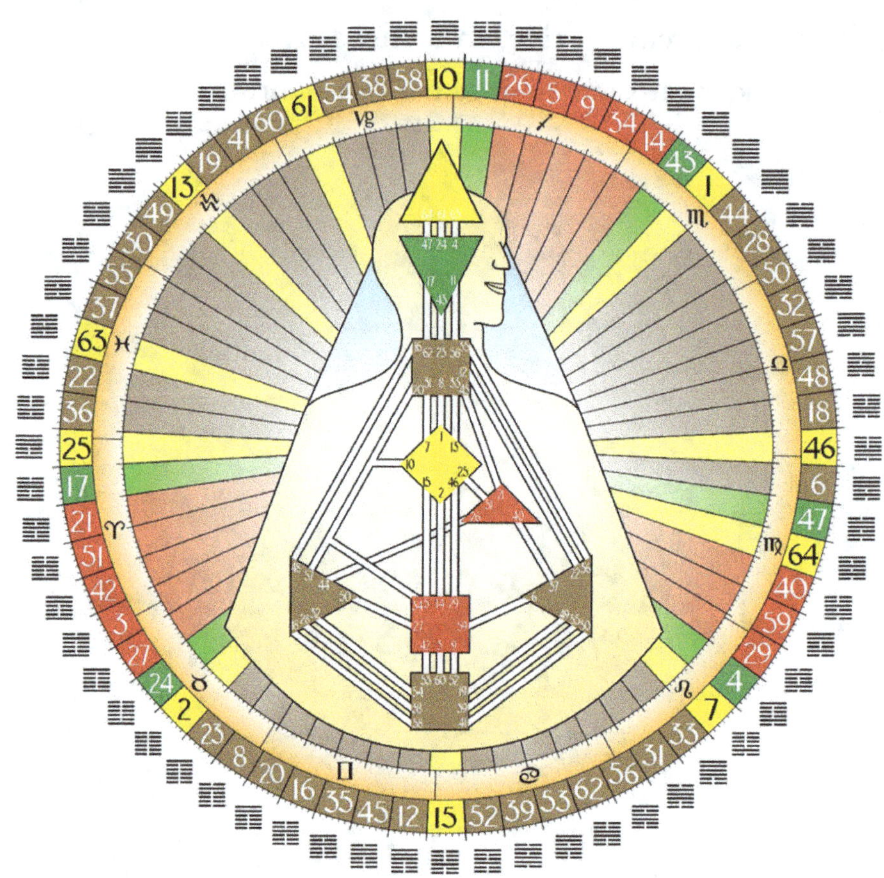

CHAPTER 4

LIVING IN A SACRAL WORLD

"There is a vitality, a life force, an energy, a quickening, that is translated through you into action, and because there is only one of you in all time, this expression is unique."

— MARTHA GRAHAM

The world is busy. Whether we're commuting to a nine-to-five job or working from home with the day job spilling into our personal lives, the hours slip by. Before we know it, it's time to collect the children from school. Time always seems to be at a premium. Then comes the need to go to the gym or head out for a run, before restocking the fridge or cleaning the car. There is always something waiting to be done. And yet, when we meet up with friends to relax over a drink or a meal, we often feel a renewed sense of well-being and camaraderie. Our energy is buzzing, especially when we're doing something we enjoy. This is life for around 70 percent of the population – those with a defined Sacral Center.

Once he understood that different Human Design Types had different energy needs, Rob, a primary school vice-principal, decided to try an experiment with the most difficult class at the school. A group of ten-year-olds was given extra breaks so that no working period was longer than 90 minutes, and during those breaks the children were allowed to do whatever they wanted — within the bounds of safety. About three-quarters of the class headed outside and raced around the school grounds to burn off the excess physical energy that was pent up after a period of sitting still and concentrating. The remaining children found a quiet corner, often by themselves or just with one other, and read, played video games, or even offered to clean off the whiteboard. They had picked up excess energy simply by being stuck in a room with all the others and needed to allow that energy to dissipate gently. The experiment was so successful that after two weeks it was extended throughout the school.

Rob had learned that those without a defined Sacral Center do not have the consistent energy that Sacral Beings have. Sometimes they will be highly energetic, especially when around others with defined Sacral Centers, but they will also need more downtime and rest compared to others.

Take Paul, a Projector child with parents who are both MGs, neither of whom could believe that he wasn't "like them" because he always had so much energy around them, almost literally bouncing off the walls, flitting from one activity to another, and rarely sitting still, not even long enough to finish a meal. Yet that same child was the one sitting quietly in a class learning about butterflies and choosing to stay in at break time rather than race around the playground with the others.

A defined Sacral Center indicates that an individual has access to a consistent and reliable source of life-force energy and vitality. The Center is associated with fertility, creativity, and endurance. People with a defined Sacral Center benefit from using their gut response or visceral reactions for guidance. You will often hear this in the responses from young children — "ah-ha" meaning "yes, my energy is rising at the prospect," or "nuh-uh" meaning "no, my energy is dropping." Generators and MGs alike can find satisfaction and avoid frustration by waiting for a response from their Sacral Center before taking action on anything.

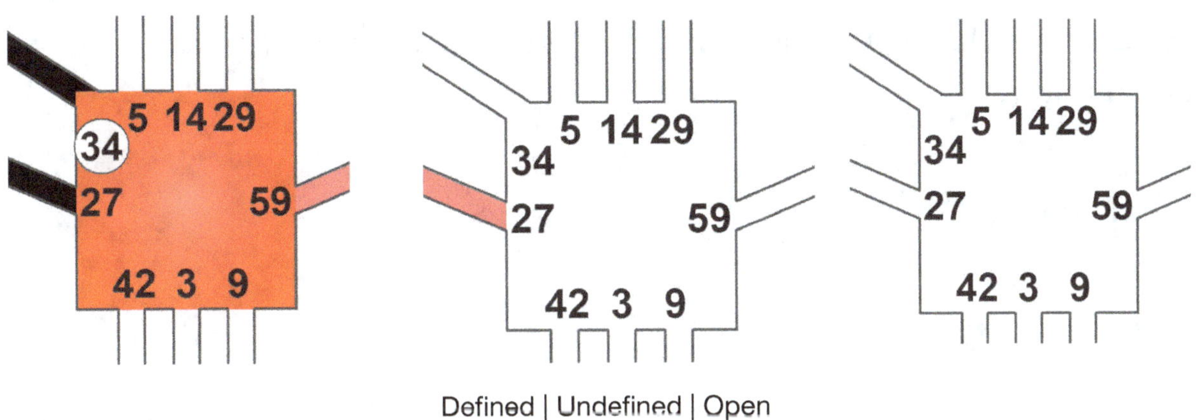

Defined | Undefined | Open

Children might express their defined Sacral Center in several ways. They tend to have a natural abundance of energy and vitality with high levels of physical stamina, allowing them to engage in various activities with enthusiasm and endurance. By virtue of their *gut feel*, they can cultivate a strong sense of what aligns with their unique design and personal desires, exemplified by a sense of authenticity and self-trust. They often have the knack of balancing work and play, engaging in activities with dedication and focus, while also knowing how to relax, have fun, and enjoy leisure time. Good at collaborating with others, they can coordinate and engage others effectively while respecting individual contributions. They can find joy in pursuing their passions and sharing their excitement with others.

Be they Generators or MGs, sacrally-defined youngsters may need help with boundaries, unintentionally disregarding the boundaries and needs of others due to their energetic nature. They can experience significant frustration, struggle to wait or persevere through longer-term endeavors, or give up prematurely. In addition, they can become impatient with slower-paced individuals who can't keep up with their abundant energy. They may struggle to understand and adapt to different energetic dynamics.

Knowing who has sacral energy in the family helps shape expectations, communicate styles, exercise routines, and more. The following paragraphs look at how each of the 9 Gates on the Sacral activate the Center differently, grouped by circuitry (see Chapter 12), and with examples to help you see what this might look like in reality.

COLLECTIVE

Gate 5 – Waiting

A child with this Gate is likely to thrive on routine and find comfort in predictable patterns, like a consistent bedtime or mealtime. That same child can become very distressed if routines are broken and may struggle with unpredictability. That said, as they grow, they may find it difficult to work within other people's time-frames and need to set their own.

Caitlin's mom gave up chivvying her daughter to school and simply waited until she was ready, having learnt from experience that whenever Caitlin arrived would be just in time – even if they were "late," class would have been delayed by something else, and Caitlin would slip in unnoticed just as everything began.

Gate 9 – Applied Details

A child with Gate 9 may well show an ability to concentrate on detailed tasks, such as puzzles, and take pride in perfection. This child can also become fixated on specific details and struggle to shift their focus to other tasks or activities.

For example, Tim, at six years old, was getting into trouble with his teacher for ignoring her call back to group work, and he was returning home upset with no idea why she was cross. The issue was finally resolved by a teaching assistant who spotted that Tim was so deeply engrossed in whatever task had been set that he simply was not hearing her – no disrespect or willful misbehavior intended.

Gate 29 – Commitment

This is sometimes referred to as the Gate of the automatic "Yes!" A child may exhibit enthusiasm and dedication in activities or relationships, like sticking with a hobby or maintaining friendships. They may also have difficulty setting boundaries, overcommitting to activities, or trying to please friends at their own expense. These are the children who need to learn that it's okay to say "no" and may need to be taught how to do so elegantly and politely.

As a teenager, Peter was having a tough time at home because his dad was ill and short-tempered. He explained this to his teachers and they agreed to his request for leniency over homework – this then enabled Peter to say "yes" whenever his dad requested he stop practicing his flute, or needed his help. "Haven't you finished your homework yet?" was met with "yes, just now" as Peter placed a period in the middle of a sentence and put his pen down.

Gate 42 - Increase

A child with this Gate is likely to show eagerness to learn and grow, being enthusiastic about achieving new milestones. They may also have difficulty letting go of things, such as old toys, and may hoard or be possessive. As youngsters, they may need to be taught how to share, by, for example, being shown that there are more toys to play with if a group shares than if they each hoard their own toys.

Joe has this gate as well as Gate 3 (see below). So, one of the ways he was encouraged to complete tasks was by recognizing milestones – this was a child who loved getting new badges and certificates and pinning them up on his bedroom wall.

TRIBAL

Gate 27 – Nourishing

A child with Gate 27 is likely to be naturally nurturing, taking care of toys or pets, and showing empathy toward friends and family. They could also be overly protective of those they hold dear and might neglect their own needs in favor of others. They may well need to learn the art of balancing care-giving with care-taking. It can be easy to assume that, having taught them the value of brushing their teeth, eating a balanced diet, and exercising, children will know how to nurture themselves.

As a child, Phoebe was indeed taught all this and still exhausted herself entertaining and serving others before herself. As a Projector with this Gate, she needed her Generator parents to allow her some downtime and teach her the value of a quiet few minutes even in the midst of a family gathering.

Gate 59 – Intimacy

A child with this Gate may form deep bonds with friends, showing loyalty and a desire for connection. They may struggle with boundaries, either being too clingy or too aloof, and may have trouble understanding social cues. Demonstrating a healthy connection with others will help these children in particular, as they notice who you hug, kiss, or shake hands with, who is invited in, and who remains on the doorstep.

Ian's family moved to a different part of the country when he was one term short of finishing primary school, so his parents left him in the care of friends to join them and his siblings once school was done. While this made logical sense to his parents, Ian needed more nurturing and understanding, frequent visits and letters or gifts from home, to show him that he wasn't "out of sight, out of mind." Even years later, Ian felt left behind and, in some way, pushed out of the family, because of those three months apart when he was eleven years old.

INDIVIDUAL

Gate 3 – Innovation

A child with this Gate is likely to exhibit resilience and adaptability, quickly picking up new skills or adapting to changes in their environment. Encourage them to be comfortable as natural innovators. Alternatively, they may be overwhelmed by the complexity of new beginnings and struggle with transitions, such as starting a new school or changing routines, and may display resistance or anxiety. These children can be helped by gaining a clear perspective, being supported to persevere, and being taught how to organize themselves to minimize any stress associated with change.

Joe (who also has Gate 42, see above) starts new challenges or projects with great excitement and really gets stuck in, quickly encouraging his classmates with his enthusiasm. Then he struggles to maintain his interest through to completion, and it all becomes something of a slog. This is when he needs help, breaking the task down into manageable chunks with interim rewards for completing a section and (sometimes!) harnessing his enthusiasm afresh for the next chunk.

Gate 14 – Prosperity

The potential wisdom inherent in Gate 14 tends to develop and grow throughout the lifetime as those with this Gate learn to embody an ease in dealing with resources of property and wealth. They are likely to develop the capacity to transform and empower themselves and/or others through commitment and perseverance. In a child, you might see this in how they manage their toys or pocket money – collecting things, allocating their things in a very deliberate manner, or hoarding for a rainy day.

Luca's brothers were perplexed by his tendency to mix different toys – for example, Lego, Meccano, and Playmobile – because he felt free to interchange anything to achieve a satisfying result. His parents encouraged him to play as he saw fit, regardless of his brothers' more pedestrian approach, thereby reinforcing Luca's natural ability to use his resources creatively and on his own terms.

Gate 34 – Power

This is the Gate of raw power and strength. A child with this Gate activated is likely to be highly energetic, taking initiative in play, and keen to make things happen. They may need help to understand the balance of power in relationships, especially with peers, to avoid being overly assertive or bossy.

Melissa was always in the middle of everything and loved nothing more than to be in the playground with her peers, whether they were engaged in make-believe or throwing a ball around. When her mom started to notice play-date invitations were drying up, she realized that Melissa was often both overly enthusiastic and throwing her weight around with the other children. This was greatly improved by encouraging Melissa to consider teamwork in her play and involving her in more sports to burn off more of that energy.

If you are a parent with a defined Sacral Center, you have a wonderful opportunity to show your children how to do the following in particular:

- **Listen to your gut.** The Sacral Center is known for its gut responses – a simple yes-no energy. Parents with a defined Sacral can rely on their gut instinct to give them a sense of what's best for the family, even more so if they also have Sacral Authority (see Chapter 10).
- **Cultivate energy.** As parents, you are likely to be the energy hub of your family. Use this strength to create a lively, active, and positive environment in your home. Remember, this doesn't mean you have to be 'on' all the time. Not every demand gets a "yes." Rest and recharge when you need to.
- **Demonstrate resilience.** Your defined Sacral may equip you with a consistent level of energy and resilience. Demonstrate this resilience to your children and let them learn from your example.
- **Engage in physical activities.** The Sacral Center is associated with physical energy and health. Engage in activities that involve movement with your family, such as sports, dancing, or hiking. This will not only help you use your Sacral energy but will also promote a healthy lifestyle within your family.
- **Foster open communication.** Listen to your children's needs and teach them to listen to themselves, too. This will encourage them to tap into their own Design and foster open communication within the family.

For those of your children who also have a defined Sacral Center, these ways of being will naturally resonate, and you will do them a huge service by helping them tune into their Sacral response.

UNDEFINED OR OPEN SACRAL CENTERS

Those of your children who do not have a defined Sacral Center may appear to have a rather different "operating system" than the Generators and MGs, a system that is less in tune with the ways of the world – remember 70 percent of the population has a defined Sacral Center. This will be covered in detail in Chapter 9, which discusses Manifestors, Projectors, and Reflector Types.

An undefined *and clear* Sacral Center easily offers guidance and wisdom in right use of Sacral energy, being committed to join in, and to stand apart according to their own inherent Authority, or personal guidance.

Children with an open or undefined Sacral Center may exhibit different characteristics or behaviors, notably having inconsistent energy levels. Sometimes they will be highly energetic, especially when around others with defined Sacral Centers (which can, of course, include their parents!), but they will also need more downtime and rest than other children. They may be more adaptable in different environments or situations, as they are taking in and amplifying the energies of those around them. This can make them very responsive and versatile, but also sometimes unpredictable in behavior.

Children with an open Sacral Center will be most sensitive to the energies of the people around them. For example, if they are in a high-energy environment, they might become more active and excited, whereas in a calm environment, they might be more subdued. They are likely to have trouble understanding their own limits regarding energy and activity levels. This can sometimes lead to overexertion as they might try to keep up with the energy levels of their peers. Often, these children are also keen observers. They might spend more time watching and learning from others' experiences. This can sometimes be mistaken for shyness or introversion.

For example, two Projector children, already friends, joined a Montessori nursery school at the same time and sat on the sidelines, holding hands and watching what was going on for the whole first term. Only then were they ready to join in!

Naturally, this is all also true of parents with an undefined or open Sacral Center for whom the following can be especially important:

- **Setting boundaries, especially around time and energy.** Parents will benefit from recognizing when they need to take a break and allowing themselves the space to recharge without feeling guilty.
- **Creating a calm environment at home.** This includes keeping the living space organized and perhaps using calming colors and décor.
- **Scheduling regular quiet time.** This can include meditating or reading a book, which can help release any energies that have been picked up from others and reconnect with yourself.
- **Engaging in social activities.** This can be both fulfilling and fill your tank with positive energy. Sometimes parents can become isolated, and interacting with uplifting friends or participating in social groups can be revitalizing, as can engaging in creative hobbies, such as painting, writing, or any other form of art.
- **Paying attention to physical cues.** If feeling tired, it's important to rest. Conversely, if feeling energetic, it might be a good time to engage in physical activity or play with the children.
- **Delegating tasks.** If feeling overwhelmed, reach out to a partner, family member, or friend. This is important in preventing burnout. You want to nurture your family from a full tank rather than try to run on empty.

Those with an undefined or open Sacral Center that has become *conditioned* often get caught up in others' activities, using energy that is not sustainable and rarely finding satisfaction in their efforts. An open and *clear* Sacral Center mirrors all the facets of Sacral life-force energy without necessarily committing to joining in others' pursuits. They become fascinated by life itself, but might seldom join in with group activities.

Whether other Centers are defined or not has an equally powerful impact on your Design as we shall see in the following chapters.

CHAPTER 5

THE QUEST FOR IDENTITY

"The privilege of a lifetime is being who you are."

—JOSEPH CAMPBELL

The most important and enduring question we can ever ask is: Who am I?

And as life unfolds, if we keep the question alive, the great mystery continues to expand. The next question is: Who are you? (Followed quickly by: What the heck is going on here? Or something similar.) Only we can answer these questions for ourselves, but the more we are able to witness our life, our behaviors, patterns, thoughts, habits, and feelings, the closer and closer we come to the answers.

For children, the early years give the possibility to keep that question alive if they are encouraged to explore their uniqueness through the gifts and talents they naturally bring with them. All of us carry traits that are intrinsic to our Design, and knowing our Human Design charts gives us the means to recognize, indulge, and honor these traits.

Everyone is subject to peer pressure, societal pressure, family pressure, traditions, expectations, fables, and, increasingly through social media, pressures to either "fit in" or be estranged. In times past, it was easy to identify as someone's child, grandchild, school kid, jock or nerd, and shift these identities over time to doctor, secretary, nurse, lawyer, factory worker, etc. In these and coming times, many such titles and trades are going to morph into something completely different. Much identity has been placed on what we *do* by giving ourselves labels, none of which, by themselves, give a complete picture of who we are. We forget that we are human *beings*, rather than human *doings*, and as many *doing* labels dissolve, it is essential to recognize and live out the *being*, instead.

Tattoos, body piercings, jewelry, cosmetics, hairstyles, and colors are all things that children can be aware of as ways of expanding a sense of personal identity. For adults, personalized number plates, exclusive club memberships, designer-label outfits, and rejuvenation efforts can consume much attention and expense in promoting or maintaining an identity.

There are entire lexicons of descriptions in a few letters in slang terms on social media that encapsulate complex gender scenarios, and many children are exposed to these terms with the expectation that they know what they mean and how to appreciate them in their own lives. What was once considered "normal" was that you were either a boy or a girl. But nowadays, there are many variations on the theme that carry multiple degrees of sensitivity, and, at the same time, many stigmas with them.

In the quest for our personal identity, in the middle of the chart is the Self Center, also known as the "G" Center that mirrors the shape of the Nautilus spiral, or the expansion of what is called the Fibonacci sequence and the perfect geometry that connects us to all life in our Universe.

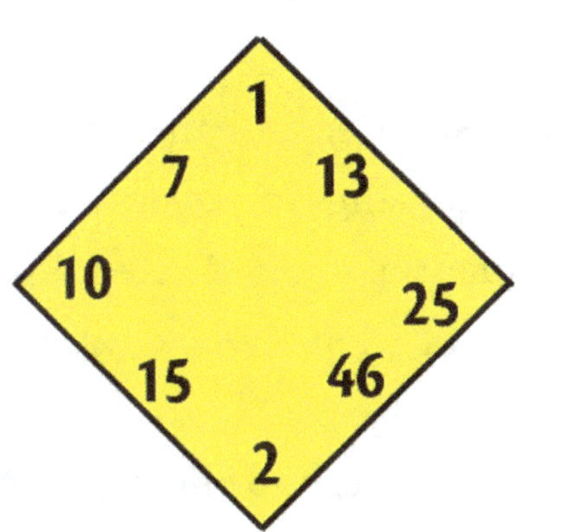

The Self ("G") Center

In this chapter, we go deeper into the Gates and influences in identifying who we are and what our life is all about.

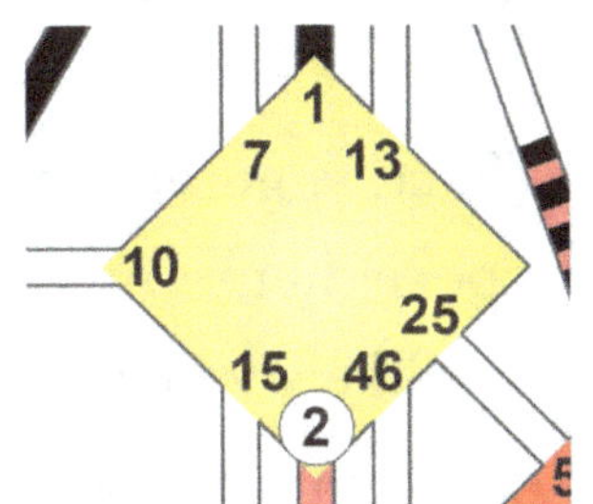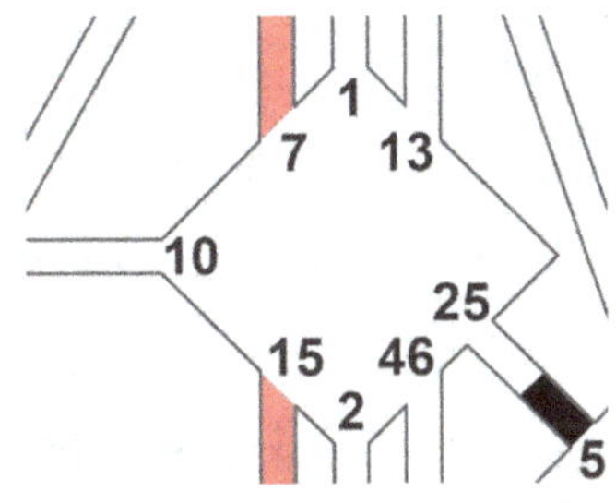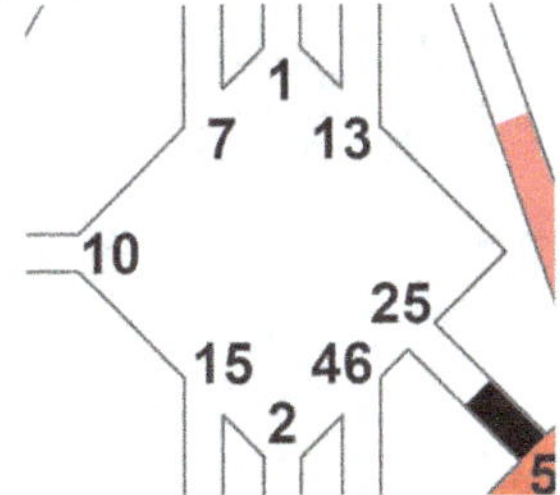

Defined | Undefined | Open

For those with a defined Self Center, there is a consistency in how you go through life according to the Channels or Channels that connect from the Self to other Centers. It is highly unlikely that someone with a defined Self Center is going to be mistaken for someone else.

An undefined Self Center has a degree of freedom to play many roles in life, gathering wisdom from the multitude of ways in which life is lived, without necessarily having a consistent one, particularly finding out the significance around the Gate or Gates that are marked in, but dormant in the Center. There is great freedom of expression in all its forms, which is not beholden to any particular identity.

An undefined or open and conditioned Self Center can easily take on other people's roles in life, habitually living according to ideas, suggestions, and concepts borrowed from the media and influential people. Often, life will be filled with places, associations, and objects that, in their own ways, provide a false sense of stability and consistency.

For those with an open Self Center, there is a lifetime of playing multiple roles, being all things to all people, fitting in and out of all kinds of groups and relationships. There is a close comparison that resembles a chameleon that constantly shifts from one identity to another. Life is a play, and there is great freedom in realizing this. An open and clear, undefined Self Center reflects the world and the people in it back to themselves. There is no fixed identity or particular way in which things must happen all the time. Identity is not of the greatest importance, but freedom to be is.

Those with a clear, undefined or open Self Center offer reflective guidance to others without having an unwavering direction or sense of purpose themselves.

If you have an open or undefined Self Center yourself, you are likely well aware of your capacity to be all things to all people. If your child has an open or undefined Self Center, they may well experience fluctuations in their sense of identity, direction, and love, and can easily feel lost or unsure about who they are. It is especially important for these children to explore various activities, hobbies, company, and interests, allowing them to discover what truly resonates with them. Since their sense of identity can shift based on their surroundings, teaching them techniques to ground themselves can be invaluable. This could be through mindfulness, meditation, or simply taking quiet moments to breathe and reconnect.

Try to avoid putting rigid labels or expectations on your child, such as "You're the smart one" or "You're the athletic one." These can be limiting and, for more than most, create pressure for the child to mold their identity around these labels.

Recognize that your child is likely to change their interests, hobbies, or even life goals. This is part of their journey in exploring the nature of identity and they will value your presence, support, and encouragement through these transitions long into adulthood.

Mark's final year studies at school were math, chemistry, computer studies, and English literature. With a science bias and a reputation for being something of a computer nerd, everyone expected him to study computing at university. During a gap year, Mark concluded that he much preferred the arts and so studied English literature while teaching computing at holiday camps and participating in a university gaming club, much to the bemusement of his peers. Meanwhile, he realized a newfound passion for philosophy, so he took a course of study on Stoicism on the side.

On graduating, Mark decided he wanted to help young men become the best version of themselves and so enrolled in a master's degree in positive psychology and coaching. Each step has seemed clear to Mark, but to an outside observer, this isn't an obvious path ... and yet with his open Self Center, he is exploring his identity and "trying on" different roles, a practice that is likely to be lifelong.

If you have a child with an open Self Center, like Mark, recognize that their identity is naturally fluid. They are chameleon-like, adjusting their colors to suit the moment, the setting, or their current interest. In younger children, this can be joyfully embraced through dressing up and role-playing games. As they grow older, they may express this through wanting a variety of clothing or styles so they have options – rather than moving through fixed "phases" as some of their peers might. The key is to ensure they never feel any sense of shame or inauthenticity for showing up differently in different environments or with different people. Instead, we can help them trust that this adaptability is part of their unique design.

There may never be a simple answer to "Who am I?" until the end of life, when all scenarios are completed. In the meantime, what you can do is live authentically, playing a part that is true for you in any moment of your life. That involves being present, aligned in your Design, and paying attention to your Type and Authority. This is all something that's quite natural to us before we start engaging with the world around us, and the instilled patterns, belief systems, and dictates society upholds, which we are persuaded or coerced to take on.

We can describe the Self Center as the place within us that aligns us with a sense of purpose, connection, direction, and love. Within the Self Center, there are eight Gates, four of which have an implied direction associated with them in how we navigate through life.

And four that align us with how love plays out in our lives, through relationships and attitudes.

THE DIRECTION OR "SPHINX" GATES

1 Creativity

As the name implies, anyone born with this Gate in their Design has a natural *creativity* to include in their life. *Creativity* can be applied in infinite ways – from art to music, writing or pointing out the unusual, to simple everyday activities like cleaning and effortlessly sparking other people to be more creative in their lives. Taking the less obvious approach to life, or recognizing beauty in what appears mundane to everyone else, having a different, even heightened, sense of acoustics or an ability to see beyond limiting horizons are all qualities of creativity. All these and more characteristics can be applied to any person born with Creativity in their Design; they will enjoy having the tools, time, and space to expand their interests.

Give Molly a pencil or crayons and she immediately starts drawing and coloring inspirational pictures and portraits. Her sister, Georgie, however, likes to draw, but would much rather be involved in stage productions, helping behind the scenes with costumes, makeup, and props. Both sisters have Creativity in their Designs and exercise their creative gifts in different ways. Encouraging creativity is a gift for all children. Humans are inherently creative; those with this Gate have an extra "dose"!

2 Receptivity

There is a simple expression: "When you know, you know." And those born with *Receptivity* as a part of their Design have an uncanny knack for knowing things without necessarily being able to explain how, or even exactly what they know. They will often find themselves telling people something off-handedly that, in time, completely rearranges something profound in those people's lives. In their own life, being receptive to an inner guidance can reveal some unusual aspects of life. Somewhat akin to Creativity and Gate 1, Receptivity can indicate unusual pathways and activities that defy generally accepted ones. Thus, anyone with this in their Design often needs to be encouraged to follow their own truth, even if it defies the commonplace.

From an early age, David found that many of the things he said would cause his listeners to raise their eyebrows or look away. For example, "You're different when they're not here," "Why would you do that if you hate it?" and "You're smiling, but you don't look happy." He found himself becoming less keen to say anything until later, when many of the people who'd heard his off-the-cuff statements told David how what he'd said had changed their lives in profound and positive ways.

7 Uniformity

In the traditional I Ching, this Gate is called "The Army," as it provides a way for people to follow a logical, future-oriented pathway in lockstep. It does involve getting people "on the same page," and moving toward an agreed goal together. It is convincing in its own way, especially when everyone around someone with this Gate appears to be a bit lost. However, there are certain instances when someone with *Uniformity* comes to realize that it is not necessarily their job to constantly be herding everyone else, even if they could. It is enough to point the way and encourage others to work it out for themselves. So long as Uniformity shares and holds a common interest, particularly offering others guidance toward an assured future, it will find satisfaction.

Imani has no problems captaining her soccer team and getting everyone to focus and work together to set up and score goals. When play becomes scattered or tempers start to fray, she is often the one who calmly names what's happening and reminds the team of the plan. She doesn't need to shout or dominate; a simple, "We're losing shape; let's reset and do what we practiced," is usually enough.

13 The Listener

One of the most sensitive Gates in Human Design, the *Listener* hears things that are not even spoken. Someone with the Listener in their Design empaths and sometimes telepaths, attuning directly to the experiences in their own and others' lives. They can pry secrets from the most hidden sources, and as children, be exposed to situations, hard luck stories, and complaints way beyond their years. People, often total strangers, who have somehow lost track in their own lives, through some trauma or disappointment, will track down the Listener to hear their tale of woe. Often, the Listener will feel compelled to stand and listen, but also must learn that they have this magnetic quality, and it is quite appropriate to make conversation because it is interesting to listen and speak or to walk away because their Type and Authority are not engaged.

Jen was reduced to tears sometimes after listening to the stories of some of the other children in her class. When her mother found her crying one day, she realized that Jen was being overwhelmed trying to console children with difficulties in their lives. Jen's mother went to the school authorities and asked that counsellors were made aware of what was going on so they could intervene as necessary.

Those born with the Direction or "Sphinx" Gates are the natural directors of life on earth.

THE "VESSEL OF LOVE" GATES

10 Behaviors

When we are confronted by a challenge, we either deal with it, or we fold and give in. Gate 10 is unusual in the Human Design chart because it can connect to three different Gates: 20 The Now, 34 Power, and 57 Intuitive Awareness. Challenges can come in different ways, and it is important that anyone with the Behaviors Gate is present, centered, and ready for whoever and whatever shows up. Many times, a challenge is an opportunity in disguise. It is something that might require a complete change in plans, but ultimately, as a *Love* Gate, it highlights our inner trust that life would not give us something that we cannot handle on one level or another. Overcoming a challenge can lead to celebration and a confidence to embrace life on a different level – encouraging a child with Gate 10 to step into challenges with self-assurance is highly recommended.

Final exams were coming, and Shirley was feeling out of her depth with all the information she had to know. She was sure she was going to flunk. Her mom helped her review all her class materials, and by remaining calm and centered on the day, she passed easily. In this instance, Shirley "borrowed" her mom's self-assurance when she'd lost her own. Her mom guided her to focus on the material in question rather than anything else.

15 Humanity (Fellowship)

This particular Gate is common to all living things and can relate to everyone and everything as equally important. Life exists in so many diverse and extreme forms and climates, and all of it is connected. *Humanity* gives us the means to interact and to engender trust in life itself and everyone and everything taking part in it. On realizing its connectedness to all of life, Humanity can be humbled in appreciating its place in the overall scheme of existence. It comes to appreciate that everything has its seasons and inherent timings. Anyone with Humanity in their Design finds they can make friends and connections in all strata of society, from the aristocracy to the janitor, without considering anyone more important than anyone else. This aspect can also cause a reluctance to be dependent on or controlled by anyone.

Sam made lots of acquaintances everywhere he went and was friendly with almost everyone he met, often without establishing meaningful or deeper friendships. His parents worried about his apparent lack of discernment. Even when he got his first girlfriend, he insisted on being available to other people, and she quickly moved on — not because he lacked warmth or loyalty, but because he did not instinctively place one relationship above all others. Over time, Sam had to learn that honoring humanity as a whole does not preclude intimacy and commitment; it asks for the courage to choose them, rather than keep everyone at the same distance.

25 Innocence

We are born innocent and die innocent. But in between, we face all kinds of complications throughout our lifetime.... And yet, those born with *Innocence* in their Design somehow have an almost uncanny connection to a blameless, trusting, even naïve attitude to life. Innocence represents a universal love that goes beyond what is generally considered "love." As such, those with Innocence in their Design are not equipped to deal with some of the offensive behaviors played out in the world. They have almost no defenses against angry, bombastic, mean, argumentative, and violent people, and are advised to leave immediately when confronted by such people and situations. If leaving is not possible, then at least to distance themselves from such an environment.

Stella made absolutely no sense out of people who insisted that life was a serious business and that arguments involving shouting and displays of anger were appropriate. Rather, she preferred to spend time with her cat, read books, and play music.

46 Serendipity

If there was ever a Hexagram in the I Ching that could be related to being lucky, *Serendipity* is the one. However, attracting luck involves three things: being in the right place, at the right time ... and the third essential ingredient, with the right attitude! Certainly, it is essential to show up, but Serendipity shines when self-assurance, self-love, and self-confidence are present. Following from this comes the recognition that the body is the vehicle that carries us through life, and the greater care we take of it, the more the body serves us on our journey, allowing us to be ready for whatever life presents. In the I Ching, Gate 46 is literally translated as "pushing upward into heaven," with the image of a germinating seed thrusting through the soil with sights set on the sky. Serendipity can accomplish much and be immensely fulfilled by being present and available to anything and everything.

Adrian found himself with a lot of resentment working three jobs with a family to support. One day, while going about a mundane task, he suddenly realized his negative attitude affected everything in his life. In that moment, he decided to shift his attitude, and the rest is history. He is now a self-employed multimillionaire.

Those born with the "Vessel of Love" Gates are the natural ambassadors for the expression and expansion of love on earth.

If you are a parent with a defined Self Center, you have a wonderful opportunity to show your children how to:

- **Be consistent.** You know who you are and you show up consistently. There's a solid, reliable quality about you that can be deeply reassuring – people know what to expect when they are in your company.
- **Follow your purpose.** You tend to move with purpose: you have a sense of direction, an inner true north. This can be immensely settling for children, who take comfort in feeling that the adult in charge knows where they're going. Just remember to explain if and when you change course, so they can follow your lead without confusion.

For children who also have a defined Self Center, these qualities will naturally resonate. You will support them greatly by helping them align with their own sense of inner direction and identity.

UNDEFINED OR OPEN SELF CENTERS

Children without a defined Self Center may be a mystery – sometimes even to themselves!

An undefined and clear Self Center offers guidance and wisdom by reflecting other people back to themselves. People who like the traits they see mirrored will feel comfortable with your child; those who don't may pull away. It is crucial to understand that this isn't personal, even though it can feel deeply so. Those who like what they see are often appreciative of the particular reflection of themselves, just as those who do not like what they see are getting a reflection of themselves that they find uncomfortable.

Children with an undefined or open Self may show different characteristics or preferences from day to day, sometimes even hour to hour, depending largely on the people around them. As a parent, you may want to keep a gentle eye on their friendship groups. They will inevitably begin to mirror the group they're with, whether that's a crowd of sporty kids or a gathering of gaming enthusiasts.

Children with an open Self Center are especially sensitive to the people they interact with. Naturally, the same is true for parents with an undefined or open Self Center, for whom the following can be particularly helpful:

- **Create clarity by naming your roles.** Explain to your children the different roles you inhabit – that you are always their parent, but they may also see you as a daughter or son, a manager, a friend, a partner. This helps them feel safe and allows them to relax into being themselves, too.
- **Choose your company with intention.** Be aware of the people you surround yourself with, especially when your children are present. Ask yourself whether this is the "version of you" that you want them to remember.
- **Encourage identity play.** Support your children in exploring different roles – dressing up, pretending, role-play games. These are all wonderful ways for them to learn about themselves and the world around them.

Children with an undefined or open Self Center who become conditioned often try to be who they think they *should* be, or who they were told to be, rather than who they naturally are. This can limit their sense of joy, satisfaction, and, ultimately, freedom. A clear open Self, however, is a gift: It allows them to mirror and learn from the people they admire and to choose, moment by moment, who they want to be, guided by their Authority (see Chapter 10).

Throughout life, we are all asked, explicitly or implicitly: *Who are you?* How we answer depends as much on our communication style as on whether our Self Center is defined or open – and on what we choose to give our time and attention to.

CHAPTER 6

OUR VOICES

"And as we let our own light shine, we unconsciously give other people permission to do the same."

— MARIANNE WILLIAMSON

The way we express ourselves is one of the clearest windows into who we are. After exploring the Self Center and the different ways identity is shaped and experienced, it becomes easier to see how naturally our voices – spoken and unspoken – may reflect that inner landscape. Some of us communicate with a steadiness that comes from a defined sense of self; others speak from the mind or from the heart, quite literally in Human Design terms, while some share their fears or feelings openly. Before we look more closely at the Throat Center and the many voices within it, it's helpful to understand how uniquely we each arrive at our words – and why our communication can feel so distinct from one another.

As we've seen, those with a defined Sacral Center have a ready sense of energy rising or falling in response to something. Does this excite me? Is my energy rising? Oh, yes, please! Does this give me that sinking feeling? Is my energy falling at the very suggestion? No, thank you, not now. Conversely, the Manifestors, Projectors, and Reflectors amongst us can be put on the spot by questions requiring a yes or no response – they have a subtler energetic indicator – and can often find it easier to reply to open-ended questions. These non-sacral types may need to reflect inside and find their own attunement or talk it out and actually hear themselves in order to reach a conclusion. Those with a lot of Tribal Circuitry and/or a fourth Line in their Profile will communicate through touch and gesture more than those without. We, humans, are distinguishable from other animals, however, through our extensive use of language as our primary means of communication – maybe it's no accident that all the Gates in the Human Design Throat Center occur in the quarter of civilization!

As a parent, it is helpful to understand your own natural style of communicating, not least because you can guide people on how to listen to you.

Sue can sound very definite (she has the 17–62 Channel) and folk around her will respond accordingly, so there are times when she has literally said: "I may sound definite, I'm not, this is one possibility, and I'd welcome yours too: indeed, I may change my mind before settling on something." It gives her listeners permission to challenge when they might otherwise have taken what she'd said as the only possibility when she's simply sounding out thoughts.

A defined Throat Center is able to speak out at any time and expresses according to the particular Channel of Channels connecting it to (an)other Center(s). For example, Channels from the Mind Center express potentially useful concepts, thoughts, and beliefs.

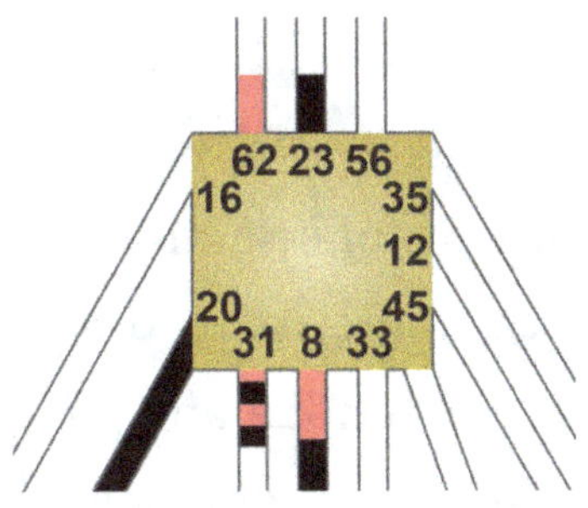 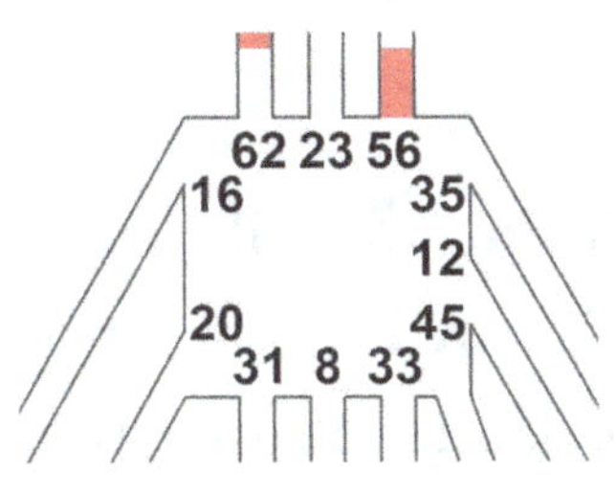 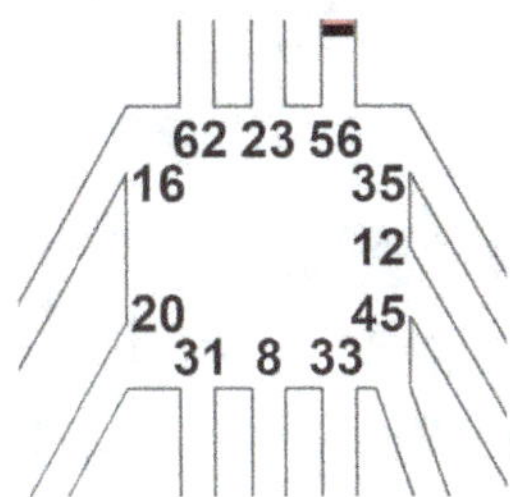

Defined | Undefined | Open

An undefined and clear Throat Center expresses potential interests for other people's situations. The expressions are for the audience, and not the speaker.

An undefined or open and conditioned Throat Center often speaks out of turn and in ways others don't want to, or cannot, hear.

An open and clear Throat Center can express in many different ways, and in many ranges of voice if trained correctly, mirroring expressions to one and all.

Understanding your children's different voices from the Gates of their Throat Centers allows you to help them communicate in ways that honor their authenticity and, consequently, allows the child to be more easily heard and understood.

COLLECTIVE VOICES

The majority of Gates in the Throat Center are voices of the collective – they are not personal, but shared, seeking to express something for the human species as a whole. This can be hugely useful to remember if you feel triggered by someone's expression. Children with any of these Gates may be the ones doing the triggering unless they are taught *how* to express themselves, without diluting the message. For example, rather than "Don't be sarcastic," you might try, "That sounded sarcastic, which can upset people. Let's see if we can find a better way for you to make your point." The collective voices are either future-focused – let's experiment – or learning from the past – let's look at our experience.

16 Selectivity

This is the Gate of enthusiasm and skill – *let's try* – as a means of selecting the best course of action. This voice will comment out loud on the merits or drawbacks of any proposal. Their excitement for a project will be infectious and they will gather others as a result. If this is you, or your child, beware those who negate you saying, "I'll try …" with a retort about not *trying* but succeeding. They are caught in a belief that *trying* is a way of avoiding success or completion. It is likely a learned expression from someone who does not have this Gate.

As a child, Emma would often get into trouble for pouring cold water on ideas with comments like, "I don't see how that would work." Parents might describe her as "always turning things into a battle," language that can be both tiring and emotionally charged.

What was easy to miss was that, in her own way, Emma was not being obstinate; she was trying to identify the best option. As she grew up, her parents helped her learn how to temper her delivery. Now, she is more likely to ask a question such as, "How would that work?"– a small shift in phrasing that tends to open conversation rather than shut it down.

62 Expressed Details

This is the Gate of clarification and expressed details – *I think* – as a means of gaining objectivity. This voice will express the salient points from a complicated mass of information with a sense of logic and command of the details. School has taught many of us to say what we think – or more often repeat what someone else has already thought – and only those with this Gate will say "I think …" with the conviction of authenticity that allows others to hear and take note.

Pippa was taught that it was redundant to write "I think…" on the basis that this was self-evident in her writing. It took some years for her to unlearn this approach because on many occasions she was distinguishing her thoughts from her feelings, beliefs, hunches, and so on. Had her parents understood this nuance, they could have helped her gain clarity much earlier.

31 Influence

This is the voice of influence and is the most authoritative voice of them all. It is logical and future-oriented, and if you have this Gate, where you lead, others will follow, confident in what you say. This voice carries, so be aware of who is listening. If your child has this Gate, to avoid misunderstandings or upset simply from being overheard, they may need to learn the art of discretion in what they say, when they say it, and where, earlier on in life than others.

Michael was confused when his friend Mohammed suddenly stopped playing with him. It later emerged that Michael had made an offhand comment about immigration while talking with his dad on the way home – not about Mohammed, and not in a derogatory way – but it had been overheard and misunderstood. The words were never meant for Mohammed's ears, yet once heard, they took on a meaning Michael had never intended.

35 Progress

This is the Gate of progress – *let's change* – with a restless nature that wants to try new things and experience all that life has to offer. *Progress* is in pursuit of growth and enjoyed for its own sake; it can be inhibited by goals and deadlines. Children with this Gate may love learning and be bored silly with the need to demonstrate their learning through homework or examinations. Cycles of Progress can become spirals of life experiences if they are nurtured well by adults who recognize that growth does not always require completion.

Louis found it frustrating always to have to finish projects; it seemed to him that if this one was better than the last, why bother? What mattered was not completion, but movement. There was always the next excitement to chase....

33 Retreat

This is one of the two storyteller Gates, in this case, the Gate of retreat and expressed memory – "I remember ..." or "I've heard...." Those with this Gate need time to step away from too much activity and withdraw into the privacy of their own shell to digest an experience, and then return to present their conclusions to the world. These stories may well be factual accounts with little embellishment.

Gus's mom could tell something was up when he returned from school, but he shut himself in his room until he was called down for dinner. Only after their meal was he able to explain that two of his friends had been fighting in class. Gus's mom had learned to wait, knowing that when Gus was ready, he would speak and that her job was then to listen.

56 The Wanderer

This is the other storyteller Gate – the Gate of the wanderer who speaks to make sense of the experiences themselves – "I believe ..." or "You'll never believe what just happened...." The search for stimulation will include a desire for feedback from their audience to challenge their own perceptions. Their stories may well be presented as fairy tales, opening with "once upon a time" and closing with a moral. Those with this Gate have an eye for a good story and may both embellish their own and be quick to spot when others have done the same!

Anna loved creating stories and would weave fantastic tales based on the lives of her pets – her dachshund became a mighty warrior and her rabbit his trusted accomplice as they fought off an invasion of alien gerbils. However, she was terrified of public speaking, which was an enormous shame, as she could hold any audience entranced with her tales.

If you have either of these Gates, 33 or 56, you are likely a great raconteur. Children love a good story, and often the more fanciful, imaginative, and expansive, the better. Some well-loved children's books started out as bedtime stories, notably *Winnie-the-Pooh, The Hobbit,* and *Percy Jackson and the Lightning Thief.* If your child has either of these Gates, encourage them to speak and write their stories as much as possible. We, humans, are hard-wired through ancient oral tradition to learn through storytelling so it is a wonderful gift to have at your fingertips and hone through practice.

THE TRIBAL VOICE

The tribe, which you might define as your family, your business, your church, or your community, has one voice – that of the King or Queen – that both speaks for the tribe and is interested in gathering resources for the tribe.

45 Gathering Together

This is the Gate of rulership, gathering the tribe and its resources together – "I have ..." or even "We have...." Those with this Gate can sound quite regal and are likely to be concerned with material resources, the wealth and well-being of the household. Children with this Gate will likely want to unpack all your shopping to see exactly what is going in the fridge. They may also be able to make surprisingly astute contributions to conversations about family well-being and decisions about whether to save or spend (and on what) from a comparatively early age.

It's long been a family joke that Kai seemed to have a mental inventory of everything in the workshop – from nails to screwdrivers, he would know exactly what resources the family had to hand.

INDIVIDUAL VOICES

Gates in the Throat Center in Individual Circuitry offer a degree of freshness or novelty. Those with any of these Gates are speaking personally, and with a unique take on life. Consequently, their expression may provoke significant shifts in others' perceptions.

23 Assimilation

This is the Gate of Assimilation and speaks with a stabilizing "I know …" that results in the audience of anyone with this Gate thinking that you're brilliant or weird, largely depending on their readiness to hear what you say. This is the most acoustically attuned of all the voices and people will hear how you say something as much as what you say. If your child (or you!) has this Gate, it is wise to invest in some kind of training in speech skills, so they learn timing and pitch and how to avoid blurting things out to the unsuspecting listener.

In the middle of a noisy playground debate about whether a teacher was "mean," Jonathan listened for a while and then said, quite calmly, "I know why she does that. She's trying to keep everyone safe because she gets blamed when things go wrong." The group went quiet. A couple of children looked at him with new respect; others felt awkward and wandered off. Jonathan hadn't meant to end the conversation or sound important – he had simply said what had landed for him, in the same steady tone he always used.

8 Contribution

This is the Gate of Contribution and bringing people together. You'll hear people with this Gate asking, "What can I bring?" or "How can I help?" Far from sitting passively on the sidelines, people with this Gate tend to galvanize others, uniting them and then guiding them toward potentially creative outcomes. They like to be in the thick of things, so if your child has this Gate, try to include them in whatever is going on, especially if they are trying to engage.

The night before visiting her grandparents, Sofia would always ask Grandma on the phone: "What are we baking tomorrow?" On the ride over to her grandparents', she would proceed to engage the whole family with her plotting and planning of delicious treats that were decided on the night before. "Dad, can you help Grandma and me with that thingy that grinds the hazelnuts into tiny bits?" "Milo, I'll let you lick the entire bowl once I'm done making the frosting. Grandma says she trusts me to do it on my own today." And one by one, every family member would become an active participant in the making of dessert.

12 Standstill

This is the Gate of Standstill, creating a pause to take stock before taking action. This can frustrate some and inspire confidence in others who rely on their discrimination. If this is you, catch yourself in the moment – what's your hesitation telling you? If this is your child, ask them what they are cautious about. This can offer wonderful teaching moments, and/or you may learn something yourself as they consider the world afresh. Often, those with this Gate have a clairvoyant ability; they tend to see things ahead and need to find ways to be accurate, sensitive, and comfortable telling of them.

Jose always paused on his way into Judo. When asked why, he explained that he needed a few breaths to gather himself and switch into the new activity. Actually, he realized he paused before most things – not just Judo.

20 The "Now"

By contrast, this is the Gate of the present moment – the Now! If you have this Gate, you will be aware of your capacity to see what is relevant in the moment while disregarding other actions. There is no pressure in this, rather a contemplative impression of what is important right here, right now. Those with this Gate can offer a real gift to others by drawing them into the present tense and away from the overly busy mind, which many of us are prey to.

Even when she was a toddler, Hannah would embrace the moment, whether she was finger painting, jumping in the waves, or playing with her cuddly toys. Her parents were delighted that this continued, as she seemed able to give 100 percent to whatever she was focused on at the time – be it schoolwork, playing her clarinet, or looking after her younger siblings.

If you are a parent with a defined Throat Center, you have a clear way of speaking, which your children may come to rely on as a source of comfort and strength. Children who have a defined Throat Center will also have specific ways of speaking – and they may be different from yours. You can do them a great service by recognizing their unique expression and encouraging them. You can also help by directly "tuning in" to your child's Throat Gates, asking, "What do you *think* about this?" "What do you *know?*" "What do you *recall?*" as appropriate.

REFLECTING OTHERS

If you or your child have no Gates in your Throat Center, you have unlimited ways of expressing yourself and will likely find yourself matching the voices of your audience.

Pippa became very aware of her son, Mark, "using" her 17–62 Channel of the organizer, to work out what he thinks. Mark has an open Throat Center and for many years has outlined his ideas to her before committing them to paper, for his university coursework, for example. When he is away travelling, Pippa won't hear from him for a week or two, and then he will phone and talk for an hour or more as he "digests" his experiences with her, as a listener, facilitating his thinking simply by being present with him. Knowing this has made her much more patient with him and less likely to interrupt; once he has downloaded what's in his mind and calibrated the information to his own satisfaction, he is ready to inquire about other things, with the capacity to hear what she has to say.

With an open Throat Center, it is also entirely possible that your audience simply hears what they want to hear because you are literally reflecting something of themselves back to them. The trick is not to take it personally yourself — it's their stuff, not yours. Indeed, Pippa taught her young son to retort to playground jibes with "You are what you say," little realizing at the time that he had an open Throat Center, so this was especially apt!

It is most important that regardless of whether the Throat Center is defined, undefined, or open, we speak in turn. Undefined and open Centers, particularly, can reflect great wisdom. However, when this wisdom is unloaded out of turn, no one will be able, or want, to hear it.

Much conversation can be devoted to our perceptions, checking them with other people's as a way of calibrating ourselves and the things of which we are aware. Our voices may express what we think, feel, or intuit — yet beneath every word lies the source of those perceptions. Awareness is the quiet engine behind much of what we speak aloud.

To understand our communication more fully, we now turn to the Centers that shape how we sense, feel, and interpret the world.

CHAPTER 7

UNDERSTANDING FEAR AND FEELING

"You are the sky. Everything else – it's just the weather."

— PEMA CHÖDRÖN

Three of our Human Design Centers are known as Centers of Awareness. While grounded in reality, they can sometimes feel like a sixth sense, as our intuition prickles, our emotional radar pings, or we just know something without being told. These three Centers are the Spleen, the Emotional Solar Plexus, and the Mind. And like all the other Centers, they operate differently depending on whether they are open (picking up the energies around them), undefined (similarly picking up surrounding energies but with more potential to create definition with others), or defined (operating 24/7 in a consistent way depending upon the Gates activated as part of a Channel connecting to another Center).

THE SPLEEN

The Spleen Center is associated with intuition, instinct, health, and well-being. One of the key aspects of the Spleen Center is its connection to fears – it holds awareness that is rooted in survival instincts and, as a consequence, it is connected to primal fears. These fears are thought to be evolutionary in nature, having developed as mechanisms to keep human beings safe from threats.

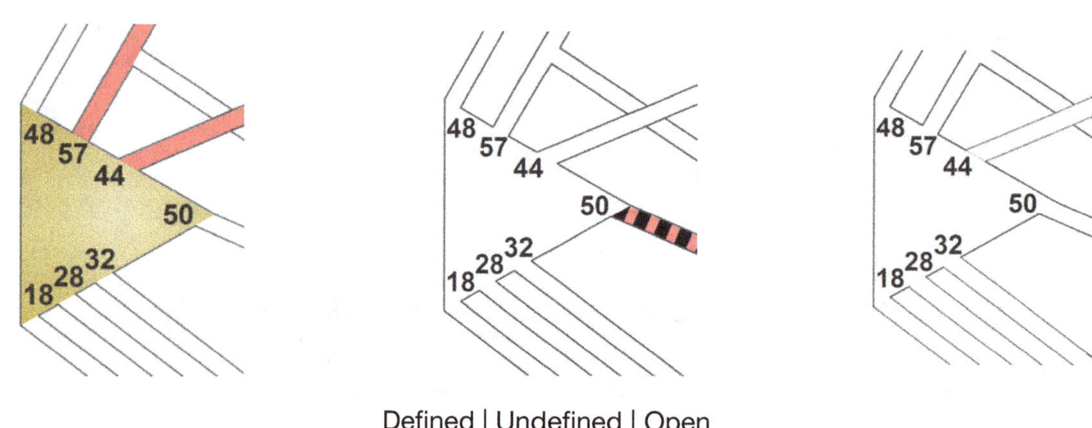

Defined | Undefined | Open

A defined Spleen Center is on guard for any sudden changes to its environment that concern overall health and well-being. It has the means to attune to changes in patterns through the senses of taste, intuition, and instinct. It can be quick-witted; however, if overly sensitive, it can live in constant nervousness.

For people with a defined Spleen Center in their Human Design chart, these fears can be consistent and somewhat manageable. However, for individuals with an undefined or open Spleen Center, there might be a tendency to pick up on the fears of others and magnify them, causing these fears to be more erratic and overwhelming. In understanding the nature of these fears and recognizing them as primitive survival mechanisms, we can avoid being controlled by them. It's about learning to differentiate between intuitive instincts that are there to guide and protect you, and irrational fears that can limit your growth and happiness. A child with an open or undefined Spleen may have irrational fears, such as dragons under the bed, whereas a child with a defined Spleen may have more grounded fears like changing school.

Josie was nine years old and at school when her grandmother died. She felt her leave in the middle of a science lesson and got into trouble for being distracted. Unusually picked up from school at the end of the day by her dad, she blurted out, "It's Granny, isn't it?" "What do you mean?" he countered, "Just wait until we're home." Josie tried to tell him that she already knew, but was met with disbelief. If your child tries to tell you something they can't logically already know, this may be an open Spleen Center in action with potentially psychic ability to "know" the apparently unknowable. In Josie's case, she pushed her knowing underground, thinking she was something of a freak, until long into adulthood, when her gifts were met by others with similar gifts.

In general, children with a defined Spleen Center might express this in their day-to-day life by being health-conscious, even from quite a young age. They may show a heightened awareness of their own health and well-being and be drawn to activities that promote wellness, prefer certain foods, or exhibit a keen sense of what's good or bad for their health. These children are also likely to be very intuitive and instinctual. They might seem to have a knack for making the right choices without needing a lot of time to think about it.

Children with a defined Spleen Center are likely to live "in the now," enjoying and fully experiencing the present moment rather than being overly focused on the past or future, and may show resilience in stressful or scary situations. Depending upon which Gate or Gates activate the Spleen Center, children may express associated fears, highlighted in the following paragraphs. Remember, each of the seven Gates in the Spleen Center has an inherent potential fear ... and also an inherent potential wisdom.

COLLECTIVE

Those with these Gates activated are expressing something almost universal, part of the human experience, if you will.

18 Improving (Fear of Authority and Not Being Perfect)

This Gate can be as much about finding remedy as it can be about improving. There is a need to review what is healthy and wholesome in life to ensure well-being and take steps to maintain it. Children with this Gate may be very hard on themselves, especially in school, and may be fearful or overly respectful of teachers and coaches.

Dinah was so determined to be best in class that she'd work on her homework under the bedcovers long after she'd been sent to bed. Once her parents found out and put a stop to this, she became so stressed that she resorted to pulling out her eyebrows. Over time, it became clear that her body was signaling distress long before she had words for it, and that learning how to care for herself would be just as important as learning how to improve at school.

48 The Well (Fear of Inadequacy or Not Knowing Enough)

Gate 48 seeks replenishment, as its name suggests, from the depths and preferably with an unending source of knowledge. A child with Gate 48 may be thirsty for knowledge and become the archetypical bookworm or Google-aficionado. They might equally be scared to answer questions in class or try new things because they are afraid that they don't know enough or aren't smart enough.

Marco always tried to get a seat at the back of the class, hoping his teacher wouldn't call on him to answer questions. When that didn't work, he tended to blurt out everything he knew on the topic, whether it answered the question or not. Over time, it became clear that both responses came from the same place – a fear of not knowing enough, paired with a deep hunger to draw from a well that never seemed quite full enough.

TRIBAL

The fears associated with activated Tribal Gates in the Spleen are to do with belonging, our primordial need to be part of a group.

32 Duration (Fear of Change/Failure)

The old phrase that the only certainties in life are death and taxes implies another certainty – the certainty of change. The need to adapt to new circumstances can be challenging for children trying to make sense of the world. Children with this Gate defined might be afraid to try new activities or hobbies, fearing they might not be good at them, and they may need extra encouragement to take part in sports or arts. They may also be very wary of big life changes, moving house or changing school, for example.

Matthew hated the idea of trying new sports. He worried about not knowing the rules, being bad at them, and looking foolish in front of other children. When his parents signed him up for a club where the activities kept changing, he felt anxious at first. Over time, though, being new became normal. Matthew learned that he could have a go without having to be good, and that unfamiliarity didn't last forever. Gradually, his fear of trying new things softened – not just in sport, but elsewhere too.

44 Patterns (Fear of the Past or a Repetition of the Past)

We teach babies and young children pattern recognition with shapes and colors before moving on to letters and numbers. This Gate is about pattern recognition, especially in relation to other people and their interactions – the tribe or group will thrive where there is acceptance and mutual tolerance. A child with Gate 44 may be fearful of situations that remind them of a past negative experience, such as avoiding a playground because they once fell off the swing.

Pat was playing on a gravel driveway when the neighbors brought home a new puppy who bounced over to join in and unintentionally toppled Pat over. His parents recalled the moment as if Pat had made a split-second decision that dogs were dangerous. Dogs being sensitive to humans largely lived up to that idea – stealing Pat's ice-cream, snapping at him, growling – until his uncle and Labrador had the patience to play gently one afternoon so Pat learned that not every dog was dangerous. To this day, Pat is wary of dogs until proper introductions are made.

50 Values (Fear of Responsibility and Sometimes Fear for the Well-being of Others)

The well-being of any group is enhanced by a sense of stability and values that have continuity through the generations, enriching the local community and society at large. Children with this Gate may be unduly concerned about their parents or siblings and feel responsible for their parents' or siblings' happiness. This can lead them to take on adult-like responsibilities.

Kiara adored having a baby brother, so much so that she made it her mission to ensure that he was happy, playing with him at the expense of her own friendships, sharing her pocket money so he could get the next collectible, and sticking up for him at the play-

ground. She was indeed mini-mom even when it was not in her own best interests, and their mother was being fully competent.

INDIVIDUAL

Those with either of these two Gates activated may be more than usually concerned with their own personal survival and well-being.

28 The Game Player, of Life (Fear of Death)

Courage and tenacity are required to meet life's personal challenges and persist in the experience of life. Celebrating our nature, milestones, even the glory of life itself can be important in maintaining our well-being. Out of balance, adults can manifest existential crisis, where they are searching for the meaning and purpose in their lives. While children might not experience existential crises, they may question the purpose of certain rules or activities. They may seek meaning by often asking *why*.

For some months after a holiday with another family whose father had died the previous winter, Will clung to his dad, especially just before bed. He repeatedly asked for particulars of why the other dad had died, seeking reassurance that he wasn't in danger of losing his own.

57 The Gentle (Fear of the Future)

This Gate is often likened to the penetrating wind where intuitive clarity arises unbidden, with a simple knowing. Intuition defies logic or previous experience and can so easily be dismissed, especially coming from children. Yet, those with this Gate need to be encouraged to listen to their intuitive gifts. Children with this Gate may dislike the unpredictable and fear changes in routine or unknown events, such as a school trip or visiting a new place. They may need reassurance and detailed explanations of what to expect.

As a teenager, Bruce was devastated by the breakup with his first girlfriend, partly because he knew he was "meant" to be in a relationship. Bruce was utterly inconsolable until his mom asked him which of their family friends were with the same partner from their teenage years. Between them, they found just one such friend. Bruce was still upset, but with a newfound perspective that most people enjoyed spending time with several girlfriends before finding "the one," life became more manageable for him again.

Parents with a defined Spleen can model the following for their children:

- **Trusting your intuition.** You have a consistent and reliable intuitive sense. Trust your instincts, especially when assessing situations for your family.
- **Establishing healthy boundaries.** You may have a robust sense of what is healthy and safe for you. Utilize this to establish healthy boundaries for yourself and teach your children to do the same.
- **Promoting well-being.** With your keen sense of health and well-being, foster a healthy lifestyle for your family, sharing your instincts with your children as soon as they are old enough.
- **Acknowledging your fears.** With a defined Spleen Center, it often happens that your fears, once identified, remain consistent. Acknowledging these fears and working on ways to manage them can be a powerful lesson for your children, too.

Similarly, parents can support a child with a defined Spleen Center by helping them trust their intuition, encouraging them to honor their senses: Do things sound right, smell fishy, feel tasteful or not? These children may have a keen sense of what is healthy and safe for them. Respect their boundaries when they express discomfort or unease and help them articulate this. With the Spleen Center's connection to the body's health and vitality, regular physical activity is important to keep the child's energy balanced and promote overall health, as are good nutrition, sleep, and hygiene. They are likely to be naturally inclined toward understanding these concepts. Help your child connect with their body and its signals. This could be through mindfulness exercises, yoga, or simply talking about the sensations they feel in their body. Similarly, help your child understand and navigate their fears rather than ignoring them.

By contrast, a child with an undefined or open Spleen Center may need more help with:

- **Health awareness.** Teach your child about healthy habits, hygiene, nutrition, and the importance of physical activity. Consistent habits can help maintain their health, because their innate sense of well-being will fluctuate.

- **Letting go.** Children with an open Spleen Center may hold onto things, situations, or people longer than necessary. Teach them the importance of letting go and provide support if and when they struggle with this.

- **Energy protection.** Because they're sensitive to the energies around them, it's essential to teach these youngsters about energy protection and how to shield themselves from overwhelming situations.

- **Understanding their fears.** An undefined Spleen Center may lead to inconsistent or unfounded fears as they pick up on the fears of those around them. Help your child understand these fears and discuss them openly rather than brushing them aside.

Jeremy used to imagine himself stepping into a purple circle where his sister, Bethany, preferred to don a green bubble much like a space suit, before going out, as a way of setting the intention that they be safe and secure.

If you're a parent with an undefined or open Spleen Center in your Human Design, you may have a tendency to absorb and amplify the energy of others around you, too. This can be particularly challenging when managing the dynamics of family life. You can support yourself by managing your own energies with regular self-care routines, meditation, or energy clearing practices.

An undefined or open and conditioned Spleen Center can become frozen in others' fears and concerns. It may be prone to taking on an unhealthy lifestyle, even catching one illness after another without ever making a full recovery. You may simply experience inconsistencies in your health and sense of well-being, so maintaining a balanced diet, regular exercise, and adequate sleep can help create stability. Undefined Spleen Centers can hold onto fears even when the perceived danger has passed or was unfounded to start with; mindfulness techniques, journaling, or speaking with a trusted friend or counsellor can be helpful if you're feeling stuck. You might tend to hold onto things, situations, or relationships that are no longer serving, so practice the art of letting go. This could involve decluttering your physical space, reassessing commitments, or even reassessing relationships.

Notice how your environment and the people around you influence your well-being and make adjustments as necessary. This could mean spending less time with energy-draining individuals or creating a calm, peaceful home environment, for example.

An undefined and clear Spleen Center can offer insights regarding health and well-being through being able to "diagnose," or pick up what is going on in someone else's life. Prone to catching illnesses in crowd situations in early years, immunity is boosted throughout the lifetime by mostly lightweight medicines and rest.

An open and clear Spleen Center reflects others while picking up on their fears, agendas, and life circumstances. The open Spleen Center often indicates psychic abilities and complete fearlessness, even in situations that, for other people, create intense worries and concerns.

THE EMOTIONAL SOLAR PLEXUS

A defined Emotions Center indicates a life of drama that can be small- or large-scale, as waves of emotion ripple from within. Producing and living in waves of emotion requires great responsibility, because the waves can cause huge upset. Therefore, establishing emotional clarity is vitally important, especially in these more turbulent times.

Many believe that thoughts always precede emotions. And sure, we can have a sudden flash of irritation as someone pulls out in traffic in front of us and we think: *What a moron, they could have caused an accident.* There is, though, another process within us: a felt sense that arises in the body that is distinctly different from thought. It might be that moment when the hairs on the back of your neck stand up – an intuition coming from your Spleen Center. Or it can be a sudden desire to dance as a burst of happiness randomly pours over you, as your emotional wave rises from your Emotional Solar Plexus. Those with a defined Emotional Solar Plexus are always riding this wave; it is distinct and personal to you. You may experience emotional highs and lows, or waves of emotional energy, that need to be acknowledged and processed over time. Your emotions can be very strong and have a significant impact on others around you, especially those with an undefined or open Emotional Solar Plexus. You may notice how your own emotional waves impact your family.

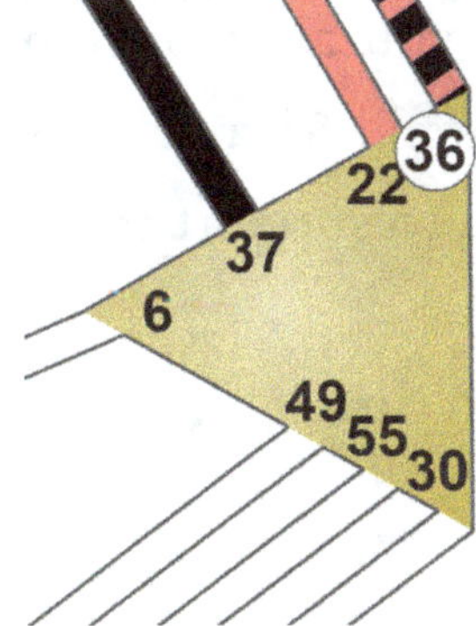
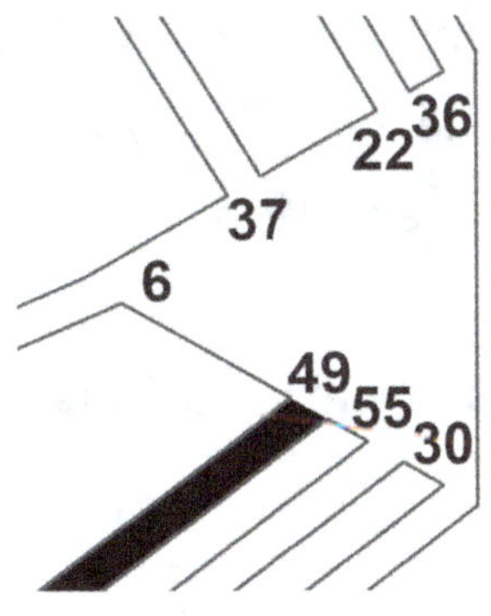
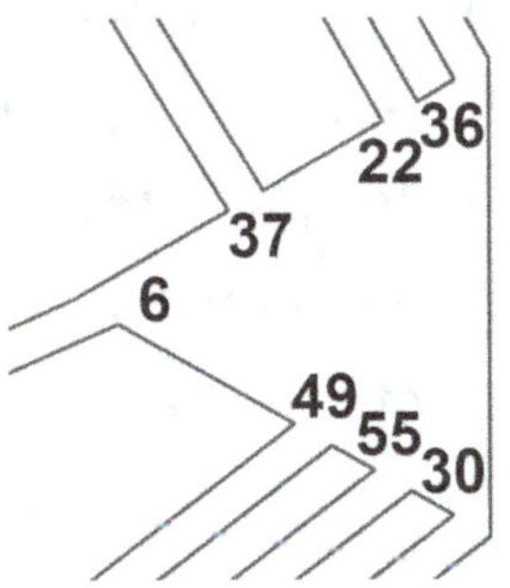

Defined | Undefined | Open

Having a defined Emotional Solar Plexus is a little like having emotional weather – it's always present in the background, and sometimes it sweeps in like a sudden storm.

This was very clear when Kate was a teenager. Some mornings, she would wake up all sweetness and light, as if the sun were shining inside her. On other days, she'd roll out of bed already grumpy, the emotional clouds firmly in place. It became a family joke that the later Kate woke up, the brighter the forecast was likely to be. Early starts, however, often came with a storm warning. None of this had anything to do with what was happening in Kate's life – aside from the usual arrival of teenage hormones – and everything to do with her emotional wave.

By contrast, an undefined or open and conditioned Emotions Center doesn't generate its own emotional weather. Instead, it can be swept up in the emotional storms around it, often amplifying upsets or arguments and resulting in a heavy, uneasy feeling in the belly. If your Emotional Solar Plexus is undefined, you may be aware of your tendency to absorb and magnify the emotional energy of others. You might often find yourself riding on other people's emotional waves, feeling their joys and sorrows profoundly. You need to learn how to protect your energy and set emotional boundaries. An undefined and clear Emotions Center learns how and when to commit to an emotional environment and the people in it. It reflects wisdom in ways that emotions are played out responsibly or not. It's vital to distinguish between your own emotions and the emotions you absorb from others, including your child. Understanding your child's Emotional Solar Plexus can also provide insight into their emotional world, helping you to support them more effectively.

Let's look at each of the Gates of the Emotional Solar Plexus in turn.

COLLECTIVE

The emotional wave pattern for those with the following Collective Gates activated tends to rise to a crescendo and then drop precipitously before rising again. Once they are old enough, children benefit from understanding their wave pattern and knowing that it is okay, it's in the natural order of things. Those with collective circuitry are often very visual, so inviting perspective can be helpful.

30 Desires (Unquenchable Desire to Simply Enjoy the Experience)

There's a kind of "all or nothing" quality attached to this Gate. And there's power in using desire as a motivator, so long as one doesn't become consumed by it or even addicted to it. Those with the Gate may have to be reminded to enjoy the journey. Children with this Gate might have intense desires for certain toys or experiences and may throw tantrums or get very upset if they can't have what they want.

To this day, Pippa remembers seeing the older sister of a friend wearing knee-high white boots (yes, it was in the 1970s!) and badgering her mom to let her have a pair of her own. It never happened, but Pippa's love of boots – of all colors – continues unabated!

36 Crisis Resolution (A State of Permanent Crisis to Compassion)

A sense of crisis can precede a new experience, and this Gate is about the potential to move from a sense of turbulence to compassion. Children with Gate 36 may be thrill-seekers, always looking for new experiences. They may be more prone to accidents or emotional upsets as they learn through trial and error, growing emotionally through the experience of highs and lows.

Lizzie's ambition to become a vet was sorely tested when she volunteered at an animal shelter as a teenager and witnessed both the successes of a pet recovering from injury and those that had to be put out of their misery. She realized that if she were to pursue this ambition, she had to find a way to become more comfortable with the cycle of life and honor her experiences with these animals for their own sake, whatever the outcome.

TRIBAL

The emotional wave pattern for those with activated Gates in the Tribal circuitry tends to be a fairly consistent, gentle wave without extremes. For children with any of these Gates, reassurance is often given by the familiar tribal senses of taste, touch, and smell; for example, a hot chocolate or a cuddle with a significant person or toy (catching both touch and smell in one).

6 Conflict Resolution (Everyone Is a Problem to True Diplomacy)

Those with Gate 6 have the capacity to take the emotional temperature at any given moment and, with a figurative (and literal) deep breath, identify the real needs of the situation. Children with this Gate may either seek conflict as a form of interaction or avoid it at all costs. They might need help learning how to manage conflicts constructively. They have the potential to become truly diplomatic and help others understand the emotional climate.

At about five years old, Eleanor had a complete meltdown at school over a conflict with her teacher. Discovering that this didn't work, she concluded that emotions were useless and shut down. Without support from home, she grew up to be a mild-mannered, passive-aggressive adult needing years of therapeutic help to make peace with her feelings and learn how to manage conflict in a positive way.

37 Family (Weakness to Balanced Giving and Receiving)

Family bonds are recognized by touch and food, and those with this Gate are likely to have, or seek, a strong sense of belonging to the family, be it by blood relationship, community group, or business. A child with this Gate may be very focused on friendships and can be deeply affected by any conflicts with friends. They are likely to need help learning to balance the art of both giving and receiving.

Ruth always wanted everybody to be invited to her birthday party – not content with inviting her classmates, she always lobbied her mom to include her cousins and her dance troop too, regardless of whether she was included in their parties.

49 Revolution ("No!" as a Reaction to "No" as a Response)

Gate 49 is all about the power of emotions to bring about change – out with the old and in with the new – according to particular principles. It is also a transpecial Gate that attunes with mammals (see Chapter 14). Children might be very black-and-white in their sense of fairness and can become very upset or angry if they feel something is unfair or if someone breaks a promise. Their default reaction may be "No!" and they may need help to learn how and when this "No" can be an appropriate response rather than a knee-jerk reaction.

Years later, Rebecca still talks about her outrage at having a brown bear in her own birthday party bag when she'd specifically asked her mom for one of the white bears. She felt betrayed by something that to an adult was simply an administrative hiccup.

INDIVIDUAL

The emotional wave pattern for those with either of the Individual Gates in the Emotional Solar Plexus is erratic, with the highest highs and the lowest lows forming no discernible pattern. Music, being out in nature, and getting creative can all help someone with these Gates return to a place of greater emotional calm.

22 Grace (Dishonor to Gracious Sharing)

Those with this Gate tend to have a natural elegance and charm born of clear emotional alignment with Consciousness. Children with this Gate may be highly sociable and very sensitive to beauty (e.g., art, music). Naturally gracious, even at a young age, there is always the potential for *dis-grace*. Being prone to emotional highs and lows, they may need extra help understanding and managing their emotions.

Graeme was inconsolable after watching a film; he knew it was a story and not real, but it triggered a deep well of sadness within him. His mom cuddled him close until his sobbing abated and then suggested a walk or cooking to help him find his equilibrium again.

55 Abundance (Victim to Spirit, Outside the Expectations of Others)

Those with Gate 55 have the capacity to access abundance in many different forms as part of their spirited nature and will experience both melancholy and bliss through their lives. A child with Gate 55 will have apparently unreasonable emotions with intense moods; it may seem like they're in their own world sometimes. Notwithstanding these highs and lows, they tend to be especially resilient, and, as children, they may be drawn to spiritual ideas.

Fascinated by history at school, Nina would enter into the world of some of the characters she encountered – Lady Jane Grey was a particular fascination for a while, as she felt for the young woman being such a victim of circumstance and admired her courage and spirit, wondering how she would cope in that situation.

Whether your child has a defined Emotional Solar Plexus or not, they will benefit from learning about emotions, especially at home:

- **Create a safe space.** Ensure your child feels safe to express their emotions and experiences without judgment. This can help them process their emotions and understand their empathetic nature better.
- **Emotional validation.** Validate their feelings and emotions and encourage them to express themselves openly in a safe space. Encourage empathy to help them understand others' feelings better, too.
- **Teaching emotional management techniques.** Skills like deep breathing, mindfulness, meditation, and journaling can be particularly helpful for managing and understanding their feelings better.
- **Fostering self-care.** Emotional energy can be exhausting. Whether your child is processing their own emotions or releasing the emotions they pick up from others, it's important that they learn to prioritize self-care and rest.

In addition, a child with a defined Emotional Solar Plexus is likely to need help learning how to process their emotions and "ride the wave." You can help your child understand emotional cycles by teaching them that it's natural to experience ups and downs in their emotional state. As they get older, you can explain that this is part of their unique design, and it's okay to feel different emotions at different times. These children often need time to process their feelings before making decisions, so it's well worth encouraging patience and giving them the space to understand their emotions before rushing into any big decisions.

If you're a parent with a defined Emotional Solar Plexus in your Human Design, it means you have a consistent and reliable emotional wave that is distinct and personal to you. Your emotions can be intense and can influence others around you, which can make for some tricky interactions if your partner or child has an undefined Emotional Solar Plexus. Left unchecked, those around you can absorb your emotional energies and are less well equipped to process them.

You can help by:

- **Understanding your own emotional wave.** Acknowledge your emotional waves and understand their patterns. This will not only help you manage your emotions but will also assist you in explaining your feelings to your children when necessary.
- **Having patience in decision-making.** With a defined Emotional Solar Plexus, it's beneficial to wait for clarity before making decisions, allowing the emotional wave to pass. Teach this to your children as well – those who have the same definition (and therefore Authority) will benefit from following your example, and those without will need to master such patience with others (a little over 50 percent of the population have this defined). See Chapter 10.
- **Modelling healthy emotional expression.** Show your children that it's okay to experience strong emotions and that there are healthy ways to express them. Teach them about the importance of emotional balance.

A child with an open or undefined Emotional Solar Plexus in their Human Design chart might experience the emotions of others quite intensely, as they tend to absorb and amplify these emotional energies from their surroundings. In particular, they need to understand emotional empathy and learn that their strong emotional reactions might stem from those around them. Help them understand that they can empathize deeply with others but also that they may need to distinguish between their own emotions and those they are absorbing. Teaching them about emotional boundaries and how to protect their own energy when others are experiencing intense emotions will help them avoid emotional overwhelm.

Similarly, parents with an open or undefined Emotional Solar Plexus in their Human Design can absorb and magnify the emotions of those around them. This sensitivity can be both a gift and a challenge, especially when it comes to navigating family dynamics and managing your own well-being. An open and clear Emotions Center often avoids emotional dramas altogether unless they perceive emotional awareness and intelligence in evidence. They move from one drama to another without absorbing another's emotional chaos and mirroring what is playing out without absorbing it.

In addition to modelling emotional boundaries and empathy yourself, both you and your family will benefit from you:

- **Promoting open communication.** Encourage your family to communicate openly about their feelings. This can not only help them process their emotions but also give you insights into the emotional energies you may be picking up.
- **Practicing mindfulness and emotional release.** Incorporate mindfulness practices into your daily routine to help manage absorbed emotions, especially deep breathing at regular intervals during the day.
- **Having patience in decision-making.** You may reach decisions more quickly than those with a defined Emotional Solar Plexus so you may need to be patient with others.
- **Seeking support.** If navigating your emotional energy becomes overwhelming, seek support from a trusted friend, family member, counsellor, or coach. They can provide tools and strategies to help manage your empathetic nature.

THE MIND

The Mind Center (sometimes also called the *Ajna*) is connected to how we conceptualize, analyze, and process information. It's about our thinking processes and how we form opinions and ideas. Here, beliefs and doubts coexist, worries can take hold, and our capacity to rationalize and make sense of the world around us is born. Society has conditioned most of us to try to use the Mind for decision-making, which can lead to anxiety and getting lost in our own heads. Human Design teaches that decision-making is in the body, *not the mind,* which we'll come to in Chapter 10. Once we have made a decision, the Mind is brilliant at helping us execute it. Once we have the "what," the Mind is a fabulous tool for working out the "how."

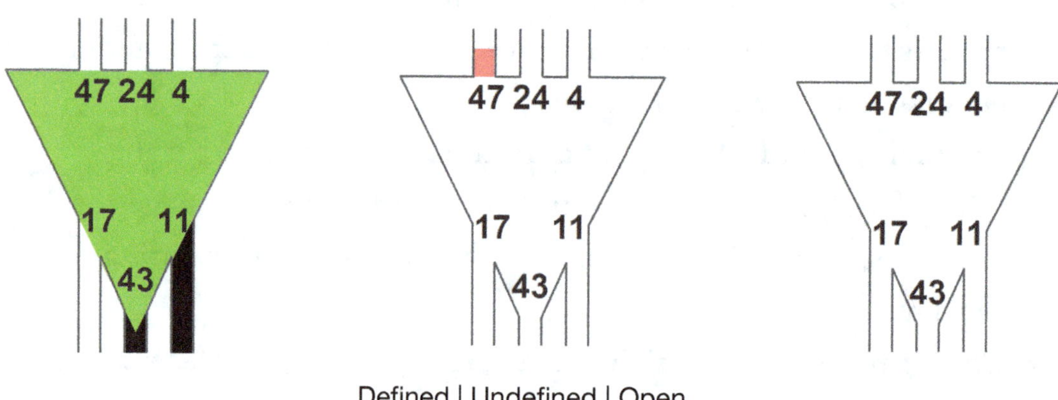

Defined | Undefined | Open

A defined Mind Center is constantly processing thoughts by logic (looking toward the future), making sense (joining the dots), or through insights (perceptive downloads).

If you have a defined Mind Center, you have a consistent way of processing information and thinking. You're likely to have fixed opinions and beliefs, and a reliable way of weighing up the pros and cons of any given course of action. You may also have a constant thirst for knowledge and enjoy learning new things or, conversely, find yourself caught in a cycle of worries and anxieties with a mind that doesn't shut off easily.

If your Mind Center is undefined or open, you have a flexible and adaptable mind that can understand and process information in various ways. However, you might also feel societal pressure to be certain or to maintain consistent ideas or beliefs, even though your natural strength lies in your adaptability. You're likely to be open-minded and able to see multiple perspectives on a single issue. If your undefined or open Mind has become conditioned, you'll likely try to apply the mental solutions of others to your own personal circumstances, as well as pick up the worries of other people and magnify them.

If your child has a defined Mind Center, it is likely to show up in their consistent way of learning and processing information. They may prefer certain types of learning activities over others or show a strong preference for a particular problem-solving approach. These children can form strong opinions and beliefs. Once they make up their mind about something, they tend to stick to it. They may be persistent or stubborn in their viewpoints. They may be highly analytical. They like to delve deep into topics, dissecting and understanding information in detail. They may enjoy subjects like math or science, where this analytical thinking is advantageous. They may have a strong interest in intellectual activities, such as reading, puzzles, or games that require strategy and thought. They enjoy the process of thinking and understanding.

Frank and Philip puzzled their parents. The brothers were great friends and loved playing together despite their three-year age gap. Frank excelled at school and genuinely enjoyed his classes (except drama – why was that even a subject?!). Philip, meanwhile, dragged his feet and counted the days until the next school holiday. When asked what he thought about something, Frank would quickly supply an answer, while Philip did his best impression of a goldfish before mumbling something he hoped no one would catch.

Everything fell into place for their parents when they had Human Design readings and discovered that Frank had a defined Mind Center, while Philip was literally open-

minded. They began encouraging Philip toward drama (despite Frank's eyeroll), design and technology, and the sciences – subjects where he could learn in a hands-on, kinesthetic way rather than relying solely on his mind.

As with every Center, the way a child expresses their defined Mind Center will also be influenced by other aspects of their Human Design chart. As a parent or caregiver, understanding this can help guide them in their learning process and personal growth.

Let's look at each Gate of the Mind Center in turn.

COLLECTIVE

4 Mental Solutions (An Overly Busy Mind)

In adults, this might manifest as a strong ability to create hypotheses or theories, often used in problem-solving, sometimes looking for solutions to problems that don't even exist yet. In children, it might appear as an innate curiosity and love for questions, often asking "why" or "how" about everything around them. They may also appear to go looking for problems to worry over as if they need to keep their Mind busy at all costs.

Jack tended to get slapped down both at home and at school for "being too clever for his own good," because he questioned everything, including his dad's assessment of whether something was even an issue – "But what if it gets worse?" or "How do you know that won't happen?" He wasn't trying to challenge authority; his mind just didn't switch off easily, and thinking things through, even problems that hadn't fully formed, was how he made sense of the world.

11 Harmony (The Search for Nirvana)

This Gate is about having a multitude of ideas and the ability to visualize them at the same time as promoting social harmony. In children, this might manifest as a vivid imagination or a constant stream of ideas and inventions, including a concern that "real" life might never live up to their ideal. They enjoy activities that allow them to express their creativity and can often be found daydreaming or coming up with intricate stories or plans.

Mira adored her dollhouse and would happily spend hours arranging the house and the dolls with detailed stories to go with each new "renovation." As she became a teenager, this continued, although her dollhouse was replaced with a computer game. Much of her creative writing was inspired by ideas that started as virtual family dramas.

17 Following (Does This Compute?)

People with this Gate active in their Design often have a keen sense for what's fair or correct, logical or illogical, beneficial for all. In children, this might show up as a strong sense of right and wrong, a worry that no one can see what's what, a tendency to express their views freely, or a desire to debate or discuss topics of interest.

On hearing her mother complain that "every time the cat comes in, he brings half the garden with him," aged about eight, Pippa cheekily responded, "that's okay then, he can only do it twice." Her logic was irrefutable.

47 Realization (Mental Exhaustion)

Often thought of as the "Eureka!" Gate, those with this Gate can wrestle with problems only to have the solution present itself in moments of relaxation – much like Archimedes, who finally solved the question of whether the King's crown was genuine gold as he rested in the overflowing bath. Children with this gate might show a talent for understanding theoretical concepts, often making connections that others don't see. They can also get lost in the abstract and drive themselves into mental exhaustion, as they over-conceptualize everything.

While staying with a cousin whose house overlooked the sea, Toby's dad showed him an app that enabled him to identify all the ships. Realizing that he could also spot light aircraft from a nearby airport, Toby soon discovered another app that enabled him to identify planes too.

INDIVIDUAL

24 Returning (Can This Be Rationalized?)

This Gate is so called because the Mind can (re)cycle thoughts repeatedly. Eventually, the limits of rational thought are exceeded by innovation, often found in silence. Children with this gate have a drive to grasp things fully, often returning to the same thoughts or ideas again and again until they make sense. This can manifest as a tendency to ask "why" repeatedly (worrying at something much like a dog with a bone), a curiosity about how things work, and an inclination to think deeply about things.

Jess's mom realized her seven-year-old daughter had been a little "off" for a while. So she sat Jess down to inquire what was up. After some coaxing, Jess explained that she didn't understand why her friend Beth hadn't invited her to her birthday party ... unless she wasn't her friend anymore? After each piece of understanding, Jess dug deeper – Beth hadn't had a birthday party. Why not? Her mom had taken Beth and her sisters to the cinema. Why? To celebrate without it being expensive. Why? Because Beth's dad wasn't working so money was tight for them. Why couldn't he work? Because he wasn't well. Was he going to be okay? Hmm, Jess's mom wondered just how much more she needed to explain to her young daughter and tried distracting her by making some cookies for Beth. The question just resurfaced a few hours later....

43 Breakthrough! (How Do I Explain?)

Those with this Gate often have an inner knowing that does not always readily translate to language so there can be frustration in communication. Children with this Gate defined may often have sudden, unexpected insights or ideas, and have a marked capacity to think outside the box. They may also become anxious if they know something and no one is listening to their insight.

Aaron regularly got into trouble for not showing his working out of a math problem in school. He usually understood the method taught, but often came up with his own solution and arrived at the answer through his own ingenuity. Having got the right answer anyway, he couldn't fathom what his teacher's problem was!

Parents with a defined Mind Center can use these qualities to support their children in a variety of ways:

- **Encourage curiosity.** Use your natural analytical abilities to foster a love of learning and curiosity in your children. Encourage them to ask questions and seek answers.
- **Share your insights.** Your defined Mind may bring unique insights. Share your thoughts and perspectives with your children, but also make sure to listen and value their insights as well.
- **Help with problem-solving.** You can guide your children in solving problems by sharing your thought processes with them. Show them

how you analyze situations. This can be particularly useful for older children who are starting to resolve issues by themselves.

- **Support their learning.** With your defined Mind, you may have an ability to grasp complex concepts more easily. You can use this strength to assist your children with their schoolwork, especially subjects that require abstract thinking.

Supporting a child with a defined Mind Center means understanding that this child has a consistent and fixed way of processing information and forming opinions. It is helpful to recognize and validate their perspective, even if you don't always agree. They may need a sounding board to express their thoughts and opinions and an opportunity to articulate their ideas in the safety of their home environment, as they learn the art of sharing their insights. While having a set way of thinking can be a strength, it can also be limiting if the child becomes too rigid. Encourage them to be open to other people's viewpoints and ideas without necessarily adopting them.

A defined Mind can lead to overanalyzing or excessive thinking, so if you notice your child becoming too wrapped up in their thoughts or overly stressed by trying to figure things out, teach them grounding and relaxation techniques. Periodic breaks from constant mental activity are beneficial – encourage activities that are more physical or hands-on, like sports, arts, or just playing outside, to rest the mind and gain perspective.

Understanding and supporting your child's unique design can make a world of difference in their development. It's about celebrating their strengths and providing guidance in areas where they might face challenges.

A child with an undefined or open Mind Center in their Human Design can have a more flexible and adaptable thought process than someone with a defined Mind. However, they can also be influenced by the energies around them, making them sensitive to other people's thoughts and ideas, so allow them to explore different ways of thinking and understanding. Expose them to diverse learning styles and methods so they can discover what resonates with them. Since they can take in thoughts and beliefs from others, they may sometimes be unsure about what they truly think or believe. Validating their experiences can help them in distinguishing between what is truly theirs and what they are amplifying from their surroundings. Let them know it's okay to change their mind or perspective.

The flexibility of an open Mind is a strength, allowing multiple viewpoints. Being open to so many perspectives can sometimes be overwhelming. So, ensure these children have downtime and aren't overloaded with information. Practices like meditation or simply spending time in nature can be grounding. As they grow up, let them know they are especially likely to be influenced by the thoughts and beliefs of those around them. This awareness can help them navigate peer pressure and external influences as they grow, particularly important in the teenage years.

By understanding the nature of an open or undefined Mind and offering consistent support, parents can help their child navigate the complexities of mental processing and belief formation in a way that celebrates their unique strengths and capabilities and potentially avoid the effects of conditioning to some degree. An undefined and clear Mind Center provides intellectual input toward others' dilemmas. An Open and Clear Mind Center offers perceptive answers to others' life situations, by literally being "open-minded."

If you are a parent with an undefined or open Mind Center, you have a wonderful opportunity to share your mental flexibility with your children by:

- **Embracing learning.** Show enthusiasm for the ever-evolving journey of learning. Let your child see that you're always open to new perspectives and that you don't have to know everything. Your genuine curiosity can be infectious.
- **Admitting when you're unsure.** It's okay to tell your child, "I don't know, but let's find out together." This models humility and the

willingness to seek information rather than pretending to have all the answers.

- **Discussing peer pressure.** Since an open Mind can be influenced by external beliefs, have open discussions about peer pressure and the importance of staying true to yourself.
- **Addressing overwhelm.** If you feel overwhelmed by the myriad of thoughts and perspectives, share this with your child once they are old enough to understand. Share coping mechanisms you use, such as journaling or talking things out, meditation, deep breathing exercises, or simply spending quiet moments in nature.
- **Staying curious.** Demonstrate a genuine interest in understanding where others are coming from, even if you don't necessarily agree with them. This teaches empathy and the value of listening.

It can be easy for all of us to get lost in our own minds and allow thoughts to become worries, whether we are blindsided by new insight, stuck in a loop of consistent yet unhelpful thoughts, or simply unable to "switch off" the mental chatter. For everyone, defined or undefined Mind, young or old ... it's hugely beneficial to share our thoughts in a safe space – the adage "a trouble shared is a trouble halved" comes to mind. Revisiting Chapter 6 on our voices may offer additional approaches. It is easy to over-identify with our Mind – after all, we've all been taught that way – so whatever helps you and your children tune into your bodies will also help enormously, whether that's time in nature, yoga, meditation, or your sport of choice.

Just as there are three Centers of Awareness, there are three Centers that push us to *do*, to *act*, and *to make things happen* in our lives, which we'll explore in the next chapter.

CHAPTER 8

DRIVE, WILLPOWER, AND PRESSURE

"The gem cannot be polished without friction, nor man perfected without trials."

— CONFUCIUS

The three Centers of the Crown, the Heart, and the Root can all provide a sense of drive in their different ways — with a busy mind, a determination, or an adrenal push to make things happen. If you have any of these Centers defined, you will be familiar with the push-and-pull, and this can come from any or all of them. For a child, it becomes a life skill to know how to navigate these energies so that they are used in service of their Type and Authority, rather than through habitual behaviors.

HEART, WILLPOWER CENTER

The Heart Center is the seat of willpower, so people with this Center defined have consistent access to determination and an inbuilt means to move mountains, if they so choose. They have the capacity to see things through come what may, but they don't necessarily have endurance unless they also have a defined Sacral/Generator Center.

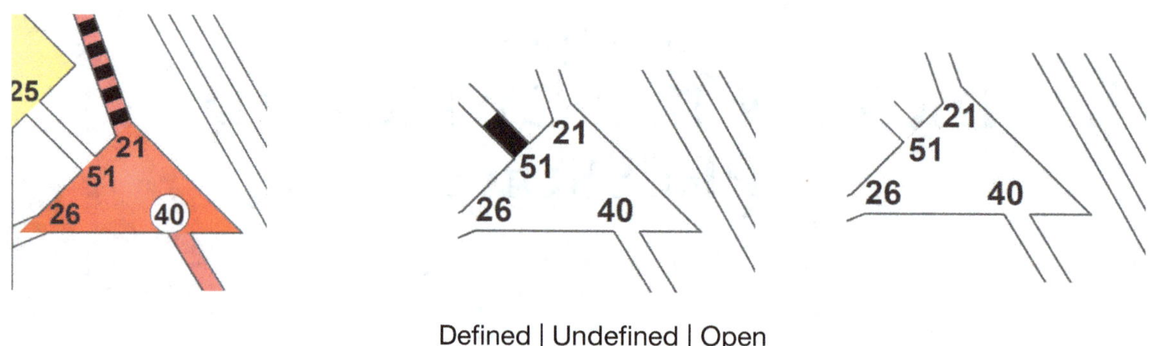

Defined | Undefined | Open

A defined Willpower Center has the power to push through, to achieve, to manage in a short time what might take much longer for others. It is efficient, gets things done ... and then is advised to rest.

An undefined and clear Willpower Center has nothing to prove. It has no need to be in permanent competition but rather is wise about who and what holds value and how to honor and offer that wisdom.

An undefined or open and conditioned Willpower Center can wonder why it takes so much effort to achieve what it pursues, and in achievement, rarely finds a complete sense of satisfaction. Without using awareness, habitually chasing or supporting others' wishes and ideals can become a way of life.

An open and clear Willpower Center is "open-hearted," and potentially generous to a point of foolishness. It witnesses a world in which almost everyone is chasing after things that often hold little or no value, and reminds others of this foolishness in simple ways and clear reflections.

The Heart-Willpower Center involves who and what holds value to us, and who and what does not. As only around 30 percent of the world's population has this Center defined in their Design, and therefore consistent and reliable, it is vital that we comprehend that most people do not have a consistent sense of who and what holds value for them. They can only establish these values through trusting their own Type and Authority in any moment.

For those with a defined Heart Center, it is important to appreciate how powerful it is, and how important it is to evaluate who and what you hold dear. Doing things that might be easy for you is probably going to be much more of a trial for someone with an undefined or open Willpower Center. For someone with defined Willpower, something that takes 5 minutes might easily take 25 minutes or longer for someone with an undefined or open Center. "Give it to me!" "I'll do it for you!" "You're taking so long doing the simplest things!" or "I'll take it from here!" are easy things for someone with defined Willpower to say, without necessarily knowing the potentially debilitating effect they are having on the person to whom they are talking.

Young or old, those with a defined Heart Center make following through on a decision look effortless, and they can be genuinely puzzled that others find it so difficult.

When Fatima was about seven, she decided that all her dolls should be dressed in blue. She spent hours making new outfits for each one and refused to turn her attention to anything else until the very last doll was wearing a shade of blue. It was incomprehensible to her that she should pause for games with her siblings before the task was complete.

In some circles, the Willpower Center has been called the "Ego" Center because it has a forceful energy that is used to take charge or speed things up, often by trampling on everyone involved. Such behavior may be completely unconscious. However, it can cause great damage to everyone concerned, including the perpetrator, if used indiscriminately and not recognized and toned down.

The Heart Center really appreciates rest after exertion. Again, it is not like the Sacral/Generator Center that can recharge as it goes. Those with a defined Heart Center have the means to "get it done," and then need to rest. It has been clearly established that heart disease is one of the leading causes of premature death or unnecessary and limiting illnesses across the world. Understanding the nature of the Heart Center and the right use of willpower is essential, and it is not complicated when everyone trusts their Type and Authority.

Here's a look at each of the Gates of the Heart Center.

TRIBAL GATES

21 Control

Children with this Gate activated may have a strong drive to control their environment. They could display leadership traits and a desire to take charge in certain situations. They might be competitive, with a strong need to win or come out on top.

Although he was the middle child, Ben always seemed to be the boss with his brothers, sometimes controlling the games they played with a laugh and sometimes teasing and taunting to get his way. On more than one occasion, his mom intervened to teach the difference between working for the common good, so they all enjoyed the game, and merely for personal advantage, whereby Ben always came out on top.

26 Accumulation

Children may be focused on the expression of truth and authenticity. They might also be persuasive and good at negotiation. They may demonstrate a keen sense of their worth, what around them is worthwhile, and a strong desire to be acknowledged for this quality. One-half of the Channel of Enterprise, children with this Gate may also embody an entrepreneurial spirit.

From a young age, Sarah was a collector of Pokémon cards, trading wherever she went, school, clubs, and with her siblings. Her parents stepped in when they realized she was even trading her lunch for new cards!

40 Deliverance

Children with this Gate are likely to use their significant willful energy to accomplish many things and will also need personal space and alone time to regroup. They may also feel a strong responsibility toward their community or family but will need time to recharge on their own.

Kay was a straight-A student and fiercely protective of her younger siblings and yet it was a family joke that every so often she would disappear, only to be found up a tree in the woods at the back of their house. Fearing for her safety, her dad built her a tree house of her own so she could retreat from the world whenever she needed.

INDIVIDUAL GATES

Gate 51 Arousing

This Gate is associated with the initiation of the Spirit. Children might be naturally adventurous and willing to step into the unknown. They may also have a knack for keeping others on their toes with their unpredictable actions, or they might handle sudden changes and shocks better than most.

For example, Susanna often surprised her parents and close friends with an unexpected response to some difficulty or other, frequently identifying a "silver lining," while everyone else was still stuck in the issue itself.

A child with both defined Heart and Sacral Centers can exhibit a kind of "perpetual motion" that is impossible to copy or keep up with, and in fact, is worth reviewing when over-exertion becomes apparent. The "keep on doing" of the Generator Center combines with the "willingness" of the Heart Center to accomplish, and all sense of what is worth doing evaporates into massive random activity. Again, in this kind of situation, it is worth reminding the child to go back to their gut response to find out if they are on the right track or just busy being busy. Ask them to pause for a moment to check if their Authority is aligned with the activity. It is tricky stopping any Generator in mid-flight, let alone one who also has willpower to push through anything, but it is very important for a child with this kind of Design to appreciate the quality of their exertions and activities, rather than just their capability to be busy.

For a child with an undefined or open Willpower Center, it is important that they be encouraged to understand that their nature is not willful. There is nothing to prove ... nothing! At least until they are in a situation in which they are crystal clear through engaging their own Type and Authority to commit. What they will find is, if they are in contention with someone who has a defined Willpower and they are not clear in themselves, then on some level, they have already lost whatever argument or issue that seems to be so important at the time. The same applies to parents who have undefined or open Willpower Centers with a child or children with defined Willpower. For the parent, there really is nothing to prove. Try taking a different approach than constantly straining to assert yourself. Often, there is no rhyme or reason to willpower. "I want" has no real justification. Trust in your own Type, Authority, and wisdom to find another way to be in charge.

An undefined or open Heart Center naturally grows in wisdom as it encounters multiple willful-oriented situations in life, being around other people's wants and needs, their pushiness and demands, and recognizing what someone is often chasing after ... love and appreciation.

"What do you want?" "Make up your mind!" can be two of the most confounding statements ever heard, especially for someone with an undefined or open Heart Center. It is almost guaranteed they will make a wrong choice, or at least a choice that is out of alignment with their life, which, therefore, causes issues at some later point. "I don't know!" can be a perfect response when a clear choice has not been established. "Please ask me in a different way, so I can find my own clarity," your child might want to say, or rather, you might pause and say, "Let me ask you in a different way," because it's the kinder way to approach apparent indecision. This pause and different approach may cause frustration to parents and children alike. However, it gives a child the choice to find their own Authority and learn to trust it. It can also take the pressure away from hasty and rushed situations, and potential regrets later.

PRESSURES

The Crown Center and the Root Center are each known as Centers of Pressure – the pressure of unending ideas and inspirations, thoughts that crowd into your Mind, demanding attention from the Crown and the pressure to make things happen *now* as our adrenal system kicks in, activating us to do something, anything, so long as it happens *right now!* To look at each in turn:

The Root Center

The Root Center in Human Design relates to adrenal pressure and is often associated with drive, impulse, and stress. There can be an urgency from the Root Center as our adrenals kick in, demanding action – any action, right now – or conversely providing a significant pause, even a complete lack of motivation to gather any momentum for a change.

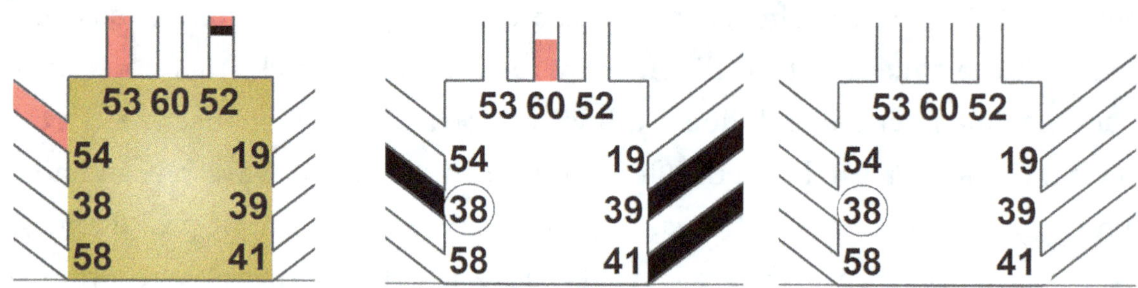

Defined | Undefined | Open

A defined Root Center lives with an ability to handle stressful environments, bringing an urgency to get things moving, but also a stability that is able to be calm yet committed in the middle of chaos.

An undefined and clear Root Center offers guidance in how to bring calm and ride out stressful situations. It finds ways to be grounded, present, and inactive unless there is an inner certainty that involvement is truly necessary.

An undefined or open and conditioned Root Center is restless, impatient, and easily stressed by habitually committing to others' pressures.

An open and clear Root Center is calm, grounded, and present in the middle of confusion, untouched by the pressured agendas playing out around them.

With nine Gates in the Root Center, statistically, most people have it defined, active and turned on all the time. The implied "urgency" that exists within the adrenal glands can be directed in three potential ways:

- **Toward the Spleen Center.** This is connected to our health and well-being and alertness to that well-being through the senses of taste, intuition, and instinct. Any child with a connection from Root to Spleen is encouraged to be active to remain in good health, as they physically engage to "pump" their lymph system by doing so.
- **Toward the Sacral Center.** This means the Root is directed toward "Generator" Life-force energy through what are called "Format"

Channels (See Chapter 12 on Patterns of Human Connection), that override any alternative ways in which the Design is set to engage with life. Here, the Sacral gut response is an essential feature for any child to know whether they are moving in their own ways or are subject to the pressures and timings of the world around them ... and hence the stress that the world mostly considers normal.

- **Toward the Emotions Center.** Remember, this is the whole arena of "life as drama," where there's the pressure to feel connected into the greater family and community through Tribal Circuitry; the unlimited parts of life itself, through the Individual Circuitry; or the desires to fulfill any and all experiences that life can offer through the Collective Abstract/Sensing Circuitry.

For children with a defined Root Center, there is the possibility to engage with life in two different ways: life can be a constant pressure in which there is a compulsion or adrenal energy to keep pushing as a habit; or the defined Root Center can be experienced as a cushion that rests on Mother Earth in a way that consistently provides the vitality to aim toward fulfillment in accord with an inner awareness or sensibility.

"Come on," shouted Archie, drawing out the word in that particular whine children seem to perfect – the one that can send a parent's patience wobbling. He was desperate to get to the swimming pool and found it almost unbearable to wait while his baby sister was changed and made ready. This was the Root Center's impatience in full force: the urge to move now. Sensing the rising pressure, Archie's mom redirected his energy by giving him a job, collecting all the swimming towels from the linen cupboard, buying herself a little time and a moment's peace.

The Gates within the Root Center might show up in children in the following ways:

COLLECTIVE GATES

41 Imagination

Children with this Gate might have a rich inner world of dreams and fantasies. They can be innovative and are often the initiators of new experiences, sometimes holding a vision that unfolds into a rich lifetime. They might feel driven to turn their fantasies into reality, and quite easily inspire others to see beyond any limited horizons.

For example, as a youngster, Rachel had many imaginary friends, much to the irritation of her older brother, who saw this as a form of lying. As Rachel became old enough to write, her imaginary friends started to show up in her stories rather than at the dinner table!

52 Mountain, Stillness

Children with this Gate may have a natural inclination toward meditation and delight in quiet time. They might show a preference for calm environments and have a natural capacity for stillness, and you'll see that they bring a certain calming quality wherever they go.

Rachel also had this Gate and excelled in the children's party game "Sleeping Lions," frequently winning as other children simply couldn't stay still for as long as she could.

53 New Beginnings

A child with this Gate may always be looking for something new and different, embracing new experiences with excitement and showing curiosity in exploring new environments. This child could also be impulsive, wanting to try many things without necessarily finishing them, or being instrumental in getting everyone else started on their own projects and experiences. As they mature, there is a great gift in teaching them to review what they've learned, especially about themselves, even as they move onto the next excitement.

Not content with everything he was learning at school, James wanted to be involved in after-school clubs every day of the week and was deeply frustrated when two things he wanted to try were on the same evening. He lobbied his parents to allow this, and the eventual compromise was that he could do two clubs on a Tuesday, so long as Thursday was a club-free night.

58 Joyous Vitality

Children with this Gate might naturally seek joy and happiness. They might show a strong desire for improvement, wanting to perfect things for the sheer joy of the process. If fostered well, they can be deliberate in not committing to anything without being able to find the joy of being involved in it.

Diana adored performing as a child and maintained her enthusiasm through long hours of rehearsal while other children were flagging – many years later her "Queen Bee" costume still hangs in her wardrobe, eliciting a smile of remembrance every time she looks in her closet.

TRIBAL GATES

Gate 19 Approach

This Gate is associated with sensitivity, and children with this Gate might be highly attuned to the needs, desires, and feelings of those around them. They might display a strong desire for inclusion and can be very sensitive to being excluded. They may have a natural inclination to support and care for others, driven by their acute awareness of what others need or want, sometimes going way beyond what their Authority is trying to tell them.

Farah was eleven years old when her dad was in hospital for the best part of the summer. Rather than play with her friends, she lobbied her mom to spend visiting hours at the hospital, sometimes simply reading a book alongside her dad, allowing conversation to swirl around her unless something specifically caught her attention. Thus, she was both included and able to offer moral support.

54 Ambition

Associated with aspiration and ambition, children with this Gate are likely to have a strong drive for social and material success and it is important that they are guided to trust their own Authority when being involved with those who can help them. They may have a keen awareness of their position within social hierarchies.

At boarding school, it was important to Martin that he be seen as a mover and shaker within his year group and yet not at the expense of his own principles. This was evident when he organized a high-profile year-group fundraiser, successfully rallying influential peers and staff support. When encouraged to sideline a quieter student for the sake of effi-ciency and optics, he chose inclusion over advantage, learning how to pursue recognition without compromising his own inner sense. He embodied both the material and spiritual ambitions characteristic of people with this Gate.

INDIVIDUAL GATES

38 Opposition

This Gate is associated with the energy to persevere. Children might show a fighting spirit, with a drive to overcome challenges and a determination not to give up in the face of struggle. Children with this Gate benefit from learning to pick their battles.

Amy had a blanket curfew of 9 p.m., which she kept missing, staying out later, especially at weekends. She ended up being grounded ... a lot. Tired of the constant battles between Amy and her dad, Amy's mom explored her daughter's reluctance to be home on time, discovering that a local ice cream parlor she loved didn't close until 10 p.m. The conflict was resolved by agreeing to a 10.15 p.m. curfew on weekends and staying home Sunday to Thursday unless Amy asked for permission.

39 Provocation

Gate 39 is linked with the energy to provoke change. Children may have a knack for challenging the status quo and disrupting routines. They might challenge others to elicit change and progress, or it may be entirely unconscious, and they elicit a reaction without trying!

As a child, Mateo was often left puzzled by other people's reactions. When he offered practical suggestions – such as organizing a systematic search for his parents' misplaced car keys or recommending an alternative textbook to help a friend struggling with history – his input frequently triggered irritation or defensiveness rather than relief. Over time, those around Mateo began to recognize that his comments were not personal challenges. Instead, his energy had a way of exposing what wasn't working, often before people were ready to acknowledge it.

60 Limitation

This Gate is about dealing with limitations and the pressure to change. Children with this Gate might show an understanding of how to work within restrictions and an ability to accept and deal with significant changes in life. Indeed, they may find limitations become a springboard for advancement.

For example, Eddie surprised his parents by getting a weekend job cleaning cars soon after he turned thirteen. He explained to his parents that his pocket money was insufficient to purchase the new bike he wanted so this was his solution. Needless to say, they were delighted!

For children with undefined or open Root Centers, relaxation techniques are essential. Potential pressures and stresses are everywhere: at home, in school, in public and also on social media and casual interactions. Teaching a child meditation and how to find an inner quiet is a gift that can last a lifetime. Sports, walks, and playgrounds followed by rest can ease away stress. Showers, baths, and swimming can quickly disperse built-up pressures. Yoga and other gentle physical exercises can be tailored to stretch a young body and join body and mind together.

THE CROWN CENTER

The Crown Center in the Human Design life chart is unique in that it only contains three Gates, only connects to one other Center, (the Mind Center), and is shown to be partly in the body and partly outside. Energetically, it relates to the pineal gland, attunes to its current environment and is the source of flashes of inspiration that come on multiple levels.

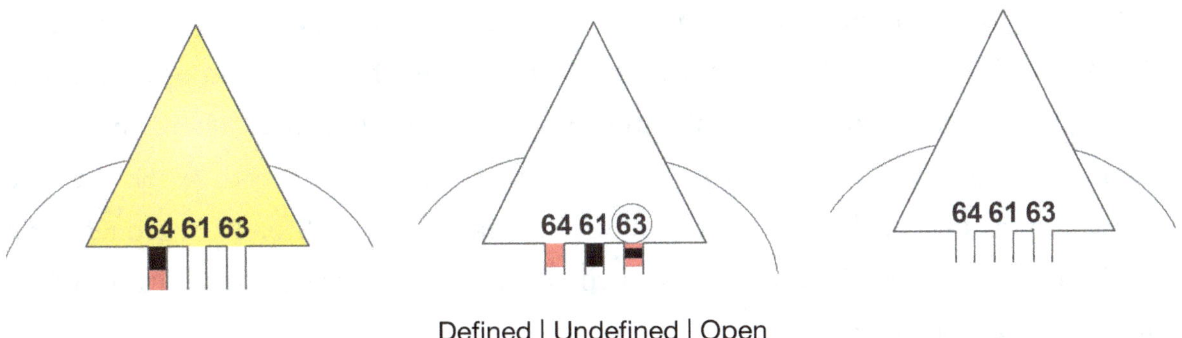

Defined | Undefined | Open

Present-day science says that the pineal gland has certain functions within the body, including regulating the production and release of melatonin, an important hormone that relates to sleep cycles and reproduction. Mystics will indicate the association between the pine-shaped pineal gland and visions and abilities connected with the third eye.

Most people do not have a defined and activated Crown Center, and therefore are open to inspirations coming through interactions with other people, or exposure to art, architecture, music, nature, and other potentially moving or interesting aspects of life. As to whether any inspiration becomes more than just a passing fancy is always reliant on Type and Authority. Often, children with open or undefined Crown Centers can get swept away on other people's interests and excitements until they have the opportunity to sit back and attune to their own nature to find out if the attraction is really theirs or not.

A defined Crown Center is constantly processing input.

An undefined and clear crown Center offers wisdom, interpreting others' life scenarios.

An undefined or open and conditioned Crown Center tries to arrange its personal life according to others' terms.

An open and clear Crown Center is fascinated by anything and everything, often reflecting this interest to others.

Those who do have a defined Crown Center also have a Mind Center that is constantly processing all kinds of information. The Crown Center exerts pressure to be mentally assured that everything makes sense, that everything is truthful and aligned or associated with a potentially successful future. There are three streams in which inspiration is processed, providing the drive to work out the significance of everything, relevant or not so that it fits in life. This process can easily become a pressure that builds until some form of mental resolution, often temporary, has happened.

Zaria's Crown and Mind were always active, even on holiday. Which university course might allow her to travel? What about a career in international relations? Where could she study that was close enough to home but not too close? Did she have a dress for graduation? Who should she invite to her birthday party next month? Even her boyfriend, who'd joined the family trip, asked her to give it a rest. She couldn't, so she simply went quiet. A little later, she was accused of being "away with the fairies" when she didn't respond to some good-natured teasing. Honestly, she thought, she could never win with this family.

When the Crown and Mind Centers are defined, there is a consistent inner pressure to think, to question, and to make sense of things, creating a mental stream that doesn't switch off. This can look like distraction or withdrawal to others, but it is simply this Design doing what it is designed to do. Parents can support children like Zaria by offering calm space and reassurance that not every thought or question needs an immediate answer.

The three Gates – 64, 61, and 63 – each access inspiration in their own ways.

COLLECTIVE

64 Diverse Possibilities

This Gate is part of the Abstract/Sensing Circuit and has a perspective that joins past experiences with present ones. In the traditional I Ching, it is called "Before Completion," as though it asks, has every possibility been considered? Has something been overlooked or ignored? It tends to look back into past references to see if it is up to date in any present conclusions. It can have a certain brilliance in pointing out to other people aspects in their plans of formulas they might have avoided or not fully considered. Children who have this Gate are inclined toward historical or religion-based references to question what has taken place before that likely makes sense now, or else needs more investigation.

Greg can always be relied on to fill in the blanks for anyone who thinks they've got the whole picture, but who he considers has taken shortcuts in their process, and needs more ideas and viewpoints, to make their adventure complete. "What about x, y, or z?" is a question he asks frequently.

63 Doubts

As a part of the Collective Logic Circuitry, Gate 63 questions anything and everything about life in a process that tries to ensure safe, future-oriented, and apparently logical outcomes. In the traditional translation from the I Ching, Gate 63 is called "After Completion," as though to question whether everything is going to work properly. Doubts are often important when certain things look to be unaligned or about to fail. However, they can become intrusive if they are a form of reasoning to always "play it safe." Being in the Logic Circuitry, Doubts is very much part of the world's science, engineering, and judicial systems, and children with this Gate can be drawn to want to check the "facts" of any process or situation. It can also be a part of a child's way of perfecting their gifts and talents, and with it, they can easily point out the potential failings in other people's plans. However, the most important thing to remember about anything in the Collective Circuitry is that it involves systems, opinions, beliefs, and processes that might find improvement, and is absolutely not personal.

George loves his science projects and is fascinated by experiments, sometimes taking things to pieces to make sure they are all working properly. He is painstaking in his ways and sometimes gets really upset when things do not turn out perfectly, or he has difficulty putting things back together again. His distress was less about the mess itself and more about the fear that something important had gone wrong.

INDIVIDUAL, KNOWING CIRCUITRY

61 Inner Truth

Gate 61 relies on an environment in which truth is considered normal, and untruth not. Any child with this Gate sooner or later is going to shun or question people who cannot be truthful with them. Even white lies will have repercussions in the future once reality has set in, unless a complete explanation is given as to why they were used. Being acoustic in nature, children with this Gate quickly attune to what resonates with them and who and what does not. Children with this Gate will have a sensitivity that goes beyond "normal" childlike expectancies, in that they might exhibit psychic and paranormal qualities that can either be encouraged or else dismissed because they challenge society's processes and are considered weird.

Cheryl tended to keep to herself, often absorbed in her own inner world. From time to time, she would say things that caught adults off guard, observations or questions that seemed to come from nowhere, yet later proved uncannily accurate. She was also the child who questioned stories others accepted without hesitation; when told about the tooth fairy, she listened politely before saying, "That doesn't sound right." In the same way, she would quietly challenge explanations that didn't ring true to her, even when everyone else seemed content to go along with them.

Children with undefined or open Crown and Root Centers are designed to be more laid back than their contemporaries. They may be unmoved when everyone else is leaping into action. This lack of motivation is not necessarily a form of laziness; it is just that they don't experience the need to work something out mentally or get something done until they have their own inner inclination to do so. On the other hand, they can be very capable of pointing out that someone else is not using their brain to full capacity, or getting things done properly.

Undefined and open Centers are places of great potential wisdom for children if they are encouraged to use them carefully. When children are committed to an activity because they are in the company of those who have the Heart, Crown, and Root Centers defined, it is important that once the company has departed or they are on their own again, they have space and time to decompress.

Having looked at each of the Centers and the Gates that activate them, let's turn to the different Types, which are identified by groups of defined and/or undefined Centers. These groups, or Types, have particular ways of being in the world. Knowing your Type, and those of your nearest and dearest, can help you maximize your gifts, live on your own terms, and enjoy your life to the fullest.

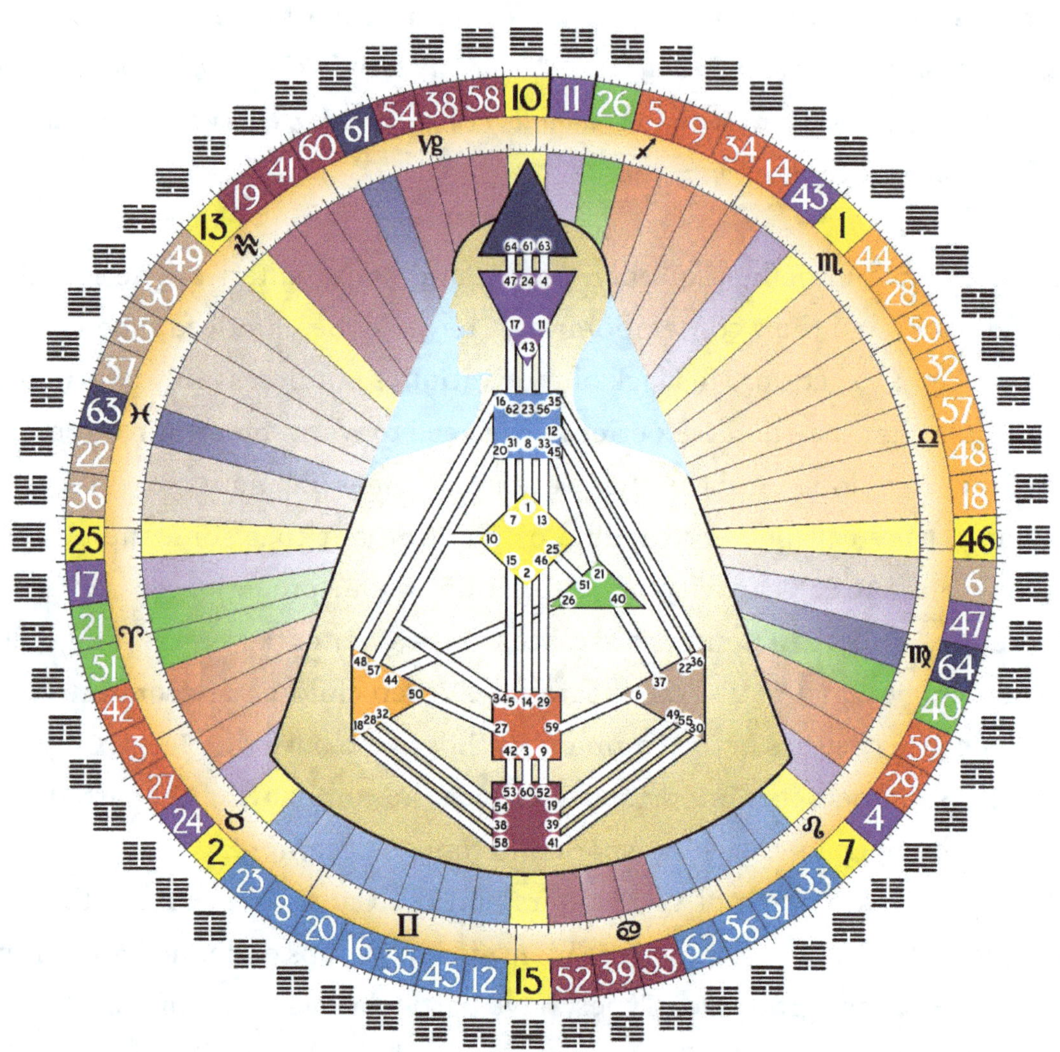

CHAPTER 9

WHY CAN'T WE ALL BE MANIFESTORS?

"It is time for parents to teach young people early on that in diversity there is beauty and there is strength."

— MAYA ANGELOU

For those new to Human Design, there can be something alluring about the idea of being a Manifestor, a kick-ass initiator who makes things happen. Yet it can be the lonelier path, forever starting things up without the staying power to see it through ... nor the need (though possibly the desire) to have a bunch of mates alongside. There can also be confusion between initiating something and creating things – we are all creators, just in different ways. While the Manifestor might decide to paint on a whim, the Generator might be drawn to paint a fabulous sunset (in response). The MG might also be drawn to that same sunset and then decide to use the colors in a new pottery glaze. The Projector might be invited to teach others how best to capture the sunset on film, and the Reflector might set up a display to show everyone's work and include a collage they created too.

This chapter takes a deeper dive into the different energy Types and how they can show up in children, and how they can be supported. You'll also have a chance to look at the different parenting challenges and opportunities for each of those Types. By understanding the nuances of your energy Type, you can harness your strengths, be aware of potential pitfalls, and create a nurturing environment where both you and your children thrive.

MANIFESTORS

Manifestors are the go-getters, the catalysts that make it all happen. The term can be confusing because, yes, we all have the capacity to manifest; indeed, many would say that we all manifest our own realities. In Human Design, it refers to the initiators, the trailblazers who set things alight with a spark that gets things going. Less than 10 percent of the population are Manifestors.

Looking at a Human Design chart, Manifestors all have a defined Throat, which is seen as the seat of manifestation. In addition, one of the motor Centers – Heart, Emotions, or Root – is defined and connected to the Throat, directly or via another Center. The Sacral Center is not defined. Consequently, Manifestors tend to work in bursts of activity and then need to rest.

Manifestor Children

As children, they might show the following characteristics:

- **Initiative.** Manifestor children often initiate activities and are inclined to act independently. They don't necessarily feel the need to wait for the approval or participation of others.
- **Innovation.** They tend to be creative, with a knack for coming up with new ideas or ways of doing things.

- **Leadership.** Manifestors often naturally step into leadership roles, even at a young age. They can rally their peers behind an activity and inspire others to follow their lead.
- **Independence.** These children may prefer to play or work on projects alone, showing a sense of self-sufficiency.
- **Impatience.** Because Manifestors are wired to initiate and act, they might become impatient when others don't move at their pace or when their path is obstructed.
- **Intensity.** Manifestor children might display an intense demeanor, with a lot of energy and passion about their interests.
- **Need for autonomy.** These children might resist control and prefer to have autonomy over their decisions and actions. This can sometimes result in power struggles with authority figures who don't understand their need for independence.

Steve, a nine-year-old Manifestor, was sitting at the counter, feasting his eyes on a cake perched out of reach in front of him. It was lunch time, and his mom had just prepared a plate and placed it in front of him.

"I want cake!" declares Steve.

"But it's lunchtime, and I need you to eat what I've put on your plate because it's all your favorite healthy food I've made specially for you," replies Mom. Undeterred, Manifestor Steve comes back: "I want cake."

Remembering what she knew about Manifestors catalyzing anything that appeals to them, she tells Steve: "Okay! You can have as much cake as you like, after you've finished your lunch plate." Without a moment's hesitation, Steve dives into his lunch. Minutes later, he's finished, gets down from his seat, and excuses himself to go play in the garden. Cake is completely forgotten.

Manifestor children, according to the Human Design system, naturally and effortlessly initiate action and make things happen. This often conflicts with society's expectations of children's behavior: to follow rules and defer to adult authority. To help Manifestor children be themselves, adults can:

- **Provide an understanding environment.** Create an environment that respects their need for independence and initiation. This might mean allowing them more autonomy in their daily routine or giving them space to pursue their interests within clear boundaries.
- **Teach them to inform.** One key aspect of the Manifestor Type is the need to inform others before initiating. Encourage them to communicate their plans and intentions before they act. This can help reduce resistance and misunderstanding from others.
- **Teach healthy ways to handle anger.** Help them learn patience and develop strategies for dealing with interruptions, obstacles, or delays in a constructive way.
- **Respect their energy.** Understand that Manifestors may have bursts of energy followed by periods of rest. Try not to force them into a steady, consistent routine if that's not what works for them.
- **Build their self-confidence.** Manifestor children may sometimes feel different or misunderstood because of their innate characteristics. Provide reassurance and positive reinforcement to help them feel confident in who they are.

Every child is unique, and these ideas may need to be adapted to fit each child's individual needs and personality. It's also important to ensure that while allowing Manifestor children to express themselves freely, they also learn to respect the needs and boundaries of others. The goal is to provide guidance that helps them navigate the world in a way that is true to their nature while also considering the well-being of those around them.

Manifestor Parents

Regardless of your children's Type, if you are a Manifestor yourself, there are some unique challenges to parenting:

- **Impulsivity.** The ability to initiate can sometimes lead to impulsiveness. Remember to consider the long-term implications of your actions, especially when it affects your family.
- **Overwhelm.** Being a Manifestor and a parent can be overwhelming at times. It's essential to recognize when you need to rest and recharge. At least a little "me time" without interruption is essential for your long-term well-being.
- **Misunderstandings.** If you're not communicating your intentions, it can lead to misunderstandings. Always strive for clear communication, especially with your children.
- **Being overprotective.** Because of your natural drive to pave the way, you might feel the urge to overly protect or shelter your kids. Allow them to face challenges and grow from their experiences.

You also have some particular strengths to offer your family:

- **Trailblazing.** You can show your children the importance of paving their own path and the value of determination.
- **Resilience.** By nature, Manifestors face a lot of resistance in life because they are often initiating new things. This resilience can be a valuable lesson for your children.
- **Empowerment.** You can teach your children to be empowered individuals who trust themselves and act on their dreams.

GENERATORS

Generators are known for their life-force energy and their ability to respond to life around them. Their Sacral Center is defined without any connection to the Throat Center. They account for about 33 percent of the population, and they are the folk who see things through to the, sometimes bitter, end.

Generator Children

The main characteristics of children who are Generator Types are:

- **Consistent energy.** Generator children tend to have a stable and consistent flow of energy, crucially so long as they are enjoying what they are doing. They are often busy and involved in various activities, constantly processing the world around them.
- **Responders by nature.** They are not initiators. Instead, they wait to respond to things in their environment. For example, they might react more positively to an activity or a task if it's presented as a question that they can respond to rather than a blunt instruction.
- **Gut responses.** Generators have a noticeable sacral response, which is an innate gut feeling of energy rising or falling. Children might show clear signs of what they want or don't want through body language or vocal sounds before they can even articulate it – the "ah-ha" or "nuh-uh."
- **Frustration.** A common theme for Generators is feeling frustrated when they're not engaged in fulfilling activities or when they try to initiate actions rather than waiting to respond.
- **Need for engagement.** They thrive when they're engaged in activities that resonate with them. You'll find that they can get deeply engrossed in tasks or play that align with their inner response.

Billy's parents were shocked to see him pick up chopsticks and use them correctly when they took the children to Chinatown for a treat meal out. Mom and Dad looked at each other and shook their heads – neither had taught him. Hmm. Relaying the story to the nursery staff on Monday morning, Rebecca laughed, "Oh yes, that'll be Billy! We celebrated Chinese New Year by laying out raisins and chopsticks and allowing them to eat each one they could pick up and move to their plate without dropping it. Once the break time bell went, all the other children grabbed their snacks and headed outside. Billy didn't move until he'd picked up every last raisin!"

The best ways to support Generator Children are:

- **Asking yes-no questions.** Instead of telling them what to do, ask questions. For example, instead of saying, "Do your homework," you might ask, "Is it a good time for homework now?" This allows them to respond, which aligns with their design.
- **Help them tune into their gut.** Encourage them to listen to their gut response. If it's not obvious by their reaction, ask them to tell you whether they feel energized or depleted by a proposed course of action.
- **Provide opportunities.** Expose them to various activities and environments, allowing them to find what truly engages and resonates with them.
- **Patience.** Understand that they need to wait to respond, and this is a natural part of their process. It's not about being indecisive; it's about waiting for their internal guidance. This will be especially true if they have Emotional Authority (see Chapter 10).
- **Handling frustration.** Recognize signs of frustration and teach them to identify what is causing it. Often, it might be because they are not engaged in what they are doing, or they are going against their natural response mechanism.

- **Encourage physical activity.** While Generators have consistent energy, they also need to deplete that energy daily. Ensure they get enough physical activity and then a good night's rest to recharge.
- **Celebrate their achievements.** Generators can accomplish a lot when they're in alignment and tend to see things through to the end, giving a great opportunity to celebrate their accomplishments.

By understanding and supporting the design of Generator children, adults can foster an environment where they thrive and develop a deep sense of self-awareness and purpose.

Generator Parents

If you are a Generator, you will see yourself in the description above, much of which may resonate from your own childhood. Generators often benefit from routines so a consistent routine can help both you and your children feel grounded and secure. Using your own gut response to guide your parenting demonstrates this capacity for your children, which will be helpful for them if they are Generators or MGs. Generators thrive when they are engaged and passionate about what they're doing, so find ways to integrate your children into activities that light you up. This not only keeps you fulfilled but also serves as a model for your children.

In essence, as a Generator parent, you have a lot to offer, most especially:

- **Stamina.** Generators have the stamina to keep up with the demands of parenting. You can handle long days and nights and still have the energy for play and engagement.
- **Modeling passion.** Your ability to dive deeply into tasks and activities you love can be a wonderful example for your children, teaching them the value of commitment and passion.

- **Getting to the finish line.** As a natural completer/finisher, you can show your children the benefit of completing tasks and seeing things through to the end.

While Generators have the energy to have a lot of fun with their children, they need to beware of:

- **Overcommitting.** Generators can sometimes take on too much because they feel they have the energy for it. Overcommitting can lead to burnout and a lack of quality time with your children.
- **Not setting boundaries.** While it's natural for Generators to wait for something to respond to, sometimes proactive steps and setting boundaries ahead of time are essential with your children.

MANIFESTING GENERATORS (MGS)

MGs have the defined Sacral of the Generator as well as a Motor Center connecting to the Throat Center, hence having aspects of both Generators (gut response) and Manifestors (capacity to initiate). Crucially, MGs need to learn to wait to respond *before* they initiate. They account for about 37 percent of the population.

Manifesting Generator (MG) Children

Characteristics of MG Children include:

- **Busy and active.** They typically have a lot of energy and may bounce from one activity to another, showing interest in a variety of things. They may be drawn to multiple things at once and have a capacity to multitask.

- **Responsive action.** Like Generators, they're designed to wait to respond, but once they do, they can move into action swiftly, often skipping steps that might seem necessary to others.
- **Impatience.** The fastest of all the Types, they often want to get things done quickly and might become impatient if they feel things are moving too slowly.
- **Changing their mind.** They may want to check out all the options before settling on a course of action, often appearing to choose at the last possible moment. This is because they are continually checking in with their Sacral to see if they still have energy for that activity. This is in marked contrast with the Generator, who has started so they'll finish. The fact that MGs can appear to change their mind can be very frustrating to those who expect them to follow through. Reminding yourself and your MG child that an initial yes is really a "yes, maybe," can help relieve disappointments and expectations for all concerned.
- **Great achievers.** Of all the Types, MGs are the great achievers, and their greatest satisfaction comes from being completely clear before committing themselves totally to anyone or anything. This clarity often involves patience and ongoing alignment with their Authority, and is not the same thing as hesitancy. Once clear, they excel!

Maya took a deep breath and dialed, smiling at the phone when she heard her dad's customary "yo" by way of greeting. Oh, but this was tough. How can she tell him she'd changed her major – again? "Um, hi Dad." Her dad chuckled, "What you got for me this time, girl?" "Well, you know I switched from law to medicine. I'm switching again to veterinarian medicine." Much to her surprise, her dad laughed, "What one species not enough to keep you busy, you need a whole lot more?! What's that going to mean practically in terms of time and money?" Maya breathed a sigh of relief and started to explain.

MG Children can best be supported by:

- **Encouraging exploration.** They will naturally want to try many different things. Encourage this exploration and allow them to find what truly engages them.
- **Having patience.** The MG process, involving checking things out before committing, often at the last minute, can require significant patience from others. In addition, since they may skip steps in their own eagerness to complete a task or move onto the next, teaching them the value of patience and occasionally revisiting missed steps is beneficial.
- **Asking closed questions.** Engage their response mechanism by asking yes-no questions. This helps them tune into their sacral response, which is their essential first step before they initiate.
- **Providing physical outlets.** Given their high energy, physical activities or sports can be a great way for them to expend energy and find focus.
- **Teaching reflection.** Due to their quick nature, they might benefit from occasionally pausing to reflect on their actions and decisions. This doesn't mean slowing them down unnecessarily, but helping them cultivate a sense of awareness.

Understanding and embracing the energy of an MG child can help adults guide them in a way that honors their Design. With the right support, these children can harness their energy and potential to achieve great things.

Manifesting Generator (MG) Parents

Carrying both sustained energy and an initiating spark, MGs often have a lot of energy. This gives an advantage in having the energy to engage in activities with your children, multitasking when needed, and being an active participant in their lives.

Your ability to juggle tasks and move quickly can inspire them, as you show your children the importance of responding by checking in with your Sacral and then taking swift action. MGs often change directions quickly, so you can use this ability to be flexible in parenting, adapting to your child's needs as they evolve.

Potential pitfalls for an MG parent include:

- **Skipping steps.** MGs tend to move so quickly that they sometimes skip essential steps. In parenting, this might mean missing key moments or not fully preparing for certain situations. It's essential to pause occasionally and reassess.
- **Impatience.** Your desire to get things moving might make you impatient when things don't go as swiftly as you'd like, especially if your children are not of the same energy type.
- **Not waiting to respond.** While you have the spark of a Manifestor, it's still vital for MGs to wait for something to respond to *before* acting. Jumping into situations without this can lead to challenges.

Your greatest strengths as a parent are:

- **Adaptability.** Your ability to change direction and adapt is an asset in parenting, as children's needs and situations change frequently.
- **Energy and enthusiasm.** Your energy can be infectious, leading to fun, engaging, and active moments with your children.
- **Multitasking mastery.** The myriad tasks of parenting can be more manageable for MGs due to their innate ability to handle multiple things simultaneously.

- **Modeling passion.** When you find something you love, you dive deep. This passion can inspire your children to find and pursue what lights them up.

Being an MG parent provides a dynamic environment for children. While challenges exist, understanding and harnessing your unique energy Type can lead to a fulfilling and active parenting experience. Remember to balance your swift nature with moments of reflection and connection, ensuring that while you might move quickly, you don't miss precious moments along the way.

PROJECTORS

Projectors wait to be recognized and invited to offer their insights or to participate in activities. They won't automatically assume that they can join in with others unless or until they are invited. Indeed, if they try to "muscle their way into something," they are likely to be rebuffed. They have neither the defined Sacral Center of a Generator or an MG, nor a motor center (Emotional Solar Plexus, Heart, or Root) connecting to the Throat, as in a Manifestor.

Projector Children

Children who are Projectors will exhibit distinct characteristics that reflect their Type:

- **Limited energy reservoir.** Unlike Generators and MGs, Projectors don't have a consistent energy source. They might have bursts of energy followed by periods of needing rest.
- **Observant.** Projectors are naturally observant and tend to watch and understand the world around them. They're often seen as wise beyond their years.

- **Sensitive to energy.** They can sense the energy of people and environments around them, making them sensitive to moods, situations, and atmospheres.
- **Desire to guide.** Even at a young age, Projector children might exhibit a natural tendency to guide or lead their peers, not through energy or initiation, but through their understanding and insights.
- **Outsiders.** Projectors are naturally "outsiders" in that to observe and then be ready to guide, they cannot be constantly involved in everyone else's activities. Once invited in, and clear to participate, they can gauge their level of involvement before standing aside once more.
- **Potential to feel overlooked.** If they don't receive the recognition they innately seek, they might feel overlooked or undervalued.

Consequently, you can best support Projector Children by:

- **Recognizing them.** Their abilities, insights, and unique perspectives. Valuing their contributions can help them feel seen and appreciated.
- **Inviting participation.** Use the language of invitation. This aligns with their strategy in the Human Design system. Ask if they'd like to join an activity or share their thoughts.
- **Encouraging rest.** Understand that they don't have the consistent energy that some other types might have. Ensure they have enough time to rest and recuperate.
- **Creating a safe environment.** Given their sensitivity to energies, creating a safe, nurturing environment where they don't feel overwhelmed is crucial. Reinforce the idea that their worth isn't tied to how much they do but rather their unique perspective and guidance.
- **Teaching them about energy.** Help them understand their energy dynamics. Let them know it's okay not to have the consistent energy that some of their peers might have.

- **Helping them navigate relationships.** Projectors can become deeply entwined in relationships. Teach them about healthy boundaries and the importance of choosing relationships where they feel recognized and valued.

Angela, a Manifestor mom, has a beautiful teenage daughter, Giselle, who's a Projector. Angela was always getting stuff done: organizing, gardening, cooking, broadcasting, and running a small company.

Giselle was living a much more laid-back lifestyle, going to college, hanging out with friends, using her smartphone ... and Angela was getting more and more frustrated in trying to get Giselle "up to speed."

When she realized her Projector daughter needed recognition of her particular qualities and invitations to be involved in her mom's frenetic life, everything changed. Angela suddenly found an ally and guide, who was also her daughter, and she started adjusting her pace and lifestyle accordingly.

What transpired was a whole new form of relating in which they honored each other's very different processes, but when they came together to combine their abilities, everything became more fun and constructive.

By understanding the specific characteristics of a Projector child, parents and caregivers can offer the support, recognition, and environment these children need to thrive. Remember, Projectors bring an invaluable perspective to the world, and with the right support, they can shine brilliantly.

Projector Parents

Raising children as a Projector offers a journey different from that of other types. Given your sensitivity to energy, it's essential to set boundaries for your well-being. Make time for yourself, ensuring you have the space to rest and rejuvenate. In a world that often values consistent output and "doing," Projectors might feel the pressure to do more, potentially leading to exhaustion. Recognize that your energy operates differently. Focus on providing quality interactions and guidance, rather than trying to match the consistent energy output of Generator types. Projectors are naturally attuned to guiding and understanding others, which can be both a boon and a challenge in parenting.

Challenges include:

- **Overexertion.** Projectors don't have the same energy reservoir as Generators. Trying to keep up can lead to burnout. It's essential to recognize your limits.
- **Going unrecognized.** As a parent, it might feel challenging when your efforts go unnoticed or unappreciated. Share this need with family members – it may not be obvious to other Types and a little recognition can go a long way to soothing a frazzled Projector.
- **Over-involvement in relationships.** Projectors can become deeply involved in the dynamics of relationships. It's crucial to maintain a balance and ensure that you don't lose yourself in the process of parenting.

That said, Projectors have some great opportunities as parents to offer:

- **Guidance.** Your ability to guide and offer insights can create a nurturing environment for your children, where they feel deeply understood and supported.
- **Deep connections.** Projectors can form profound connections with others. This can lead to a deep and meaningful relationship with your children.
- **Intuition and insight.** Your intuitive nature can help you understand your children's needs, even when they might not be able to articulate them themselves.

- **Modeling self-awareness.** By understanding and living true to your Projector nature, you model the importance of self-awareness and authenticity to your children.

In essence, as a Projector parent, you bring a depth of understanding and connection that is unparalleled. By being aware of the potential challenges and embracing your innate strengths, you can create a nurturing environment where both you and your children thrive. Remember, it's not about how much you do, but the quality and depth of your interactions that make the difference.

REFLECTORS

Reflectors are the rarest type in the Human Design system, making up only about 1 percent of the population. Reflectors have all nine centers in their Design undefined or open – not colored in – which means they sample the energies around them deeply. As they are processing so much input from the world around them, they can appear slow to others and consequently be misunderstood. They mirror or amplify the energy of their environment, which can be a challenge, especially for children.

Reflector Children

Characteristics of Reflector Children include:

- **Sensitivity to their environment.** Given their completely undefined design, they're highly sensitive to the energy of places, people, and situations around them. They can feel the moods and energies of those nearby.
- **Evolving identity.** Their identity and energy can seem changeable, shifting based on where they are and who they're with. One day, they

might be energetic and bubbly, and the next, calm and introspective, depending on their environment.

- **Gaining wisdom through experience.** They have the potential to gain deep wisdom about the human experience because they sample so many different energies. This can be apparent at a surprisingly young age.
- **Needing time and space.** Reflectors operate on a lunar cycle, taking around 28 days to make major decisions as they explore options, discuss possibilities with trusted others, and sample and process different energies.

Sally looked so dejected coming out of the school bus that her mom, Jane, what on earth was wrong. On inquiry, Sally scuffed her shoes and mumbled, "I got in trouble with Miss Jones today." That seemed so unlike her, Jane asked gently, "Why was that, love?"

Sally took her hand and explained, "I was late coming in from break-time. I'd spotted a snail with a really beautiful shell, all different colors, and the birds could have gotten it if I didn't move it. I was looking for a good place where it wouldn't be seen and didn't hear the bell. Miss Jones didn't believe me." And with that, Sally sniffed.

Jane sighed; her sweet daughter was always rescuing things, as evidenced by the now three rescue cats they had at home. "Well, I'm sure the snail was very grateful, Sally. Let's hope Miss Jones has forgotten by tomorrow. There are fresh-baked cookies waiting for you at home now." Sally looked up at her mom and smiled, squeezed her hand, and dropped it as she skipped on down the road.

Supporting Reflector Children can include:

- **Provide stability.** Given their sensitivity, a consistent, stable, and nurturing environment helps them feel secure.
- **Choose environments carefully.** Be mindful of places and situations,

recognizing that chaotic or overly intense environments might be overwhelming for them.

- **Encourage regular "alone time."** Allow them time alone or in nature to discharge energies they've absorbed and to reconnect with themselves. These are the children that absolutely need a space to call their own, be it a study area, their own bedroom or a garden shed so that they can retreat when they need to.
- **Patience with decision-making.** Recognize that they need more time to make decisions. Encourage them to listen to themselves, their feelings, and intuitions over a more extended period.
- **Educate them about their energy.** As they grow older, teaching them about their Reflector nature will empower them to navigate the world in a way that's true to their design rather than being overly swayed by their peers. Encouraging open dialogue about how their environment affects them helps them understand and articulate their unique experiences.
- **Avoid labeling.** Given their changeable nature, it's essential not to label or pigeonhole them into fixed roles or characteristics.
- **Celebrate their uniqueness.** Help them understand and cherish their unique ability to experience and reflect the world's energies.

Reflector children offer a unique lens through which to view the world. With understanding and support, they can navigate their open and sensitive design, providing invaluable insights into the human experience. It's essential to provide them with the tools and understanding they need, fostering a sense of self-worth and empowering them to embrace their unique nature.

Reflector Parents

As a Reflector, you have a unique ability to adapt and flow with various energies. Use this fluidity to connect with your children in different ways, depending on the situation and environment. Surround yourself with supportive communities, friends, and family who understand and respect your Reflector nature. The entirely open nature of Reflectors offers them a distinctive perspective on life and relationships, which can profoundly influence their parenting style.

Reflectors are so highly empathetic that they have some particular challenges as parents:

- **External pressures.** Due to your open centers, societal pressures about "how to parent" can weigh heavily on you. Trust your instincts and your unique process.
- **Misunderstanding from others.** Others might not understand your need for reflection and longer decision-making periods, which could lead to misinterpretations or impatience.
- **Overwhelm.** Given your sensitivity to environments, there might be times when the chaos of parenting feels overwhelming. It's essential to recognize when you need a break and to take time for yourself.
- **Inconsistent energy.** Unlike Generators or MGs you don't have a consistent energy source. Be aware of this and try not to over-extend yourself.

That same empathy is a huge blessing in parenting, allowing you to understand your children on a profound level. Other blessings include:

- **Flexibility.** Your fluid nature enables you to adapt to various situations and needs, offering a flexible parenting style.
- **Deep wisdom.** As you sample various energies, you gain insights and wisdom about human nature, which can be invaluable in guiding and understanding your children.

- **Model of reflection.** By living true to your Reflector nature, you become a model for introspection, patience, and authenticity.
- **Celebrating individuality.** Your unique perspective can teach your children to celebrate individuality and the many different ways people experience the world.

While there are challenges to parenting as a Reflector, the deep connections, empathy, and unique insights you bring to the family create a nurturing and understanding environment for your children. Remember to care for your own well-being, taking the time you need to reflect and rejuvenate, and communicate openly with your family about your needs and experiences.

Understanding your Type and those of your nearest and dearest is the first Key of Human Design. The second Key is your decision-making Authority....

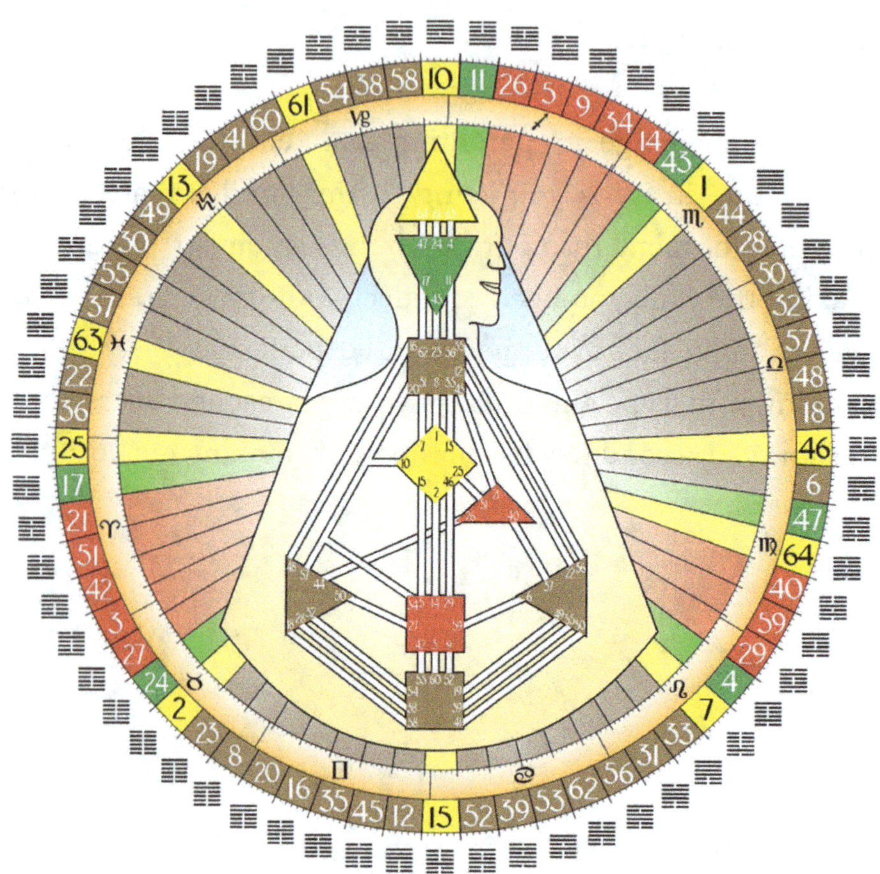

CHAPTER 10

YOUR BEST DECISIONS

"Before you tell your life what you intend to do with it, listen for what it intends to do with you."

— PARKER J. PALMER

Making clear decisions that attune exactly to our own nature and to where our own life is calling us is one of the most important capabilities we have. In Human Design, we each have a distinctive inner guidance for how we make decisions. Recognizing and enhancing these natural gifts from an early age can change the whole course of life, reduce the number of issues caused by making poor choices, eradicate years of therapy and self-doubt, and bring about a conscious evolution for children, their families, and the lives of everyone they meet.

Is it possible to find the balance between being a guardian who makes clear decisions during a child's formative years, while also encouraging and enhancing the child's own natural guidance practice? By the time we go to and through school, most of our natural tendencies have been thoroughly drilled out of us and replaced by a dependence on mental processes. It is not a bad thing that the mind develops toward being a good servant. However, if it develops in a way that this imperative takes over our lives and makes us slaves to its split pro-and-con mechanisms, then problems show up very quickly. We are bombarded by all the "shoulds," "coulds," "woulds," "mights," and "musts" of mental obligations that, when traced all the way to their origin, are often rooted in failures or dissatisfactions of one kind or another and are usually those of other people, not even our own.

As early as possible, it is important to find, recognize, and practice the clear decision-making process we've given ourselves from birth. It's clearly marked in our Human Design, and contrary to popular belief, it is not in the Mind. Knowing how other people in our lives make their clear decisions not only enhances tolerance but also opens ways in which seamless decisions can be made when whole groups or families are involved.

LET'S START WITH EMOTIONS

Emotions are unique to humans. They are a part of the grand experiment playing out on Earth. It can be argued that animals, birds, and other species have emotions, but in fact, they all "catch" emotions and emotional behaviors from us. We'll look more at this in Chapter 14 on pets and other beings.

In this age of extremes – creativity and destruction, it is essential that we humans comprehend the nature of our emotions and feelings, and how to employ them with some degree of sensitivity in our lives. Lack of emotional awareness can cause domestic violence, warmongering, digestive disorders, breathing difficulties, socializing issues, addictions of all kinds, sex problems, and has even been linked to some autistic susceptibilities.

It is not certain to be true, but it was rumored that men didn't start having feelings until the mid-1970s because up until that time it was presumed that only women did ... so, in many areas of life, there are still entrenched beliefs around feelings, as to who has feelings and how they are to be felt, allowed, or supposed to be expressed. The stereotypical British stiff upper lip and the Oriental poker face are still employed to this day, regardless of what is going on inside. It is essential to be cognizant of emotions and their vital role in life, so this part of the book is going to go into extensive detail.

Emotional Power and Emotional Awareness

Nearly half of all people born enter the world with a defined and activated Emotions Center in their Human Design life chart. What is apparent with the Emotions Center is that it is not only a place to witness our feelings with emotional awareness, but it is also an area of our life with extraordinary power, reaching states of ecstasy and agony, determining extremes of love and hate, delight and disaster, veneration and humiliation, and multiple margins of life experiences.

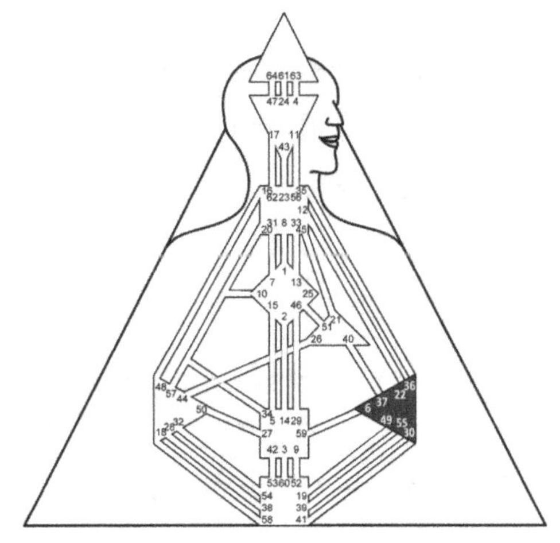

It is essential that all humans find and implement the balance between emotional power and emotional awareness. If children can comprehend and be encouraged to implement this balance in emotions from an early age, the effect on the world around us is enormous.

When we talk about the Emotions Center in Human Design, we are relating to the Solar Plexus, and an area just below the belly button on the inside. Our belly button has its own magical connection first to our mother, and then to almost everything that goes on inside us, and thus outside us too. It is estimated that our belly button has over 70,000 nerve endings, so the area around the Solar Plexus is extremely sensitive. Indeed, one of the most intimate of actions is to put your hand on another's tummy.

What becomes apparent for anyone with a defined Emotions Center is that there is a wave movement of feelings that rise and fall that are felt around their Solar Plexus. Waves of emotion go up, and great contentment, happiness, and excitement are felt ... and then the waves go down, and a disinterest, disappointment, and even a depression can follow ... and then the waves go back up again, and down again.

Emotions and Trauma

There are many different wave patterns and wave timings, just like there are waves that roll across the ocean and arrive on any shore. If shocks or accidents happen at any time in life, often emotional waves become frozen at a particular point, and a trauma is etched into the otherwise smooth emotional sequence. Until a trauma is revisited on some level and released, there will always be a sticking point every time that part of the emotional wave is reached.

Coming from a safe and supported place down the birth canal into bright lights and nervous company is almost bound to be traumatic. Being passed from one person to another, held upside down, and smacked on the *buttooski* might be a way to get breathing underway, but also introduces us into an apparently hostile world. Holding a newborn in a way that supports the release of amniotic fluid and encourages them to take their first breath also aligns the child with a natural survival instinct. Premature children might need some gentle encouragement and extra care.

Time expands rapidly for new arrivals with so many interruptions and events being absorbed by a mostly helpless being. The first days, weeks, and months of a child's life can leave them with profound impressions and stored pre-verbal memories without anyone really appreciating what's been happening to them. They are aware of all the comings and goings in their life, and can quickly register being accepted and loved, and equally sense rejection or abandonment if that exists in the atmosphere around them.

Overall, from very early days, the Emotions Center in any child is greatly impacted.

We find in Human Design that everyone, whether they have a defined, undefined, or open Emotions Center, is profoundly affected by their emotional environment. Those who have a defined Emotions Center, when encouraged, can develop a consistent means to tune into their feelings and, through awareness, resolve most issues that have become set and fixed in them.

Those who have undefined or open Emotions Centers are subjected to all kinds of emotions over which they have no apparent control. The quality of emotional awareness of their carers and companions will determine how easy it is for newborns and growing children to process emotional patterns and traumas.

Emotional Authority and Breath

For those with a defined Emotions Center, considering that emotions are highly motivational as well as a source of potential awareness requires a high degree of attention and awareness. When emotions run away with us, it can be difficult or even impossible to stop our moods and actions as feelings cycle from one extreme to another. Emotions that are combined creatively reach extraordinary heights of bliss and ecstasy. Emotions that align destructively through violent or mob actions bring horrors to our world.

One of the most essential ways to establish emotional clarity is through breathing. Helping a newborn and a young child to breathe naturally from a place of inner relaxation opens the possibility of being in touch with their feelings from the get-go. When a baby is in distress and crying, it is important (if you can remember) to watch your own breathing. Easier said than done, for sure! However, being clear and calm through conscious breathing when holding a newborn makes breathing easier for them. Breathing as though you can breathe all the way to the Solar Plexus, your own belly button, naturally puts you in touch with your Emotions Center, and can then encourage the newborn to be in touch with their own. Breathing consciously can help both you and your child synchronize your emotions while you attend to whatever is needed for them.

Life is full of emotions and all kinds of ups and downs. However, there is the potential right at the beginning of life to establish personal emotional clarity, and breath is key. The whole Eastern art of Tantra and the understanding and expansion of human consciousness commences with breath, and the energy that is available through the right use of breathing. In the West, in recent years, "rebirthing" and other breath techniques have gained recognition and importance. So, in simple terms, through meditation, exercise, singing, sports, yoga, and various other activities, all children can be encouraged to breathe well. That is, to breathe all the way to fill their lungs. Shallow breathing limits energy and ultimately access to emotional and other vital sensations.

Riding Emotional Waves

All emotions rise and fall. What is fascinating, engaging, exciting, and unavoidable in one instance can be boring, ridiculous, obsolete, and completely avoidable in another. What seems delicious at one time can be indigestible at another.... Oh, yes, eating and digestion have a lot to do with the Emotions Center, too.

Emotions are not reasonable. For those who have Emotional Authority, life is an ongoing drama. "All the world's a stage," and anyone with a defined Emotions Center, or in the company of someone who has defined Emotions Center, is going to experience life-as-drama. You find yourself in the company of a newborn with defined Emotions: Drama on!

Of all Centers, the Emotions Center is the most complex with its variety and extremes of wave patterns. Some waves pass in a flash, others may take days or even weeks to pass by. How to find clarity in all this emotional movement? If a decision is made at the top of a wave of excitement when everything appears to be wonderful, it does not necessarily include what is going to happen naturally when the wave crashes. Similarly, when a decision is made when everything appears hopeless, it does not consider what is possible when the wave rises. Between all the rising and falling of waves, there are moments in which there is no movement. There are *still points* when the breath is neither going in nor out, when the wave is no longer rising or falling, when attunement to the Solar Plexus Emotions Center can happen. In those moments, it is possible to catch and ride the wave, feeling its full movement and sensation.

For those with defined Emotions, and thus Emotional Authority, every wave is connected to every other wave, from the very beginning to the very end of life. The recognition of a clear decision comes when there is a stillness, a quiet knowing in the belly. It feels clear. There's no agenda. No attachment to highs and lows. Emotional simplicity happens in that moment, and a decision becomes clear.

When Mei's friends asked her to join a summer volunteer trip, she felt thrilled one moment and overwhelmed the next. Part of her imagined the adventure; part of her secretly wanted to stay home and rest. Each time someone asked for an answer, her response changed with her mood – an enthusiastic "yes" on a high day, a firm "I don't think so" when she was low.

After noticing this pattern, Mei told her friends she needed time. Over the next few days, she stopped trying to decide and simply paid attention to how she felt. One evening, sitting quietly in her room, a calm certainty settled in. She realized she genuinely wanted to go – not from excitement, not from pressure, but from a steady inner knowing. Once that clarity arrived, it didn't waver. She booked her place the next morning, feeling peaceful rather than pulled.

For adults, since every wave throughout life is connected to every other wave, being able to remember the sensations, the environment, the people, the stillness, and consequences of the moments of clarity opens up the potential to find clarity in all present and future scenarios. This ability to tune into our own emotional awareness through our own experience is almost magical. Having that inner belly-button sensation is extraordinary.

For children, guiding them or allowing them to find this inner clarity tied to their feelings can take enormous patience and restraint for all involved. Rushing a child with Emotional Authority can easily derail them from finding and employing one of the most essential qualities in their life. Encouraging them to breathe and be aware of their breath is a great place to start. To "take a deep breath" before jumping spontaneously into anything can give them the moment's pause to engage with their own clarity. For important decisions, encouraging your child to "sleep on it" until they are sure, rather than rushing it, will set them up well to be unhurried and clear in adult life. Making decisions at any time you know you, or your child, to be in a mood is definitely not recommended. "Time out" lets any tsunamis settle and calm.

Emotional Authority with Sacral Gut Response

Many Generators and MGs have a defined Emotions Center, and thus overall Emotions Authority. The Sacral gut response can be so strong (see below), with such an urge to get involved with something or someone. However, it is important that this urge does not override emotional clarity. Ultimately, children are looking to find their emotional clarity, their internal still point, and so the gut response can easily be an indicator of where they are on their emotional wave rather than a true reaction to the decision in hand.

A strong "yes" gut response might indicate their wave is "up" and they have a yes for anyone or anything. A strong "no" gut response could indicate they are down in their wave and not in the mood for anything. Encouraging children to be aware that there needs to be an inner still-point in their Solar Plexus to guide them to making clear commitments, and sometimes taking a deep breath, being patient, and attentive is the only way for them to be sure and clear. In essence, the decision-making process for a Generator or an MG with Emotional Authority is to pick up on a gut response that indicates interest or not and then check on the feelings ... maybe sleep on it if you are not certain ... and when the emotions are clear, listen to see if the gut is still aligned.

Nine-year-old Jasmine adored after-school clubs and usually leapt at any new activity. When her teacher mentioned a weekend drama workshop, Jasmine's Sacral responded instantly – "Yes!" – before the sentence was even finished. She buzzed with excitement all afternoon. By the time she got home, however, she was tearful and snappy for no clear reason, and when her mom asked again about the workshop, Jasmine insisted she didn't want to go at all.

Her parents had begun to notice this pattern. Jasmine's first response was often strong, but it shifted with the rise and fall of her emotions. The next morning, after a good night's sleep, Jasmine felt calm and cheerful again. When asked once more, she nodded slowly and said, "Yes ... I think I do want to try it." Her mom recognized the difference: this was a Sacral "yes" aligned with emotional clarity, not just the high point of an emotional wave.

Emotional Authority with Splenic Awareness

Children who have both defined Spleen and Emotions may find the urge to make spontaneous decisions, which is fine, provided they are clear and in touch with their emotions first. However, they can easily make choices that override their Emotional Authority, and that will almost always lead to difficulties and potential regrets. There is no getting away from the need for patience for anyone with a defined Emotions Center, or for those with a different Authority who are closely involved with and want to interact with someone whose decision-making process is aligned with having clear emotions.

Omar loved anything adventurous. When his cousin invited him to a weekend rock-climbing session, his Splenic instinct lit up instantly – a fast, full-bodied yes! He felt the familiar rush of excitement and wanted to commit immediately. Yet as the evening wore on, his mood shifted. He became quiet, tense, and unsure why he suddenly felt uneasy. His emotional wave had begun to move, and the certainty of his Splenic impulse quickly dissolved.

By the next morning, after time to settle, Omar admitted he didn't actually want to go climbing at all. He realized the idea had thrilled him in the moment, but at ten years old, he wasn't ready. His parents recognized that although Omar's Splenic responses were quick and enthusiastic, his true clarity always came from his emotions – and when the two disagreed, his Emotional Authority needed to lead.

Emotional Authority with Defined Willpower

Even though with a defined Willpower Center, energy can be applied to move something or someone, to push through and go it alone, it is the feeling clarity with the Emotional Authority that is so essential. Until the world becomes more emotionally mature, it is very easy for someone to get their feelings hurt or feel abused when they are willfully pushed aside.

The challenge for the whole world is to be clear in the living and expression of emotions. Children are the ones who can lead the way if they have Emotional Authority and know how to honor and use it, regardless of other urges or abilities in their chart, or in the influences that come at them from people around them.

When Amira set her sights on something, she threw her whole will behind it. If a friend hesitated or wanted to do something different, Amira would lean in harder, determined to make things happen her way. One afternoon, she insisted the group play a game she had planned, pushing past her friends' reluctance. Minutes later, one of them ended up in tears, and Amira felt awful without fully understanding why.

Later that evening, once her emotions had settled, Amira realized she hadn't really felt like leading the game at all – she had simply powered through because she could. Her parents began helping her notice that her strength of will wasn't the guide; her emotional clarity was. When she paused long enough to feel where she truly was, her choices were kinder, clearer, and far more connected to the people around her.

SACRAL AUTHORITY

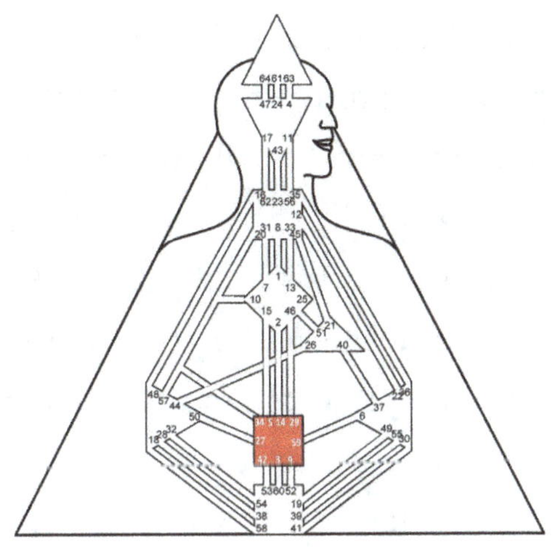

We live in a Sacral World. As mentioned previously, almost 70 percent of the world's population has a defined and active Sacral Center, which we call the Generator Center in Human Design. This Generator is always on, always available as a potential source of life-force energy just waiting for the right moment, or right interaction to be engaged. The focus is on the word "right," because the Generator is easily taken for granted. Since it has so much potential energy, it can seem boundless and capable of taking on anything. Many children born with a defined Sacral Center can exhibit two different speeds: flat out, or flat out resting. The great thing for any child, as with any adult, is to find satisfaction in using this amazing energy source consistently.

Whether we like it or not, we are all living in a response mode ... responding in multiple ways to whatever we sense or whatever appears to be calling for our attention. Unlike Manifestors, Projectors, and Reflectors, Generators and MGs have an actual physical response that is sourced in the Sacral Center. This physical response can be more or less obvious because it can either come as a sound "ah-ha!" indicating a positive and interested response, or a "nuh-uh!" indicating a negative, mismatched, or uninterested response. If Generators or MGs do not have a defined Emotional Solar Plexus, then this response is your guidance system for decision-making.

The Sacral response can also be sensed as a soundless rise of energy, indicating interest, or a fall of energy, indicating a lack of interest at that time, or no movement of energy at all. For parents, paying attention to this silent movement of energy in children can be a quick way of reading what is going on with them. Young children can certainly read their Generator and MG parents' responses and intentions.

The rising of energy indicates interest, a potential involvement and a "heads up," "tell me more" response. The falling energy or no response indicates "not now," or often a blanket "no!" All Generators and MGs are in Sacral gut response mode twenty-four hours a day. Everything, and often everyone, is trying to gain their attention and get their involvement, their potential life-force energy. Every adult Generator or MG knows exactly what this means, and the complete exhaustion and frustration that comes through indiscriminate involvement, often in work or projects, and with people and situations where there is no inherent or common interest.

All Generators and MGs are hereby put on notice: Pay attention to your gut response!

Children born with a defined Sacral Center naturally respond to life from their gut. They have not yet arrived at a way of evaluating life on a mental level and intrinsically know whether something resonates with them.

When Noah's older cousins invited him to join their football practice, he didn't need time to think. His whole body leaned forward, his eyes brightened, and a spontaneous "ah-ha!" escaped before anyone finished the question. His energy rose like a little spring inside him – unmistakably interested.

Later that week, his grandmother asked if he'd like to help her bake. This time Noah's response was just as clear. His shoulders softened, his gaze drifted, and nothing in him moved toward the idea. No sound, no spark, no upward lift, simply a quiet, natural "no," not from shyness or worry but because the activity held no life-force interest for him.

A few weeks later, when the kitchen was already warm and the bowls were out, Noah wandered in on his own. He watched for a moment, leaned against the counter, then reached for the spoon. "Can I stir?" he asked — not because he'd been encouraged, but because something in him had come alive at the right moment.

Honoring these responses made life easier for everyone. When Noah's "ah-ha" was followed, he threw himself into the activity with enthusiasm and stamina. When his "no" was respected, he stayed calm, cooperative, and open to whatever did engage him. His parents soon realized that his gut was far quicker — and far truer — than any explanation he could offer.

This is something essential to know about Sacral Authority and the gut response:

- It is not a mental process.
- It is not a moral process that accords to arbitrary rules and beliefs.
- It is pure.
- It is going to surprise you sometimes.
- It states: "I have life-force interest here, or not...."

Within half a second, the mind jumps in and starts interfering with the up or down gut response. Always ready to take over, the mind questions this clarity and often points in the opposite direction from the original response. It all happens so quickly, and we have all been programmed so perfectly to ignore what is natural. If it is possible to pay attention to and follow through with your child's gut response, it can open your eyes to things that have been taken for granted for ages. It can reveal habitual ways of life that really do not bring fulfilment for anyone. A pure gut response can open whole new horizons. It can break patterns of frustration and dreary obligations. Of course, we must be responsible, but the ultimate *response-ability* is to be true to ourselves and the lives we came to live.

Sacral Authority with Splenic Awareness

Some children have both a defined Sacral Center, and can thus be persuaded to pay attention to their gut response, and also have Splenic awareness that is constantly attuning to present environment situations. This awareness is crucial, and in instant emergencies, can be relied on to bring alertness to dangerous situations. However, we would recommend encouraging them to listen to their gut response before making any major moves or changes in life.

When Malik walked into a neighbor's garden party, he paused instantly at the top of the steps. Something in the air felt "off" to him — too much noise, too many unfamiliar faces — and his body hesitated before he even knew why. His mom recognized the look; Malik's Splenic awareness had picked up on the atmosphere long before his mind could explain it.

A few minutes later, once he'd settled and felt safe, his mom crouched beside him and asked quietly, "Do you want to stay for a bit?" Malik closed his eyes for a moment, waited, and then felt the warm upward pull of his Sacral "yes." The initial splenic pause had helped him register the environment, but it was his gut response that told him whether he genuinely wanted to be there. Only when both were honored did his energy move freely.

Sacral Authority with Defined Willpower

In a chart where you see both red centers, the Willpower and Sacral Centers colored in and defined, you are looking at someone's access to perpetual motion. It is known that willpower can accomplish much in a short space of time. It is extraordinarily efficient and capable when it is applied. Sacral energy can have a steady endurance of keeping things going, and going, and going.

If your child has both Sacral and Willpower Centers active together, it is vital that their Sacral gut response is recognized and used. Otherwise, the moment one project is completed using willpower, all of a sudden, the next project shows up and is completed, as the Sacral, Generator energy keeps on keeping on from one thing to the next. Persevering in this way, the natural conclusion is exhaustion, and the lack of opportunity to pause, rest and appreciate real achievements. Encouraging your child to tune into their gut response ensures they are clear and ready to take on the next activity.

Jamie spent the whole morning lining up his toy soldiers in perfect formation, then immediately launched into building them a fortress, and then a secret tunnel, barely stopping to breathe. His Willpower and Sacral energy had teamed up again, carrying him from one "very important mission" to the next without pause.

By mid-afternoon, he was in tears, exhausted, and confused. When his mom gently asked whether his tummy had really wanted to do all those things, Jamie realized he hadn't checked once. Learning to pause for a quick gut response helped him enjoy his projects without exhausting himself.

SPLENIC AUTHORITY

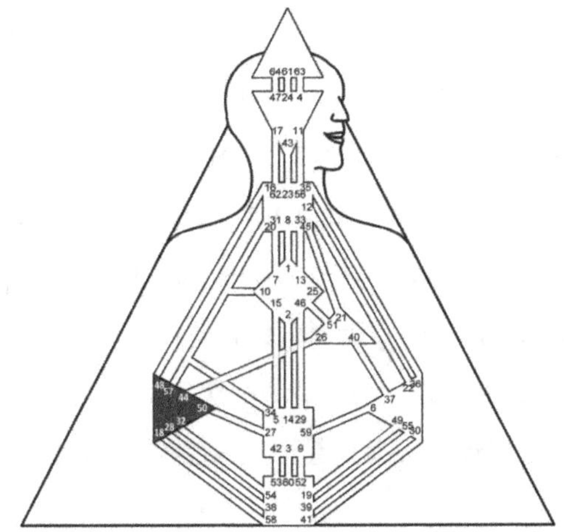

We often use the word *intuition* for that quiet inner voice or tap on the shoulder alerting us to something unseen but somehow relevant. When we consider the Spleen and those who have a defined Spleen Center, they consistently have this natural alertness and are well-advised to pay close attention to it.

The Spleen Center also has access to what we've called instinct, literally how something smells, or resides in our cellular memory and our very bones; and also taste, how something tastes, whether that is something we put in our mouth or how we identify harmony or disharmony in our immediate environment, whether it is "tasteful," or not. These senses are instantaneous.

The Spleen Center very definitely works in present tense. It is the oldest alerting ability common to all living creatures — from humans and mammals to insects, and even plants. It has a finely tuned alertness that picks up if the environment around it is in order, healthy, and safe. It does not need sacral, willful, mental, or emotional input to know whether something is right or not. In fact, emotions and overthinking can easily cloud its instantaneous clarity. Splenic awareness gives an immediate alert that is either heeded or ignored and put aside.

In simple terms, the Spleen is like the body's laundry system, keeping everything fresh and healthy through the lymph system and its T cells and other extraordinary defense mechanisms. The Spleen Center's instantaneous senses pick up on people, environments and situations that are weird, plainly unhealthy, about to change, or even dangerous. It is a bit like an internal radar that continues to scan the local and distant environment. Ignoring Splenic alerts has consequences. However, constantly scanning your environment can overstimulate nervousness and lead to an inability to relax. Learning to distinguish between which senses truly merit attention and which are background alerts is all-important for anyone with a defined Spleen Center.

Anyone with Splenic Authority is often the fastest person in the room. With their undefined Emotions and undefined Sacral Center, they get things instantly while everyone around them is still trying to work out what, if anything, is going on. Surrounded by those who cannot immediately sense a shift in the atmosphere can be daunting, especially when Generators and MGs are persisting in whatever they are already involved, and those with defined Emotions are caught up in clarifying their feelings. Consequently, anyone with Splenic Authority must learn to trust their inner senses, especially when no one around them has those same sensibilities. It is quite natural for them to live in present tense even if everyone else is stuck in the past, or constantly basing their life on an unlived future.

If you or your child has Splenic Authority, you know what it is like to live in a sleepy world. Much of the world's health revolves around you, and probably the health that plays out on other levels beyond just the physical. Reality exists in present tense and being present. Splenic Authority naturally accords to living in the now and has to be vigilant not to be put off by peer pressures, emotional dramas and time-worn habits that discourage intuitive awareness.

When Roberta arrived at a classmate's birthday party, she stopped in the doorway before anyone else noticed anything unusual. The music was loud, the room felt hectic, and her whole body gave a quiet, unmistakable "no." She didn't panic, cry, or cling – she simply stepped back and held her mom's hand, certain she wasn't going in.

For a Splenic child, this kind of clarity isn't stubbornness or shyness – it is intuition functioning exactly as designed: fast, quiet, and precise. Her mom respected the signal, and the two of them went for a short walk instead.

Everyone with Splenic Authority is either a Manifestor or a Projector; both Types are naturally non-inclusive. Manifestors are self-catalysts who can like but not necessarily appreciate support or input from others, and Projectors are natural outsiders who are alert, present, and "on-call" to give guidance, particularly to the Generators, MGs, and Manifestors.

Children with Splenic Authority may find themselves watchful or even critical of other people and the ways they behave. They are alert to possible dangers and yet may assume that they can handle any kind of sickness and bug themselves or become hypersensitive and alarmed about potentially hazardous environments. Yes, they may have an immune system that is always on, keeping the environment fresh and healthy, but there are times when surrounded by so many others who are ill that their immune system can become overloaded. When this happens, and they ignore the signals they are getting from their intuitive, instinctive or taste senses, they have the potential to get sick in a way that exceeds their immune system's ability to be able to repair itself without drug intervention and rest. The immune system is extraordinarily powerful; however, it does have its limits.

Splenic Authority with Defined Willpower

Your child might have a defined Willpower Center as well as Splenic Authority, and is encouraged to live by their wits, intuition, instinct, or sense of taste to determine who and what to engage with, and who and what to avoid. Only 30 percent of people have defined Willpower and the ability to apply it at any time. However, here, the Splenic awareness is key: to sense in an instant whether to follow through on something by applying their willpower, or not.

Liam loved a challenge. When his teacher announced a class talent show, he immediately decided he would perform a magic trick and practiced with fierce determination all week. On the morning of the show, though, he stepped into the hall and felt a sudden Splenic "no." Something in the room just wasn't right.

Liam could have pushed himself onto the stage – his Willpower was strong – but he quietly told his teacher he wouldn't perform today. There was no drama; the clarity was instant.

For a child with both Splenic intuition and natural Willpower, this is the balance: the ability to push through anything must still follow that first, unmistakable sense of yes or no.

WILLFUL AUTHORITY

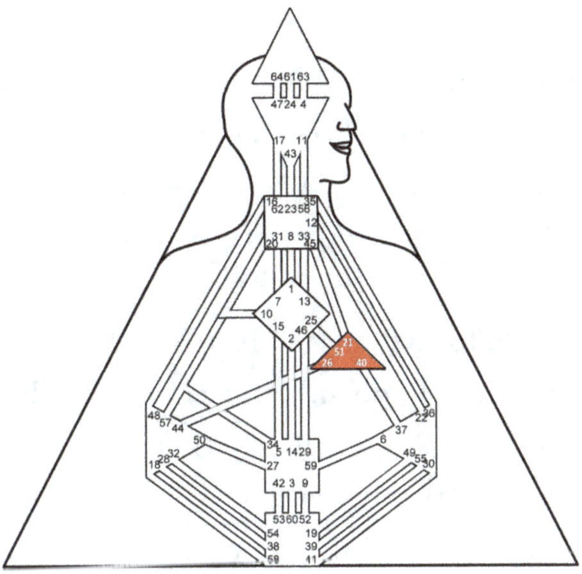

A person with an undefined Emotions, Sacral and Spleen Center, and with a Willpower Center that connects to the Throat Center (either directly through Channel 21–45, or by connecting to the Self Center through the 25–51 and then to the Throat Center through one of the four leadership Channels) is a Manifestor and has Willpower Authority.

Children with Willful Authority have a way of getting what they want, or causing a massive disturbance if they are denied.

Mason often woke up with a plan already forming in his mind. One Saturday, he marched into the kitchen and declared he was going to build a "real" raft to float on the pond in the park. His mom, caught off guard, instinctively said, "No, absolutely not." The explosion was immediate – doors slammed, a chair toppled over, and the family dog wisely left the room.

After they all took a breath, his dad tried a different approach. "You can work on a raft," he said, "as long as it stays in our garden and you use the recycling wood, not anything with nails." Instantly, the storm passed. Mason nodded once, grabbed his tool-

box, and set to work with fierce focus. By lunchtime, he had built something surprisingly sturdy, and proudly invited everyone outside to test whether it would hold a teddy bear.

For a child like Mason, the urge itself isn't the problem — it's being blocked without explanation. When his inner Willpower says, "I want this," the most effective path is clear boundaries that still give him autonomy. With that support, even the wildest ideas can turn into safe, joyful adventures rather than battles of wills.

The simple description for anyone with this Willpower Authority is: "Whatever you want is what needs to happen." For a child with this Authority, it appears obvious to them, but some coaching will help them recognize what is really worth having, what holds value, and what does not.

When you have a Manifestor with Willpower in the family, life is not going to be peaceful, especially if you use the words "no," and "don't." Vocabulary has to be rearranged! No one likes to be told what to do, and Manifestors in particular react to direct instructions and denials. Describing sensible boundaries as part of consensual agreements can work wonders.

Instead of "Bedtime," try "Stay up as late as you like, but not past 9 p.m." "Play as long as you like once your homework is done. Yes?" "Yes, go to the skate park with your friends once I can walk around your room without treading on anything except the carpet."

Combatting willpower is a losing battle, but supporting a child in making clear decisions based on what holds particular value to them is priceless. At first glance, the statement: "Whatever you want is what needs to happen" can appear completely selfish. However, given space, positive guidance, and sensible boundaries, all Manifestors with this Willpower Authority come to realize they are actually serving a greater whole, provided they trust their own authenticity and follow through on what is in their heart of hearts.

The alternative, for a child with Willpower Authority who is constantly restricted and shut down, is resentment. Such resentment easily turns into forcefulness, anger, avoidance tendencies, or despondency, which in turn leads them into the unsatisfactory role of facilitating for everyone else and not for themselves.

Encouraging your child to let you know what's calling to them, or what inner urge is wanting expression quickly defuses concerns you might have around their ability to turn the world upside down. Many Manifestors don't want to tell anyone anything for fear of being prevented or blocked. So, opening conversations to find out what's going on for your Manifestor child can bring about clarity and ease for all concerned.

Having a Willpower Manifestor in the house means things can get done. Nothing needs to become an obstruction, provided everyone is up for and open to the catalytic presence in their midst. Certainly, the Willpower Manifestor is going to want to do things on their own, and other members in the family might be very happy to have a break from the action! However, it can be tremendous fun being around a Willpower Manifestor, because who knows what's going to happen next. Some of the simplest activities can turn out to be the greatest adventures.

SELF-AUTHORITY

With undefined Emotions, Sacral and Spleen Centers, and a defined Self Center that either connects to the Throat Center or to the Willpower Center without connecting to the Throat Center, the chart is that of a Projector who has Self-Authority. Self-Authority is very gentle but also profound. Those who have it develop an enormous capacity to trust their own way through life, regardless of all the pressures, dramas, fears, and chaos played out around them.

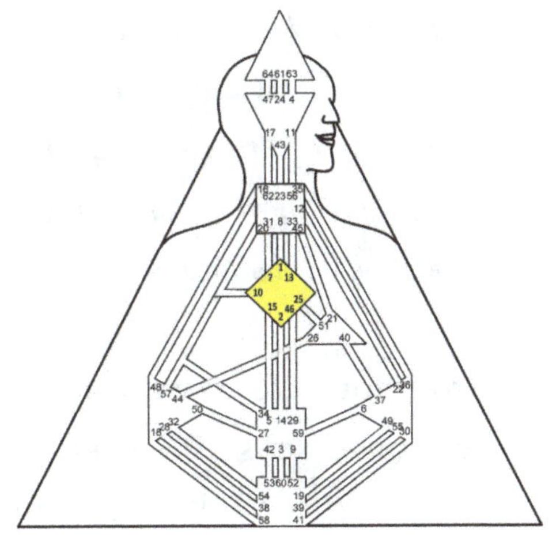

As the name suggests, this Authority really does rely on a very particular internal connection to whatever appears to be going on outside. The sensation of finding clarity with Self-Authority happens in a physical nature around the sternum in the center of the chest. There is a sensation there that either opens to the possibility of being involved or remains closed off and waiting.

When explaining to a child how to be clear in their inner knowing, you can ask them what their favorite flower is. Once they've visualized it, ask them to imagine that flower sitting in their sternum. Flowers have two easily recognized states: to be in a bud, waiting for the right season and weather conditions, or to be wide open, fragrant, and blossoming, yet also vulnerable and trusting.

Clare's parents noticed early on that she didn't rush into things the way other children did. When her class was invited to join an after-school drama club, most of her friends signed up immediately. Clare simply stood still for a moment, one hand resting lightly on her chest, as if listening for something inside her. Then she shook her head gently. "Not this time," she said, without hesitation or worry about missing out.

A few weeks later, her teacher mentioned a small lunchtime art group. Before the sentence was even finished, Clare's whole expression softened – her shoulders dropped, her face brightened, and she stepped forward as if pulled by an invisible thread. "Yes," she said quietly, already knowing it was right for her.

For a child with Self Authority, the guidance comes from this inner opening – a quiet, physical recognition that signals a true invitation. When the "flower" in the sternum opens, Clare moves with clarity and ease. When it stays closed, no amount of persuasion makes the moment right.

Projectors are always advised to wait to be recognized, and in some way invited, or to sense themselves being drawn with clarity into interactions with others. For those with Self-Authority, the right interactions happen when the sensation in the sternum relaxes, or the flower opens from a bud to a bloom. There is a natural internal recognition of the situation, indicating a "yes," and a connection and potential involvement. At other times, it does not matter how amazing an invitation or offering might be, the bud and the sternum remain still, indicating a "no," and no further involvement at this moment in time.

Children who have Self-Authority find themselves as natural leaders or inspirers of others. They are naturally Projectors by Design, since there are no "Motor Centers" involved in their chart (unless they have Willpower, see below), they will find themselves pointing the way for others. Pointing the way is one thing; they then need to be very clear if they themselves are to follow through to where they are directing others' attention.

From a parent's point of view, it can be easy to recognize what attunes to your child with Self-Authority, because you will sense their instant opening to good suggestions, and an instant reluctance when something does not align for them. You can see in your child someone who radiates delight when they are in company with people and situations that are in tune with their perspective of life, and how despondent they become when in company or situations that are going nowhere interesting for them.

Self-Authority with Willpower

A chart that has Self and Willpower Centers connected, without a connection to the Throat Center, while Emotions, Sacral, and Spleen Centers are undefined, has Self-Authority with willpower. Again, the internal guidance comes from the Self Center. However, the inclusion of willpower brings about a potentially powerful and forceful, perhaps even mystical, presence into play.

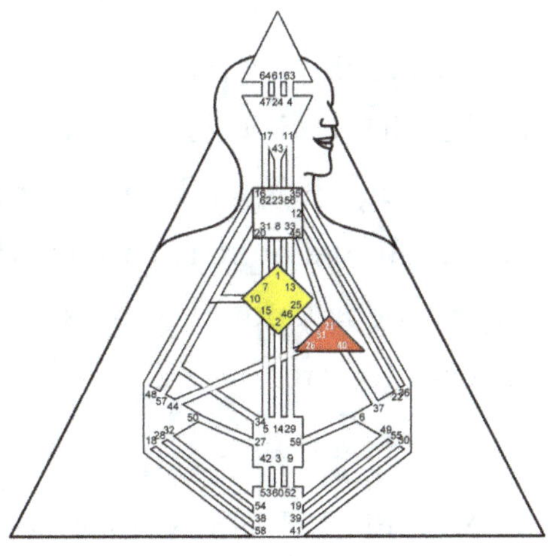

This particular expression of Self-Authority bridges Tribal, supportive qualities, with individual empowering ones. The Channel 51–25, called Initiation, can be extremely abrupt, literally shocking people out of the mundane into the real, and out of the past or future into the present.

Tessa had a knack for upending group projects with one well-timed sentence. During a group project, everyone was stuck in a mind-numbing "Poster or slideshow?" debate that had lasted far too long. Tessa, who had been quietly observing while eating crisps, suddenly felt that unmistakable click of clarity.

"We're making a musical," she said.

No drama, no sales pitch – just a statement. The room froze. Then, somehow, people started pulling desks into a makeshift stage, someone found a keyboard, and the debate was over. Tessa hadn't meant to take charge, but Willpower combined with Self-Authority tends to have that effect.

At home, the same force showed up differently. When her dad suggested she join the 7 a.m. running club, Tessa didn't even pause her scrolling. "No." Not rude, not emotional – just a conclusion delivered with the unbudging tone of someone who will absolutely not be convinced otherwise. Her parents knew better than to try.

For teens like Tessa, clarity lands decisively. When it's a yes, momentum follows. When it's a no, even the most enthusiastic pep talk doesn't stand a chance.

If your child has this form of Self-Authority, they are different (as though any child isn't), and often they might need encouragement to tread their own path, even though it is so different from what might be considered "the norm." Again, the encouragement is to consider the properties of a flower in the sternum: it either opens and blossoms when connecting with the right companies and endeavors, or remains a bud until the right opportunities appear.

NON-MENTAL "ENVIRON(MENTAL)" AUTHORITY

One of the rarer Authorities is for children born with mental definition, between the Crown and Mind Centers, and often, but not always, with a connection

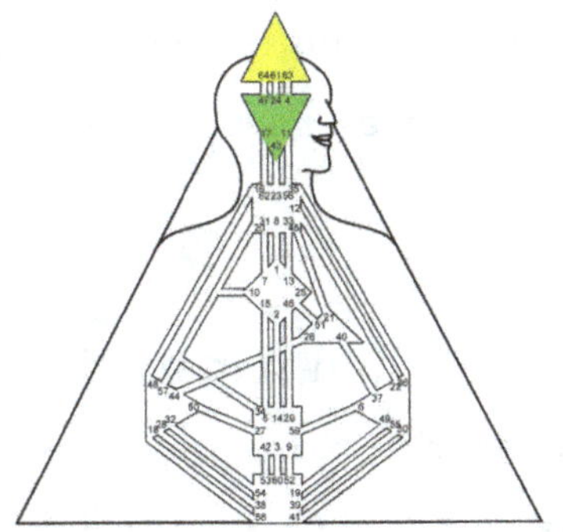

between the Mind and Throat Centers and no Centers colored and defined beneath the Throat Center. This implies the lifetime of an empath, who will be tuning into and configuring all the activities, emotions, fears, willfulness, and calmness of the world around them. Their Design is very much one of the observer or witness of life. When they attain clarity, these young people become enormously effective in giving guidance and counsel to anyone who seeks it.

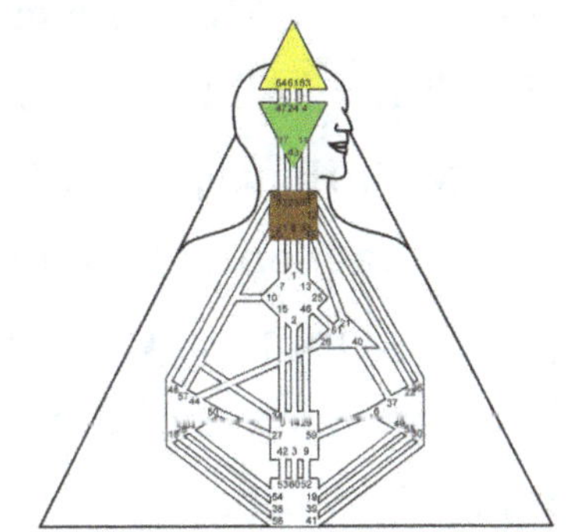

Certainly, this is the Design of a Mental Projector, or we might more accurately say Environmental Projector. And as with all Projectors, there is the great need for recognition of their gifts and inclusion in situations that really suit them. Projectors are naturally "outsiders" who attune to the world around them and are available to offer guidance and wisdom on demand. However, does anyone ever stop and ask for directions? And what does it take to hold back on giving directions when no one is asking for them?

Projectors make up about 20 percent of the world's population, completely outnumbered by the "Energy Types," and Environmental Projectors about 2 percent, so the Environmental Projectors find themselves in an unusual place in life. They have the ability to watch, observe and witness anything and everything, but how do they find their own place in the middle of it all?

When six-year-old Nora walked into her classroom each morning, she made decisions faster than her teacher. If the room felt calm, she marched straight to her seat and began drawing. If it felt "wrong" – too loud, too bright, too busy – she froze, turned on her heel, and announced, "I'll be in the reading corner," as though it were a scheduled appointment.

Once she relocated herself to a cozy spot with soft lighting, she relaxed instantly and could answer questions with surprising clarity. To her teachers, it seemed magical. To Nora, it was obvious: the place tells me what to do.

One of the most important things any parent can offer their child, and particularly their Environmental Projector child, is meditation. Meditation opens the possibility to view life objectively, starting with the mind and its whole thought process. The Mind is a great biocomputer with an extraordinary range of possibilities, but as with all computers, it operates according to the programming it has received. Hence, the Mind cannot go beyond the limits imposed by the programming that comes through family, school, social media, and other constraints. For your Environmental Projector child to find fulfillment in their life, they have to become masters of their mind and thinking process. To avoid being ruled by their mind, Environmental Projectors can use meditation to allow their mind to evaluate and direct their life through all ongoing environments.

Meditation takes three steps:

- First, to identify that the mind is a brilliant biocomputer that will run continuously and randomly if not mastered.
- Second, to move from the head to witness the heart and the whole arena of feelings and desires.
- Third, to move from the heart to the Being, and be the witnessing presence within everything.

Learned at an early age, meditation will open any child's life toward being internally fulfilled, regardless of what appears to confront them in their world.

"OUTER" AUTHORITY

Within all possible variations of Human Design charts, there are those few that have no defined Channels connecting between any Centers, the Reflector Design. As the name implies, those rare individuals who have a Reflector Design literally reflect everyone back to themselves. Sometimes it can seem to a Reflector that they are bouncing around in an ocean of thoughts, feelings, fears, actions, and dramas while everyone around them gets on with their lives.

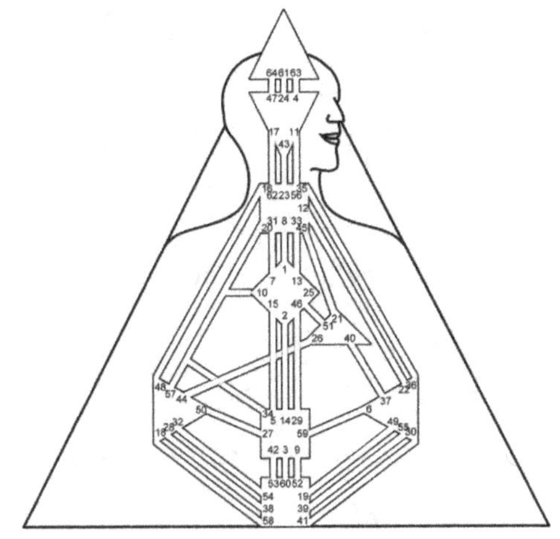

Certainly, life can be overwhelming until a Reflector appreciates how different their place in the world is. They do not have the same inner guidance as others, and might consider themselves very strange until they come to realize that they are the world and the empath who is picking up on everything and everyone. Of all people, they potentially have the purest connection with life, provided they can find a way to trust in life and their own journey in it.

Hence, Reflectors are advised to be very protective of their space and the people who come close to them. For a Reflector, there is always the potential to absorb rather than reflect, and they need to find ways to release and cleanse their body, mind, emotions, and other areas of their life. It is essential that they have a place to retreat and either process everything that they are exposed to or find ways to let it go.

There can come a time when it is all just too much, and Reflectors go into hiding, communing with animals, trees, and other life forms that present a purely natural presence for them. However, when Reflectors are at peace and balanced, and people around them are receptive and open to them, their presence is amazing. If we agree on the understanding that the Universe is created out of love, in all its multifaceted forms of expression, then Reflectors are the reflectors of love in which other people can see, feel, and know reflections of themselves from a loving and completely non-judgmental presence.

Max's family eventually stopped asking him quick questions because the answers changed depending on the day ... or the hour. On Monday, he had to play the trumpet. By Wednesday, he announced he was "deeply allergic to loud noises." Saturday morning, he wanted a hamster; by Saturday afternoon, he wasn't sure he could "emotionally commit to someone that fluffy."

When his parents asked if he wanted to join the school football team, Max gave his usual reply: "Maybe ... let me think about it." This did not mean ten minutes. It meant a month. Over the next few weeks, he tried out every possible version of himself: football-Max, chess-club-Max, dramatic-Max (that one wore a cape), and absolutely-not-sports-of-any-kind Max.

By the next full Moon, he wandered into the kitchen and announced, very calmly, "I'm going to try football. It feels correct." His parents nodded, pretending this was completely usual, and were secretly relieved he hadn't chosen "cape life" full-time.

All Reflector children benefit from a very early introduction to meditation to give themselves a means of witnessing everything that appears to happen inside and around them. It provides balance and clarity that serve them throughout their life, especially in situations where great dramas, fears, worries, and chaos unfold. If parents can also find time to meditate with their Reflector children, some very profound levels of communication and comprehension will happen.

In finding their Authority and how to make decisions clearly, it is suggested that Reflectors give themselves a month before coming to any major decisions.

A month ... !?

Yes, a full cycle of the Moon.

In a Reflector chart, there are no consistencies. There is no definition and no colored entries indicating a set pattern within the Design. It is a purely empathic

Design subject to whatever plays out in other people's Designs and lives. Trying to live according to other people's needs, wants, fears, thoughts, and emotions may work for a while, but it will become impossible sooner or later. Reflectors can put up with a lot, but they have to be clear to make decisions for themselves in their own life. The one reliable and consistent thing in their very sensitive life is the movements of the Moon, passing for about 10 hours through each of the 64 Hexagrams or Gates in their chart, regular as clockwork.

As the Moon enters each Gate, it highlights the nature and quality of that Gate, triggering a potential shift in the Reflector's chart, either by highlighting a conscious or unconscious Gate in the chart, or by completing a Channel temporarily. An attunement with the Moon's consistent orbits offers the Reflector something that is consistent in their life that is not dependent on the people around them. During the course of each lunar month, a Reflector can examine, research, and check out every aspect of a potential decision to be made. By month's end, they will be perhaps the most informed person around. Hence, given time to go through their process, Reflectors carry within them a profound wisdom.

Reflector children's parents, siblings, and friends will come to realize that they have a truly extraordinary presence in their lives, who, when nurtured and given space and time to engage with life, will bring profound blessings and perceptions with them.

FAMILY AUTHORITY

When two or more people come together, it is likely that as a group they have Emotional Authority – either because one of them does or because when you put their charts together, a defined Emotional Solar Plexus is created between them. This has profound implications for relationships.

Take two Generators, one with defined Emotions and the other with a defined Spleen. While they both have that "gut feel" of energy rising or falling, the former needs time to allow their emotions to settle on a decision, while the latter has an intuitive knowing that is ready to make a quick decision. It's very easy to fall into a trap where the Generator with a defined Spleen is naturally the first one to decide and then lobbies the other, thereby confusing their search for emotional clarity. Truly, relationships need patience, an understanding of differences, and the ability to table discussions until all parties are ready.

Let's take a mythical family of seven through a decision-making process by way of example:

At Thanksgiving Dinner, Adam, father of the family and a Manifestor with Willful Authority, announced that he would be going to Mexico next year on holiday – he'd always wanted to explore the country, and he was happy to have any family members along who would care to join him. Everyone looked very startled, wondering where this idea had sprung from, yet it was very "dad-like" to come up with unexpected ideas.

His second son, Dan, a Projector with Splenic Authority, was first to speak. "Wow, Dad, what a fabulous invitation! I'd love to go so long as it's safe at the time. I've heard there's sometimes trouble." "I've no intention of going if there's any trouble, son," Adam reassured Dan.

Next was his youngest daughter, Grace, an MG with Emotional Authority who chimed in with: "Oh, I've always wanted to go to Mexico, although I've got exams next year – can I sleep on it?" "Of course," replied Adam, "I'm going and there's no immediate rush to settle who's coming too."

The deep tones of his eldest son chimed in, "I'm a yes," a Generator with Sacral Authority, Chuck was usually clear fairly quickly whether something was for him or not.

"Well, that looks like you'll definitely have company, Adam, how exciting," said his wife, Becky, "and you know me, I'll need to research Mexico and possible travel arrangements before I'll know whether it's for me." It was a running joke in the family that his wife couldn't make a decision without a ton of research first, entirely appropriate for a Reflector with Outer Authority.

"What do you think, Ella?"

Their eldest daughter squirmed, a Projector with Environmental Authority, she often took her time too: "My mind is going a million miles an hour right now – like Dan said, is it safe? What will the weather be like? My Spanish isn't good. Will I be able to take time off work? What about our dog, Rufus? And if I say yes, can I bring my boyfriend?" The dinner table erupted in laughter. "Chill, Sis," said Dan, "you've got time to meditate on it; Dad isn't asking you to decide right now. It'd be fun if you came too, though."

Chuck turned to their youngest brother, "Freddie, what's your flower saying?" eliciting more guffaws around the table. "Now, now, don't be mean!" scolded Becky. Freddie turned pink and closed his eyes; you'd have thought with all the understanding in the family, they wouldn't still tease him. A Projector with Self-Authority, he wished he'd never shared his favorite flower was a simple daisy. At least they'd grown out of singing, "Daisy, Daisy, give me your answer – do" and yes, that gentle sense of an opening under his sternum was there. Freddie blinked up at them all. "I do believe that's a yes from me too."

"Great," said Adam, "that's a 'yes' from Dan, Chuck, and Freddie, a 'probably' from Grace and a 'maybe' from Becky and Ella. Looks like it might be a boys' trip at a minimum. Let's pick this up at Christmas and hatch a plan – hopefully by then the girls will each know whether they're in. Please share all your research, Becky, it always gives the rest of us a head-start!" With further chuckling around the table, the conversation moved on.

Once we've understood our Type and decision-making Authority, the first and second Keys of Human Design respectively, the third gives an insight into how we most readily connect with the world at large and other people. Human Design Profiles are our next area of exploration.

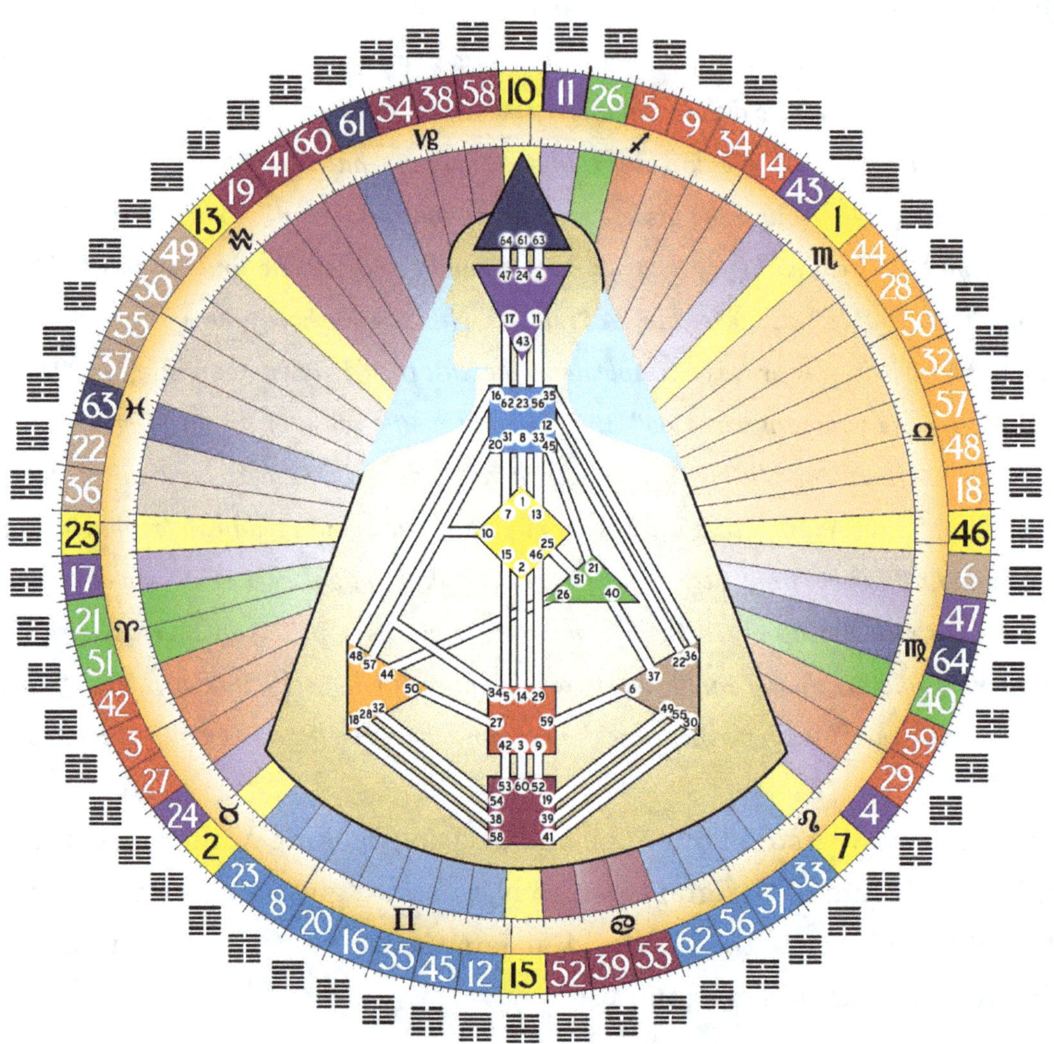

CHAPTER 11

WHO ARE "MY PEOPLE"?

"The meeting of two personalities is like the contact of two chemical substances: if there is any reaction, both are transformed."

— CARL JUNG

For those with a lot of Tribal Circuitry, this is an obvious question: Who belongs in my tribe? To whose tribe do I belong? In these instances, the tribe may be family and also workplace, church, club, or community. The question also arises in a different way for Projector Types who are here to guide those people who invite them; they are not here for everyone, so part of a Projector's way is to get comfortable with recognizing that some are, and some are not, "my people." Aside from these senses of belonging, we all have folk with whom we just seem to click, whether we have obvious interests or values in common or not.

LINE NUMBERS

The Lines are an integral component that adds more specificity and nuance to the primary information given by the Gates. As we saw earlier, each of the sixty-four Gates corresponds to one of the sixty-four hexagrams of the I Ching, and each hexagram is made up of six lines. Thus, each Gate in the Human Design chart has six possible Lines. These Lines provide additional insight into how the energy of a particular Gate is expressed, never more evident than with the Gate activated by the Sun, hence the importance of Profile, the two Line numbers associated with the Gates of the Sun.

Line 1: Grounded

This line is about foundation – the physical and bodily survival. People with Line 1 as part of their Profile are often seen as being very grounded and can be regarded as a "rock" for others. This can hide a deep insecurity lying at the physical level of the body, along with fear (notably for survival and of confrontation), which may be repressed.

People influenced by this line tend to be thorough, introspective, and need a solid foundation or understanding before moving forward. Consequently, Line 1 was originally called *The Investigator*: What is this material life all about? They like to investigate and get to the bottom of things as it affords them a sense of security. They might enjoy deep study, especially of life itself and the material world, and can be introverted, preferring to learn at their own pace.

With Line 1, people can struggle to express their feelings and experience a sense of being swamped by dread, all the while hiding and feeling trapped inside themselves to the point that they may appear secretive. You might think of this as a Root Chakra issue, and indeed, Line 1 folks can have physical problems.

If you, or your child, have Line 1, you want to get comfortable physically – with movement, out in nature, and in awe of life itself. Learning to witness feelings, rather than being swamped by them, can help people lessen the impact of their fears. Physical touch is key, so Line 1 people are often very tactile, and a hug can go a long way toward assuaging their fears, too.

Ethan would never start a Lego build until he had located every piece in the instruction booklet. If one tiny brick was missing, he'd quietly set everything aside and go in search of the missing piece. Once the piece was found and he felt secure in his foundations, he relaxed – then happily built for hours.

Ultimately, those with a Line 1 need to work on themselves to get to the core of their wound (we all carry them), to understand themselves and thereby heal to become the grounded, confident, and truthful souls they are. These children may need to be taught how to stand up for themselves, to temper their tendency to be direct, and to love themselves and their body.

Line 2: Natural

At its best, this Line is about being natural, relaxed, and playful. Where fear can be a challenge for Line 1, anger can be the most obvious issue for Line 2 (although such anger sometimes covers up a fear of everything) and can show up explosively. People with Line 2 can be oblivious or in denial and can use anger as a mask to stay in denial.

This Line represents the natural talent. Those with Line 2 can be recognized for their innate abilities. They might prefer solitude or working alone, waiting to be called out or recognized by others. There's a duality here: a need for alone time, free of pressure, but also a potential for recognition when they engage with the outer world. They may be quite self-contained, not liking interference and unable to explain their particular genius, hence the original name of *The Hermit*.

People with Line 2 in their Profile can feel an external pressure and respond with bodily denial, becoming physically careless or manifesting as eating disorders, weight problems or sexual issues. They can project their issues onto external factors or other people and remain in denial about their own responsibility.

The "answer" for people with Line 2 is in relationship, using the outer world as a mirror to see themselves and owning their part in any situation. Relaxation is key, as is learning to play without being competitive. The natural genius of a Line 2 lends itself to being able to win all the time – allowing others to do so is gracious and ultimately more fun for all.

Vikki could pick up the violin and play a tune after hearing it once, but if anyone tried to show her "a better way," she would vanish into her bedroom and shut the door. She came out again only when she felt ready – usually humming beautifully, as though nothing had happened.

If you have a Line 2 in the family, you want to cultivate a relaxed household, encouraging everyone to be themselves and allowing spontaneity and playfulness. Teaching youngsters to eat healthily and well will go some way toward mitigating any risk of eating disorders. Recognizing their gifts will not only encourage them but also allow them to relax into being who they are. Life doesn't need to be understood in order to find a state of flow, and in that flow of life, true nature will unfold through events as they occur.

Line 3: Experimental

Experimentation is the keyword for Line 3. People with this line are here to learn by trial and error. They need to embody things to know if they really work. They might make mistakes, but these are essential for their learning and growth. They challenge the status quo and can bring about innovation through their experimental nature, always seeking improvement.

Such is the experimental nature of people with a Line 3: commitment is a trigger issue, and choosing something can be a real dilemma. They are acutely aware that making one choice shuts the door on other possibilities. Consequently, they may be seen as greedy ("I want it all!") and yet this is rooted in a deep insecurity about whether they'll ever be "good enough." Addictive patterns can show up with issues of money or food, and they can become masters of avoidance and distraction.

The original name for Line 3 was *The Martyr* on the basis that folk with this Line have the capacity to call things as they see them and take the heat for it. Yet, Line 3 is deeply emotional, and these feelings can readily tip into shame. There is an inbuilt dilemma in needing to learn through experimenting and feeling shame in making mistakes, and yet true innovation is always preceded by many "mistakes."

The escapist nature of a Line 3 can be harnessed with a decision to love life and a degree of humor about your own antics and those of others. It's okay to make mistakes. It's also okay to laugh at them and your own foolishness. The capacity to experiment and innovate also makes Line 3 folk remarkably adaptable.

Rory once decided to bake cupcakes "all by his own," as he put it. After three collapsing batches and one burnt tea towel, he proudly produced a misshapen but delicious tray of cakes. He shrugged, grinned, and said, "Now, I know what not to do." His family cheered – they'd learned to celebrate the process as much as the success.

If you or yours have Line 3 in their Profile, it is so important that your family recognizes the endeavor at least as much as the achievement of goals. Laughter is key in helping Line 3 people lighten up and avoid taking things too seriously. You tried, it didn't work out this time, laugh about it (cry about it too if that's how you feel) and then recognize what you've learned – and so your store of wisdom grows.

Line 4: Heartfelt

Line 4 is all about connection, and those with this line in their Profile can be enormously kind, compassionate, and loving … unless and until they sense rejection, in which case they can become cold, hard, and even cruel. With a great fear of rejection, they can reject before being rejected themselves.

This line is about external influence and networks. Those with Line 4 are usually friendly, socially driven, and often rely on their networks or close relationships to progress in life. First called *The Opportunist*, people with Line 4 recognize and make use of opportunities presented through their relationships. As a result, they can become hugely influential.

There is a fragility about Line 4, which can show up as tears, rigidity, and the need to feel protected. Change can be unsettling for those with Line 4 in their Profile. That warm person with open arms can hide behind an emotional wall, controlling the environment, and being mean. They can look successful while they feel numb inside, desperately wanting to be accepted.

Imogen adored her little group of friends and wrote them tiny notes with stickers and hearts. If someone didn't smile back at school drop-off, she would immediately assume they were cross with her and fold in on herself. A warm cuddle at home usually melted the icy shell and brought her kindness shining back out.

Line 4 folk can be most influential as they focus on community and drawing people together. Open-hearted and kind, they can be loyal friends with a great love of people. At their best, they are tender, soft, demonstrative, and totally comfortable with others.

If you have Line 4, be gentle with yourself. If your child has Line 4, teach them to be a friend to themselves. Much like those with Line 1, a hug can go a long way toward softening the chest armor of a Line 4 and allowing them to love and be loved without constraint.

Line 5: Director

Those with Line 5 are born teachers, coaches, leaders, guides.... Originally given the title *The Heretic*, they can be objective, practical, and brilliant in far-reaching and novel ways. They can also be manipulative, delusional, and driven by guilt. Somehow, they seem to invite folk to project their own concerns onto them, sometimes hiding in the projection field even from themselves.

Individuals with this Line are seen as those who bring change or have a solution for a wider community. There is something universal in their message. There's often an expectation projected onto them, much like a mirror, and they might be seen as either saviors or problem-solvers. However, they can also face opposition if they don't meet these expectations, which may cause them to tend toward shyness. Few people really get to know a Line 5.

The mind of a Line 5 can be so clever that they believe what their fear wants them to believe. That way lies paranoia, caught in a web of their own delusion, which can be exacerbated by others who feed the illusion, and a never-ending "blame game." They are masters of "rescuing" others, all too often at their own expense, and all the while creating a false image of their own self.

Rowan's teacher once jokingly said, "I wish someone could organize this art cupboard," and Rowan took it as his personal mission. He re-sorted every paintbrush and labelled every shelf, then felt crushed when classmates teased him for being a "teacher's pet." Once he realized people simply expected a lot from him — often without explicitly asking — he relaxed into taking charge only when it truly mattered.

A love of humanity often shines through a Line 5, and in grounding their ideas in practical reality, they expand their brilliance and capacity to lead others. Forgiveness is in their nature; by forgiving everyone and everything, they can find their way out of any "Hall of Mirrors" they may have around them. Once they have clarity, they can enact their dreams.

With a Line 5 in your family, everyone will benefit from clear boundaries to mitigate any tendency toward illusion or delusion. Fostering an atmosphere of forgiveness will teach family members to live and let live and encourage that Line 5 to soar.

Line 6: Visionary

The Line 6 is about balancing Spirit and matter and living by example. It has three distinct life phases as people with this Line mature over time. Until about the age of thirty, life is about trial and error (like Line 3); from thirty to fifty years old, life is often more contemplative, learning through witnessing; and from fifty years onward, life is about coming out as a *Role Model* (the original name for this Line), and providing guidance based on life's experiences. They often appear to have a bird's-eye view of life.

People with Line 6 can struggle to be grounded on the physical plane, seemingly walking between the worlds. This can manifest as distrust and escapism, or as someone who is present, available, and authentic. The early life processes can hone an understanding of what it is to be human and embodied, so long as folk don't get lost in separation with a tendency to blame others without taking responsibility for themselves.

The Line 6 folk can get lost in the mind, sometimes as a means of escape from the physical world. They can feel excluded, without recognizing that they are excluding themselves, usually by appearing aloof, bored, and above it all. The lack of trust they feel can show up as a sense that "everyone is out to get me," along with a disconnection from the "real" world.

Ari spent most of childhood climbing trees "to think," watching everyone else play from above. He'd come down with calm, oddly grown-up comments like, "I don't think they're arguing about the game, I think they're tired." As he matured, that bird's-eye clarity slowly became his superpower.

At their best, those with Line 6 are strongly independent with a spiritual authority and a belief in the power of dreams and the joy of physical manifestation here on Earth. They are concerned with the whole planet and, having mastered the art themselves, they encourage others to transcend the mind, connect to Spirit, and turn their visions into reality.

If you or your child has Line 6, firstly recognize your process through life and be kind to yourselves! Encourage yourselves to believe in your dreams and, rather than get lost in them with your head in the clouds, manifest them here on Earth, thereby showing others how to do the same.

If you imagine a solid fence or hedge that you cannot see through, Line 1 is looking at the bottom of the fence, the foundations or roots, perhaps starting to dig to see what's down there, and what it's all made of....

Line 2 is gazing at the fence, wondering what its purpose is, perfectly happy in its own company ... perhaps there's an opening somewhere?

Line 3 is wondering if there is life on the other side and needs to find out if the grass really is greener there, and then how to squeeze through or better jump over the fence.

Line 4 peers over the top of the fence and gets a bit of the view, but not the whole picture, it wants others to join them and come see.

Line 5 has an unobstructed view and can appreciate and point out all kinds of possibilities on the other side ....

Line 6 gets the whole picture in front and behind the fence, and often feels obliged and then overwhelmed by being responsible for everything on both sides.

THE PROFILES

Before we combine the two Line numbers to create a Profile, it is worth recognizing that the first number shown is conscious and the second unconscious. It is in the unconscious that we find the default way of being, a person's "autopilot" if you will. Given that understanding our Profile is a quick way of seeing how we relate to others and can grow into our full potential, it is well worth homing in on the unconscious to offer targeted support and encouragement in the first instance.

When we look at the Lines and how they might manifest in children with different Profiles, we can begin to see patterns in behavior, learning styles, and interactions with others. Recognizing the tendencies associated with a child's Profile can be very beneficial for all those involved in their upbringing. It allows for an understanding of the child's natural inclinations and offers ways to support their unique learning and growth paths.

Lines 1, 2, and 3 are personal, singular, and the associated learning style is in relation to the self. *What does this mean to or for me?* Lines 5 and 6 are intrapersonal, learning about life in relation to others. Line 4 is almost a bridge – if you were to conjugate a verb, the pronoun would be "we," so a personal concern in the context of others. All the Profiles below are balanced between personal and intrapersonal, except the 1/3 (all personal). So, children with this Profile may need extra help to understand what something might mean for others. You could think of the individual Lines as 1 = Me, 2 = You (Thou), 3 =He, She, It, 4 = We, 5 = Y'all (You plural), 6 = They.

1/3

A child might want to explore things deeply, asking many questions and needing a solid foundation in any subject before moving forward. They may prefer depth over breadth in their learning. Coupled with their investigative nature, they learn by trial and error. They might be the child who takes things apart to see how they work ... and may not always put them back together correctly. Mistakes are crucial for their growth, putting things aside when they are no longer interesting is also part of their story. A parent can be most effective by offering steady reassurance and plenty of space – a safe base for all the questioning, and a gentle cheerleader when the inevitable experiments (and missteps) unfold.

Sebastian discovered a profound interest in Roman History at an early age and led his family on many an expedition to archaeological sites in search of a deeper understanding of the Romans. After another year in school, he decided he wanted to study Mandarin Chinese.

1/4

A child with this Profile often wants to understand things deeply. They may frequently ask "why?" and are not easily satisfied with surface-level answers. They thrive when they have a firm foundation in a subject or skill. These children are also very socially oriented and need demonstrative love to feel secure. They may seek to integrate their deep knowledge with social opportunities, possibly sharing what they've learned with friends or wanting to teach others. It helps to give them clear explanations, steady routines, and regular reassurance that you're right there with them as they learn.

Judy's primary school reports consistently referred to her being slow to grasp new concepts, but once she'd understood them, she asked intelligent questions to ensure comprehensive knowledge and potential application.

2/4

This child might have periods where they seem introverted, preferring their own company or engrossed in solo activities. They might have innate talents that they haven't yet recognized. However, they also value their close friendships and might often learn or get opportunities through friends and social connections. They could be the child who thrives in group activities or playdates, so long as they don't go on too long! It helps to balance quiet time with short, enjoyable social moments, letting them retreat when needed and rejoin when they're ready.

Stuart's school reports always had an edge of frustration with comments on his ability to turn his hand to anything successfully if only he would put his mind to it and avoid the distractions offered by his peers.

2/5

These children often have innate talents or interests that they may not be fully aware of. They might enjoy periods of solitude, where they can delve into these talents or simply relax on their own. With their natural abilities, they may often find themselves in situations where they're seen as problem solvers or leaders, even if they didn't actively seek out these roles. This can be both an opportunity and a challenge for them. They might be called upon or expected to provide solutions based on their perceived abilities, and navigating these expectations can be a learning journey for them. Parents can support a 2/5 child by giving them space to explore their interests quietly, while also helping them manage the expectations others place on them, so they don't feel responsible for solving every problem.

Richard's fascination with all forms of transport was something of a joke amongst his friends until he was able to navigate the bus timetable and get them all to the soccer match before kick-off.

3/5

These children thrive on trial and error, and provided they don't repeat mistakes, they learn at light speed. They may seem restless, constantly experimenting with new ways to do things. This can sometimes lead to them being perceived as "clumsy" or "careless," but they're just learning through their activities. Coupled with their experimental nature, they might unintentionally find themselves in situations where they're seen as challengers or rebels. Other kids might expect them to take the lead or find unconventional solutions. For a 3/5 child, this mix of hands-on experimenting and the expectation from others that they "fix" things can feel intense, so reassurance and humor at home help them stay resilient while they learn what truly works for them.

> *John seemed to be in trouble in school frequently because he always had to prove what the teacher was saying to his own satisfaction by, for example, painting around the paper, testing the gas supply to the Bunsen burner or crossing the wires to a battery pack.*

3/6

Experimentation is the key theme, and they can learn things very quickly by sometimes blundering through them. Children with this Profile love discovering things on their own. Early on, they might take more risks, but as they grow, they'll become more observational, watching, and learning from the sidelines before finally emerging with wisdom in their later years. It helps parents of a 3/6 child to remember that their experimental phase lasts well into adulthood, and that every tumble, test, and discovery is laying down the lived experience that later becomes their hard-won wisdom.

> *Never mind what she might have learned in biology or personal development classes, Hazel was fascinated to watch the birth of baby goats at a family farm at which she worked on Saturdays, and promptly asked her parents to allow their dog to have puppies so she could observe afresh again.*

4/1

These children have their own way of navigating the world and are naturally friendly and curious. They often form tight-knit groups of friends and are very social, and yet need alone time too. When they find something they're passionate about, they dive deep. Whether it's a hobby or a school subject, they want to know everything about it. They do not and cannot fit into others' expectations – they are here both to explore and to demonstrate one facet of life. Parents of a 4/1 child often find life easiest when they honor both sides of this design – giving them the security of their deep interests while allowing their social world to unfold naturally in its own time.

Serena discovered a passion for music early on, playing on the family piano before she started school. As soon as she saw the older children playing instruments together, she lobbied her parents for violin lessons so she could join the orchestra.

The 4/1 Profile is so very different from all the others – let's pause and look at a case study to understand it more deeply.

There was a time that Chetan was teaching Human Design in Istanbul, and after the classes finished and before flying home, he would do readings for students and family members. On one occasion he was asked if he could do a reading for a couple who had some issues with their son, Ahmed. Chetan had the charts ready, and when the couple arrived, we appreciated that they knew very little English, and wanted our translator to help out.

Apparently, Ahmed was very destructive both at home and at school, to the extent that school authorities had brought in doctors, psychologists, mediators, and all kinds of specialists who examined the boy, but who could find no way of placating him. The couple appeared to me to be completely in love with each other, and had arrived at their wits end, desperate enough to ask for Chetan's input. They didn't give him many details of their situation, but hoped he'd be able to tell them something useful.

Chetan started going through their charts first, and they sat attentively while the translator explained what he saw in their partnership. Then, he turned to Ahmed's chart, and described his Design, and areas in the chart that might cause issues when in the company of other people. At one point, he had to stop, because the couple were talking animatedly to each other, and after waiting for a few moments, he asked the translator what was going on. She told him that the couple were stunned that he was able to describe their son and his particular characteristics exactly, and also how he'd been reacting in ways that unsettled everyone and was causing so much difficulty.

Among other features, Ahmed had a "Fixed Fate" 4/1 Profile and a very "Individual" MG Design, which implied that he was not open to instructions or expectations that went against his nature. Most disciplines, rule and belief systems, behavioral patterns that his present society might consider "normal," were likely antithetical to his make-up, and thus caused reactions whenever they were imposed. The stronger the insistence that he behave "normally," the greater became his reactions. Of course, then came the big question: what to do about it all? What they discussed was threefold:

1. They considered how difficult it would be for Ahmed to go to a school that provided education that catered to a child's special interests, like a Waldorf School?

2. Could a personal tutor be found who would devote two hours a day with Ahmed, on the condition that he would commit to be calmer with his parents, at school and at home?

3. Could Ahmed be given yes-no questions to help guide him into making clear deci-sions that resonate within himself, and which can also be acknowledged by his parents and teachers?

The couple found an alternative schooling arrangement and also a tutor. Sometime later, when Chetan asked if the family's life had improved, he was told that now, for the most part, they had a calm and loving household, and upsets were minimal, as everyone was adjusting to their new understandings and agreements.

4/6

Social connections are vital. They might often bring friends home or always want to be involved in social activities. In their younger years, they're all about exploring and may often combine this with their social nature, like organizing group adventures. As they grow, they may become more reflective, often serving as a bridge between younger and older children. It helps parents of a 4/6 child to remember that their early social enthusiasm gradually matures into natural leadership, so giving them both connection and breathing space allows their confidence to grow in its own rhythm.

Debbie brought home friends from school much more often than her siblings and was an ace at arranging lifts and car-shares with her friends and their parents whenever they wanted to go into town.

5/1

These children might often find themselves in leadership roles or positions where others look up to them, even if they didn't actively seek it. Other children – and adults – may see what they want to see in these children, projecting their own expectations on them. They might be expected to have answers or solutions in group settings. They will want to understand things at a foundational level. They might enjoy researching or diving deep into subjects that interest them. Parents of a 5/1 child need to remember that offering steady reassurance and helping them check whether others' expectations are true or simply projections can give them the confidence to separate who they really are from what others imagine them to be.

From a young age, Matt seemed to attract strong feelings from others which he found very disconcerting. People seemed to love or hate him without any obvious rhyme or reason. He found he had to be very particular with his choice of friends and be able to move on when they had expectations he was not going to fulfil.

5/2

Even if they don't seek it out, they might find themselves in situations where they're seen as leaders or problem-solvers by their peers. Crucially, they need their downtime. Like Matt in the example above, they are often projected on and may need to withdraw from social situations to regain their equilibrium and recharge. It is in their own company that they find their peace and inspiration. They may need encouragement to share their ideas and reassurance that their insights are welcomed. For a 5/2 child, the most supportive thing you can offer is permission to retreat, recharge, and emerge in their own time, helping them stay grounded amid the projections of others and confident in sharing their quiet brilliance.

Calum was the "quiet one" in his family as his siblings jostled for attention at the dinner table. Invited to share his thought, Calum frequently brought everyone to a standstill as they paused to digest what he'd said – sometimes teased for his ideas and other times appreciated for his wisdom.

6/2

Early in life, these children are in the experimental phase. They might seem a bit reckless or adventurous, testing boundaries often. As they grow, they'll move into more reflective phases. Despite their adventurous nature, they also have periods where they prefer solitude or their own company. They might be independent learners and occasionally surprise adults with unexpected skills or knowledge. For parents of a 6/2 child, it helps to remember that their early risk-taking gradually matures into quiet competence, especially when they're given plenty of space to explore life, and themselves, at their own pace.

Maeve was the adventurous one of her siblings, never missing an opportunity for a cookout, camping trip or expedition into the woods and often came home with new "one pot" dishes to test out at family dinners.

6/3

These children are on a journey of three life phases, with the early years characterized by much trial and error. Their experimental nature is doubled down in this profile. They're bound to try things in various ways, learning from their mistakes and growing from them. Often wise beyond their years, and soon done with childish things, they can need encouragement to join in with others as they grow older. For a 6/3 child, it helps to remember that their early chaos is part of a much bigger arc – their bumps and experiments eventually ripen into unusual wisdom, especially when they're supported to learn *with* life rather than fear getting things wrong.

Freya was forever getting into scrapes as she tried one madcap idea after another. What others merely talked about, she tested out – climbing, experimenting, and learning by doing – occasionally pausing to draw breath and offering an observation that surprised those around her with its quiet insight, well beyond her years.

There is an inner harmony between Lines 1 and 4, 2 and 5, and 3 and 6. Those with a Profile comprising harmonious Lines will experience less internal push and pull than those without. They will also have fewer people in the population with whom they immediately resonate. For example:

- A 1/3 Profile will have some resonance with other 1/3 Profiles as well as 1/4, 3/5, 3/6, 4/1, 4/6, 6/2 and 6/3.

By contrast:

- A 1/4 Profile will resonate with other 1/4s, and 2/4, 4/1 and 4/6 Profiles.

Mary's parents were concerned that she didn't seem to make friends easily at school, and it wasn't until she was about twelve years old that she had a best friend. Even then, on the face of it, the two youngsters didn't seem to have a huge amount in common, and yet the strength of their friendship was undeniable. Years later, the two friends discovered that they were both 1/4 Profiles.

Unlike Mary and her friend, the "cool kids" at school likely have Profiles that resonate with lots of others!

Profiles help us understand the stance a child takes as they meet the world — whether they dig for foundations, poke at possibilities, experiment their way forward, gather friends, shoulder expectations, or gaze at life from a higher perch. Each brings its own rhythm and charm. With these patterns in mind, we now turn to another layer of Design: the energetic pathways running beneath it all. These reveal *how* a child naturally connects, creates, collaborates, or quietly observes — right down to the one who dismantles the toaster simply to understand breakfast.

Let's explore how these deeper circuits help shape the story your child is here to live.

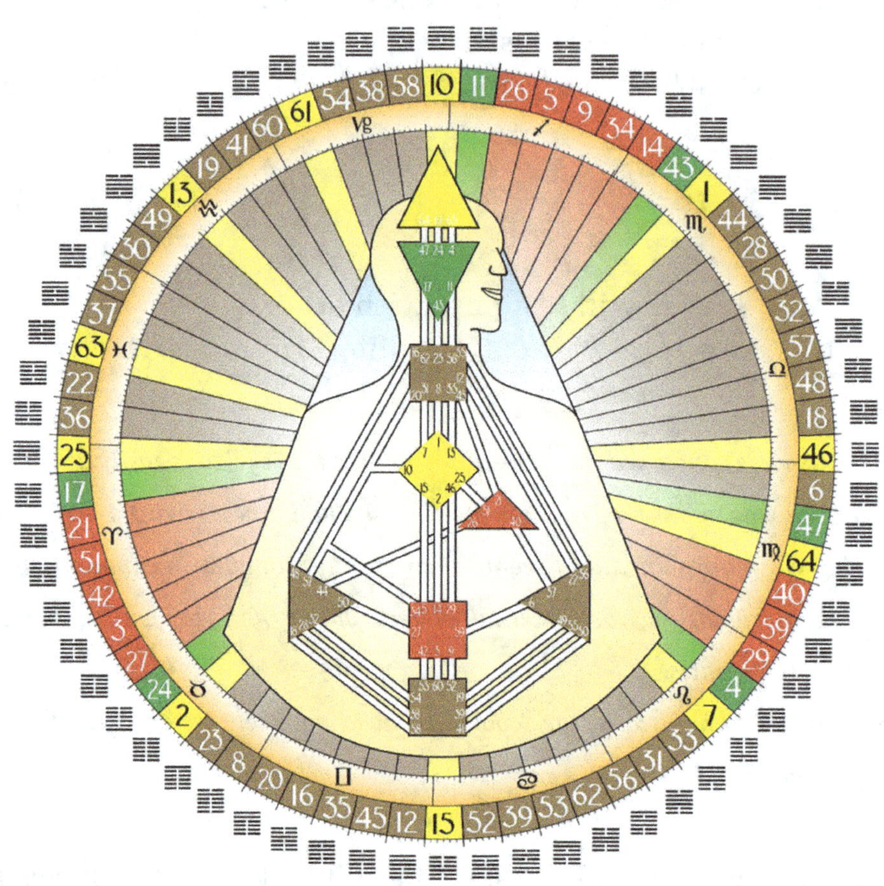

CHAPTER 12

PATTERNS OF HUMAN CONNECTION

"Connection is why we're here; it is what gives purpose and meaning to our lives."

— BRENÉ BROWN

Having explored many of the individual parts of a Human Design chart and how they shape a child's way of meeting the world, now we turn to something that weaves these parts together: the Circuits. These energetic pathways show the larger patterns running through a person's life, revealing how they connect, create, and contribute in their own unmistakable way.

CIRCUITS

There are many different Circuits in the Human Design chart, three of which are especially relevant to understanding yourself and your child. There are thirty-six

Channels that connect the nine Centers, and here we describe how these Channels are grouped in ways that contribute to particular traits within civilization. Each Channel belongs to one of these three main Circuits, and a Gate or Channel appears only once within them. The three main Circuit groups are:

- **Individual.** This group includes Knowing, Centering, and Integrating.
- **Collective.** This group includes Logic and Abstract/Sensing.
- **Tribal.** This group includes Entrepreneurial, Communal, and Defense.

In all charts, there are going to be activations in each of the main Circuits. However, a predominance of a particular Circuit can indicate a more emphasized series of gifts and abilities in a child's or parent's chart. This can mean that a parent with mostly Individual Circuit traits might have one child with predominantly Collective Logic traits, and another child with predominantly Tribal Circuitry traits, and each one of you is living life with your own inbuilt priorities, gifts, and approaches to life. Understanding these differences can go a long way toward honoring and encouraging each person's passage and accomplishments in life. The child who is encouraged to become a doctor might really be more inclined to perform music.

This table shows some of the different attributes of the three main Circuit Groups:

Individual	Collective	Tribal
Contains: Knowing, Centering & Integration Circuits	Contains: Logic & Abstract/Sensing Circuits	Contains: Entrepreneurial, Communal & Defense Circuits
Individual Traits	**Collective Traits**	**Tribal Traits**
Personal	Impersonal	Familial
Acoustic	Visual	Smell/Touch
Empowering	Sharing & Cooperative	Supportive
Romantic	Realistic	Negotiating
Depressive/Elative	Experienceful/Experimental	Willful/Heartfelt
Mutative	Progressive	Hierarchical
Individuality	Committees	Elders
New Forms	Renewing/Reinventing	Restyling
Music/Poetry	Text	Ceremony
Moody/Melancholic	Progressive/Steady	Serving
Transforming	Changing	Traditional

Even a cursory glance at the table shows how people with a preponderance of one type of circuitry might go through life in a very different way than another. Of particular note with your children is whether they have an affinity for acoustic, visual and/or sense of smell/touch – such recognition gives you an immediate insight into what will soothe your child more quickly. Do they need gentle music, a beautiful picture, or a hug most?

Each Circuit expresses itself through specific Channels – the energetic pathways that create consistent traits and behaviors. When a Channel is active in a chart, its themes become part of a child's everyday way of engaging with life. Cards for each of these Channels with an associated mantra are available from Pippa's website at https://www.dagaz.me/resources/.

TRIBAL CHANNELS

Historically, the world has grown from small groups in which families combine their intentions, efforts, and capital to enrich the lives of all in a larger group. Families expanded into tribes, and tribes expanded into communities that involved extended families, villages, sports teams, corporations, and even whole countries.

All tribes have a "King" and/or "Queen," Matriarch and/or Patriarch, elder, dictator, boss, CEO or chairman ... who generally have the last word in tribal community situations. All tribes have a "pecking order," from chief to serf, matriarch to great-grandchild, and everyone knows their place through an unwritten set of codes and priorities. Everyone "does their bit" to support the tribe or family as a whole.

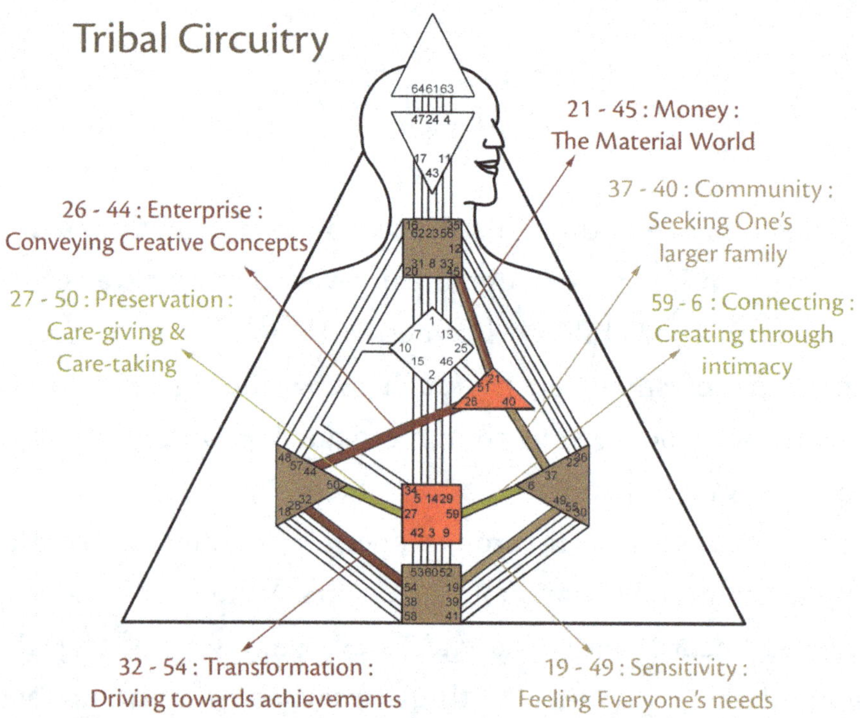

Tribes are not democratic in nature, and their elders expect (and ultimately demand) 100 percent approval, obedience, and support. If they do not receive this, the tribe splinters into factions, and a new order is established by outcasts and usurpers.

In the Human Design chart, all Tribal Channels are based on what has value, particularly on the material level. Out of four possible connections to the Heart/Willpower Center, three of them are a part of Tribal Circuitry.

The Tribal Entrepreneurial Circuit Channels

The two Channels to the left from Root to Spleen Center, 54–32, Transformation, and from Spleen to Heart/Willpower Center, 44–26, Enterprise, are entrepreneurial in nature, driven to enhance lives by reviewing, re-engineering, and updating whatever their tribe members value. These Channels and their Gates operate through the sense of smell, or an instantaneous instinctual, visceral attunement that can reveal a complete comprehension of a larger scenario from a momentary hint.

The Root Center provides pressure to achieve. The Spleen Center's input involves quick recognition of what works and what does not, what is healthy and what is not, and the Willpower Center applies perceived and material value. The connection from Willpower/Heart Center to Throat, 21–45, The Money Channel, controls and oversees agreements, investments, and resources for the tribe or community.

The Channel 54–32, Transformation, Driving toward Achievements derives pressure from the Root Center, as an Ambition, to set specific goals that are maintained throughout their lifetime by active vigilance. The holder of this Channel is motivated through personal effort or assistance from capable sources to produce and promote something that comes from an inner urge. Children with this Channel will exhibit an entrepreneurial nature that takes them into friendships and associations with those who can boost them and their objectives.

Eight-year-old Andy has already decided he wants to run his own business one day, so he carefully saves his pocket money in labeled jars and asks his aunt endless questions about how she started her shop. While other children spend freely, Andy watches, plans, and waits, quietly focused on what his effort might grow into over time.

The Channel 44–26, Enterprise, Conveying Creative Concepts has the means to shift people's priorities toward those that are healthy as well as valuable by offering alternative opportunities for their lives. Instinctual in nature, it can heal ego issues by guiding people toward constructive growth; it can also exaggerate ego issues by taking advantage of others' vulnerabilities. Children born with this Channel are always going to balance between using their instincts and creative abilities honorably and using them with self-interest as their motivation.

During a school fundraiser, Aisha moves from table to table, changing her approach each time – joking with one friend, appealing to fairness with another, promising fun to a third. By the end of lunch, most of the class has signed up, and Aisha is already turning her attention to the next opportunity.

The Channel 21–45, Money, The Material World uses direct Willpower-Manifesting abilities to control the accumulation and use of resources for their family and community. It has the power to qualify values in how education, assets, and possessions are best manifested and employed for their family or community, regardless of others' beliefs or opinions. Children with this Channel are encouraged to find what lies in their heart of hearts at any time, and then live that.

Nine-year-old Caleb insists on being in charge of the family game cupboard, carefully deciding who gets what and reminding everyone when it's time to put things back properly. When asked why, he shrugs and says, "Someone has to make sure it's fair and taken care of," already holding a strong inner sense of responsibility for shared resources.

The Tribal Community Circuit Channels

The two Channels to the right from Root to Emotions Center, 19–49, Sensitivity, and from Emotions to Heart/Willpower Center, 37–40, Community, provide the structure and requirements for tribal members through which inter-family agreements, bargains, handshake deals, and familiarities are established. These two Channels and their Gates operate through the sense of touch, and a connection that registers differing levels of familiarity through handshakes, holding hands, hugs, massage, and physically sensual connections. Each family or tribe's particular codes decide who is allowed to approach and touch whom, and exactly how familiar that touch is allowed to be. (Covid interrupted many such interactions.)

The Channel 19–49, Sensitivity, Feeling Everyone's Needs is really the Channel of Hyper-sensitivity in that it picks up on people's abilities and aptitudes, and is often ready to fulfill the needs of anyone who appears lacking or lost. It easily confuses others' degrees of sensitivity with its own and has to learn to be cautious around clumsy and insensitive people. A child with this Channel tunes into everyone and is ready to assist them, but must attune to and thrust their own Emotions Authority to avoid getting their feelings hurt by inconsiderate people.

Noor is the first to notice when someone is left out, quietly offering her snack or sitting beside them without being asked. Later, when a cup tips over at home, she dissolves into tears, as if the feelings she's held all day finally spill out too.

The Channel 37–40, Community, Seeking One's Larger Family combines Emotional energy and awareness with Willpower to expand friendship, family, and common interests through clear heartfelt agreements and appreciation. A community supports its members through handshake deals, hierarchies, and merged resources. A child with this Channel easily makes friends and comes to appreciate that some friends reciprocate time, energy, and resources more than others.

At birthday parties, Simon is often the one making sure everyone's included, naturally pulling different groups together into one shared game. Over time, he starts to notice which friends show up for him in return — who keeps their promises, who shares willingly, and who quietly drifts away when things feel less fun.

The Tribal Defense Circuit Channels

For a tribe to be successful, it must have member numbers. This means new additions — babies, as well as the ability to provide nourishment and caring for existing members of the tribe who need it. A large, healthy tribe is strong and accomplishes much in terms of wealth and well-being. To the left, the Channel from Sacral to Spleen Center, 27–50, Caregiving/taking, provides nourishment and nurturing, and the Channel to the right from Sacral to Emotions Center, 59–6, Intimacy, concerns fertility, procreation, and creative prospects for the tribe.

The Channel 27 – 50, Preservation, Care-giving and Care-taking provides support in terms of wellness-care and nourishment, both edible and environmental. Those with this Channel can assume it is their role to provide for everyone, and they must remember to follow their Sacral response and personal clarity before committing to anyone or anything. Children with this Channel are naturally caring, often going out of their way to please and comfort those they sense are unwell or lacking in some way.

Without being asked, Emily brings a blanket to her grandfather, reminds her teacher that someone forgot their lunch, and worries if the family dog hasn't eaten on time. She seems to feel responsible for everyone's well-being, even when no one has told her it's her job.

The Channel 59–6, Connecting, Creating through Intimacy's Sacral, life-force energy penetrates into the Emotional body of anyone around them, either making a strong connection, or causing emotional discomfort. Great creativity can come through contact, either through procreation or in the form of original works.

However, those with this Channel realize how their presence affects those who feel clear to engage, and those who immediately distance themselves. Children with this Channel make immediate connections with others that become more or less intimate over time.

Some children seem to connect instantly, and for Miles, that happens everywhere – within minutes of playtime, he's building a secret den with his best friend, then leaning over to share a whispered joke with the new kid. A few children hang back, but those who stay find the connection deepening each time they play together.

The keyword for any Gate or Channel in the Tribal Circuitry is *support*. Everything and everyone are involved to enhance the tribe, family, community, and team as a whole.

COLLECTIVE CHANNELS

When tribes grow too large or are forced to live in confined circumstances, a new set of rules and conditions is formed. Instead of elders making pronouncements for the well-being of the whole tribe, committees are formed, and knowledge and beliefs that go outside traditional ways are shared. This knowledge and these beliefs are used with an implied trust that they serve the majority in the best ways.

Everything that involves Collective Circuitry is impersonal and visual in nature, and through the use of eyesight ("seeing is believing"), knowledge, understandings, and beliefs are shared and assumed. Collective Circuitry is comparative in nature, ranking everything in particular orders of acceptability according to a particular society's relative standards and morals. The collective operates either through logic or an abstract/sensing process, neither of which is personal in nature, but more concerned with objects, systems, and "right" or "wrong" ways in which things get done.

Logic involves constantly experimenting, perfecting systems and techniques, and aiming life toward an assured future. Experiments can be tried over and over, aiming for a perfect outcome that sooner or later will be replaced through updated techniques, refined systems, and new discoveries. Science, Western medicine, performance excellence, and most judicial systems operate on this basis.

The Abstract Sensing Collective references the present from the past and compares experiences to make sense of them and consider whether they are progressive and worthwhile. Experiences only need to be lived out once; repetition leads to monotony and boredom. The oral tradition, travel, histories, and religions operate on this collective basis.

Wherever Collective Circuitry appears in a chart, there is the potential for freshness, imagination, joy, realization, progress, enthusiasm, serendipity, improving, listening, and sharing. However, the collective also carries with it judgment, doubts, skepticism, arrogance, grasping, flaky, fickle, sullen, concealing, guilt, shame, and other characteristics that encompass a potential undertone. The collective has the means to steer society toward adjusting to changes in practical ways, but it can also become entrenched in dogma and fixed opinions that limit freedom and the pursuit of happiness for all individuals.

The Logic Circuitry Channels

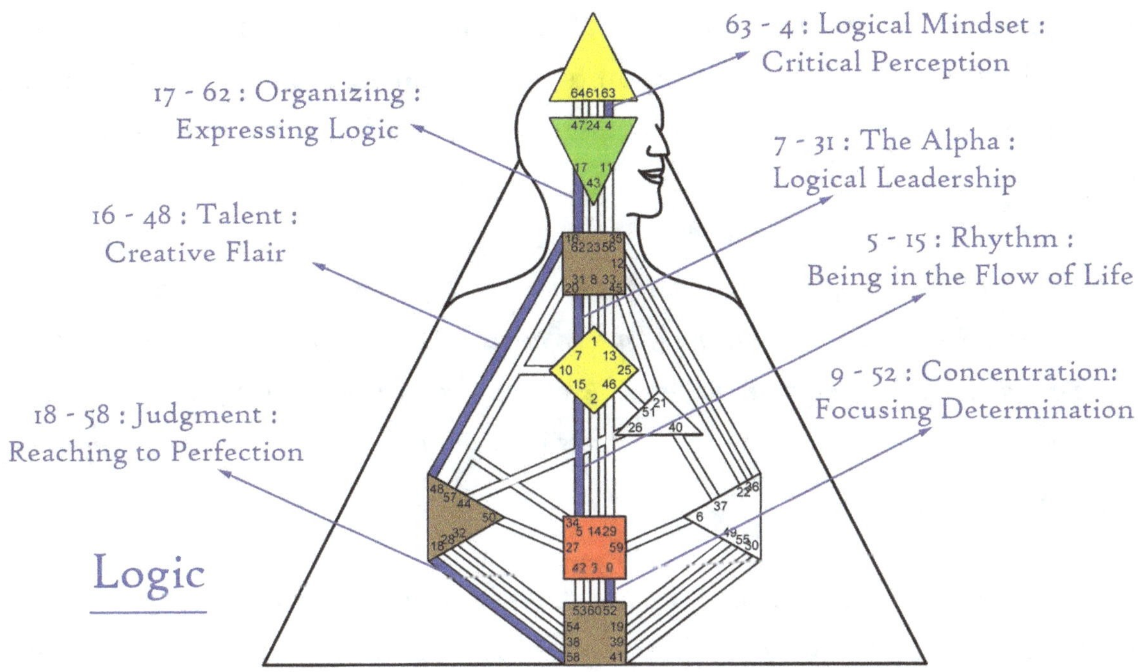

The Logic Channels pass through all Centers except for the Emotions Center (Logic is not about feelings), and the Willpower Center (Logic is not directly involved with material or spiritual values, or Tribal concerns).

The Channel 63–4, Logical Mindset, Critical Perception is constantly checking that thoughts, objects and actions are aligned logically and with attention to a safe and ordered future outcome. A child with this Channel is likely to be concerned in seeing things are "just right."

During homework time, Neil keeps stopping to reread the instructions, pointing out that the example answer doesn't match the question and asking, "Are you sure this is the right way?" He's far less interested in finishing quickly than in making sure every step actually makes sense.

The Channel 17–62, Organizing, Expressing Logic can present facts in seemingly indisputable order, again, aiming life toward a particular future-oriented outcome. Apart from being able to arrange things, this Channel gives a child a potentially strong ability to argue points in a logical way and it might be hard to convince them that their way is wrong, or not needed, from others' points of view.

While his Scout group is planning a weekend hike, Mohammed starts rearranging the plan with the others – pointing out that food needs to be sorted before routes, and routes before deciding which games to bring. Even when a few people disagree, he calmly explains his thinking until the order he sees begins to feel like the most sensible one to follow.

The Channel 16–48, Talent, Creative Flair gives its holder natural gifts that can be applied in multiple ways, although it helps when these gifts are guided, exercised, and applied creatively. Multiple talents are amazing to behold, and guiding, encouraging, and also bankrolling a child might easily become burdensome if resources are overstretched.

One week it's violin practice, the next it's coding, then suddenly Gretchen is absorbed in painting for hours, picking things up with surprising ease. She seems to have a deep well of ability that keeps revealing itself in new forms, often leaving her parents wondering how to support it all without stretching themselves too thin.

The Channel 18–58, Judgment, Reaching to Perfection can easily bring about self-judgment and criticism in its holder. When life is lived from a place of joy, the joy becomes the fuel to self-mastery. Anyone with this Channel can be hard on themselves when projects and life instances don't match expectations. It is important for a child with this Channel to appreciate that life mastery is achieved through persistence and getting over perceived personal failures.

Ten-year-old Dalia finishes a drawing, frowns, and quietly pulls out a fresh sheet to start again, rubbing out small details that bother her. Even when others say it looks great, she's already focused on fixing what doesn't match the picture she had in his head.

The Channel 9–52, Concentration, Focusing Determination gives its holder extraordinary access to future endeavors, provided they are patient enough to await their Sacral Response and inner clarity. Patience is a virtue, and when the moment comes, a child with this Channel can excel in moving toward a planned outcome.

At four years old, Tom can sit on the floor for ages, lining up his toy cars, completely absorbed, barely noticing the noise around him. When he decides it's time to move on, he does so with surprising certainty, shifting his focus only when something truly captures his interest.

The Channel 5–15, Rhythm, Being in the Flow of Life has a particular alignment with nature's timing and seasons that are common to all living things. Those with this Channel might have issues with clocks and other people's sense of time. With an attunement to a different sense of timing, any child with this Channel can be lost in their own world, or they can expand the sense of time, offering others a closer engagement with the present moment.

No matter how many reminders his parents give, Hiro's mornings follow their own pattern – shoes go on only after breakfast feels finished, and coats are forgotten until the very last moment. Yet when Hiro is outside building dens or watching ants on the pavement, he can stay perfectly engaged for ages, setting a pace that feels unhurried and oddly calming.

The Channel 7 –31, The Alpha, Logical Leadership gives forthright and convincing instruction to get others to follow it toward a shared future. All leaders need to know if it is their job or just their ability to lead in any situation. This Channel offers a child natural attunement that gives clear guidance even beyond their years, as they foresee outcomes often before anyone else.

During a school science project, fourteen-year-old Julia quickly sketches out a plan, decides who will research, who will build, and who will present, and gets everyone moving within minutes. She speaks with such calm certainty about how it will turn out that the group naturally falls into step, even when no one officially asked her to lead.

The Abstract/Sensing Circuitry Channels

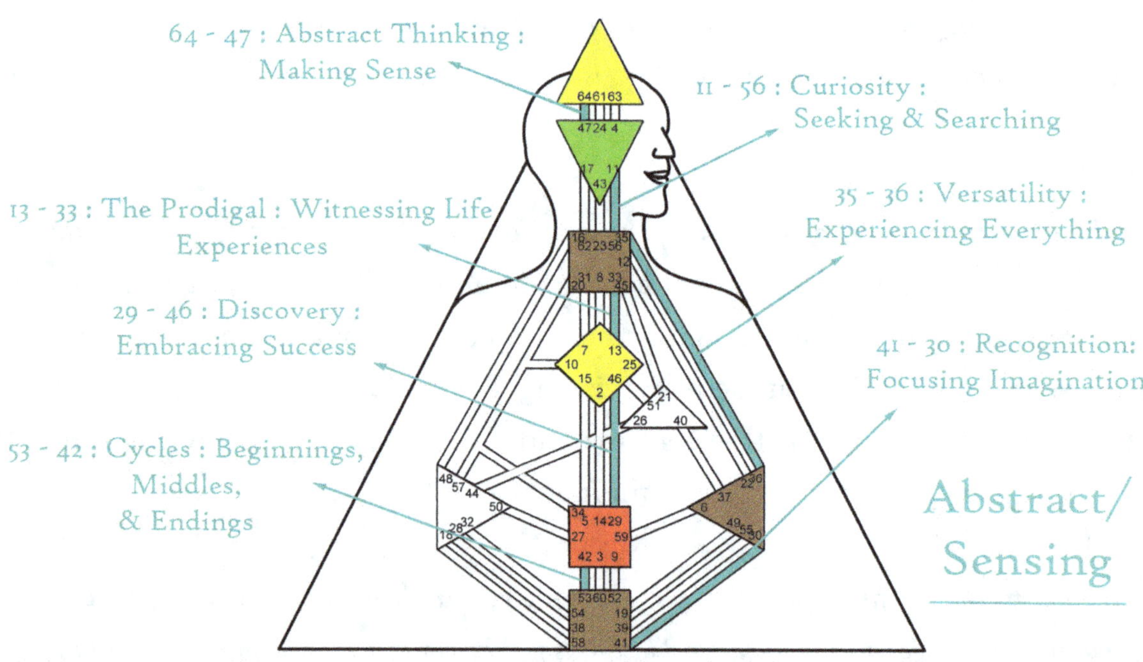

Abstract/Sensing Channels pass through all Centers except the Spleen (no direct concern for safety or physical health and well-being) and the Willpower Center (Abstract/Sensing is not directly involved with material or spiritual values, or Tribal concerns).

The Channel 64–47 is the Abstract Mindset that consistently tries to make sense out of life, with the appreciation that even though much does make sense, there are always more and more possibilities that don't. It links past information with present circumstances and often delves into histories and old religions to get perspective. Any child with this Channel has a natural inquisitiveness about life and how it works. Good luck trying to explain everything!

Lying in bed at night, twelve-year-old Iris asks questions that seem to come from nowhere – why people believed in different gods in the past, what memories are for, and how today connects to things that happened long ago. Her parents answer as best they can before leaving the room, smiling and slightly lost, while Iris keeps turning the ideas over long after the light is switched off.

The Channel 11–56, Curiosity, Seeking and Searching opens the mind to explore anything and everything to find rationale and make sense out of life. It is an endless exploration through everything life has to offer, from religious scripts, unusual diets, travels, physics, nature's anomalies, and related histories of all kinds. A child with this Channel is on a lifetime's inquiry, and will feast on ideas, stories, and adventures of all kinds.

At the dinner table, eight-year-old Theo jumps from telling a story he heard at school to asking about black holes, ancient myths, and why people eat such different foods around the world. His mind seems to wander joyfully from one idea to the next, collecting stories and possibilities faster than anyone can answer them.

The Channel 35–36, Versatility, Experiencing Everything is an emotionally charged Manifesting Channel that can hesitate and then leap, or dive headfirst into experiences of all kinds without a moment's consideration. Experiences only need to be tried once and this Channel can be lived out through a short attention span or provide the means to "push the envelope" of life's encounters ("Been there, done that!"). A child with this Channel can be a daredevil or cautious participant in all of life's offerings. It must be repeated: this Channel is imper-sonal. It is all about the experience.

One weekend, sixteen-year-old Chloe begs to try rock climbing, throws herself into it with full intensity, and declares by Sunday night that she's "done with that now." By Monday she's already talking about learning to surf, volunteering at a music festival, or signing up for a last-minute drama workshop – the rock-climbing experience complete, her curiosity is already moving on.

The Channel 41–30, Recognition, Focusing Imagination has the potential to discover a vision and open ways to live out any and all desires to achieve it. There is an inherent pressure to find meaning in life through experience, and this Channel can either move through dreams and fantasy or open the way to explore life and everything it has to offer. A child with this Channel might be fascinated by fantasy, or more practical in terms of engaging a deep drive to explore their reality through arts and activity.

Before anything actually happens, thirteen-year-old Amara has already imagined it in detail – how the play will feel on stage, how the costume will move, how the audience might respond. Whether she's lost in daydreams or pouring that vision into drawing, drama, or dance, it's the pull of what could be that keeps her energy alive and focused.

The Channel 53 – 42, Cycles, Beginnings, Middles, and Endings initiates and drives the Abstract Circuitry into and through any possible life experience. It is important to remember that the Sacral Center has an "on" switch, but no "off" switch. Once engaged, there's no stopping. So the Sacral Response and personal Authority for anyone with this Channel are essential, because once committed to a career, partnership or endeavor of any sort, there is no turning back until the cycle is completed. A child with this Channel can open a cornucopia of life experiences. However, if they are guided to pay attention to their gut response and personal

Authority, they will naturally find fulfilment. If they randomly jump into anything life offers, they will suffer.

Once Daniel agrees to build a volcano for the school science fair, it becomes the center of family life for weeks. Cardboard, paint, and half-finished ideas clutter the kitchen table as his excitement gives way to frustration and determination, until the model finally erupts on presentation day and earns a proud smile from his teacher. Only then does Daniel seem able to relax, the project finished and the cycle truly complete.

The Channel 29–46, Discovery, Embracing Success opens the possibility to a fulfilled lifetime provided its holder pays attention to their Sacral Response and personal Authority. Those with this Channel bring great levels of energy to anything they do, and yet, must learn to engage this energy only in situations that resonate with them. Once involved, the person with this Channel disappears into whatever they are doing, returning only when everything is complete. Fulfilment is the key to life, and any child who learns how to use this energy well can be the most accomplished of all.

When the school production is announced, Christian hesitates – acting, lighting, stage crew all sound possible, but none feel quite right at first. The moment he starts helping build the set, measuring wood and painting backdrops late into the evening, his energy locks in, and he gives himself to it completely, hardly surfacing until opening night. When the final curtain falls, and the stage is cleared, he's exhausted and glowing, satisfied in a way that only comes from choosing well and seeing something through.

The Channel 13–33, The Prodigal, Witnessing Life Experiences provides the means to summate any and all life experiences. Part of the Oral Tradition of talking story, this Channel can hear things at a very deep level, experience activities both personally and through others, and provide leadership that draws from many layers of human experience. A child with this Channel is drawn to living, hearing, and telling stories, and the broader their experience, the more apt they become at comprehending and relating to life.

At a family gathering, ten-year-old Rosa holds the room as she retells a story from a recent seaside trip, remembering the sudden rainstorm, the café where everyone squeezed in to dry off, and the comment her uncle made that had everyone laughing. Relatives exchange glances, amazed at how deeply she listened and how naturally she turns shared moments, her own and others', into stories that bring the experience back to life.

The keyword for any Gate or Channel in the Collective Circuitry is *sharing*. The collective distributes knowledge and beliefs directly and randomly through politics, religions, and media of all kinds. Anything lived in accordance with Collective Circuitry is impersonal.

INDIVIDUAL CHANNELS

The Individual stands in a majority of One. Individuality has no comparisons, so wherever Individual Circuit Gates and Channels occur in a life chart, there is always a quality that goes outside of Tribal traditions and expectations, and beyond Collective rules, beliefs, and systems. Tribal ways are involved in supporting the family, team, community and corporate traditions and ideals to bring about growth and improvements; the Collective involves keeping everyone up to date with the latest entertainment, news, and beliefs; the Individual ways are novel, creative, different, mutative, and often take a path less trodden.

Individual Channels have the means to break new ground and create new passages and concepts so there exists within them potential extremes in terms of elation and depression, excitement and despondency, success, and failure. In fact, melancholy is a term that can be ascribed to Individual Channels when there might be personal uncertainty in where new steps are leading.

Tribal ways involve touch and smell, nurturing and intimacy.

Collective ways involve seeing and sharing points of view and beliefs.

Individual ways are acoustic in nature and revolve around sounds, intuition, and personal empowerment. Hearing is a unique quality in that everyone can be listening to the same sounds. However, each person's appreciation for what they hear and what it means to them is purely individual.

There are three groups of Channels within the Individual Circuitry: Knowing, Integration, and Centering.

The Knowing Circuit includes all Centers except the Willpower Center. Each Channel indicates a personal expression that is unique to the person who has it.

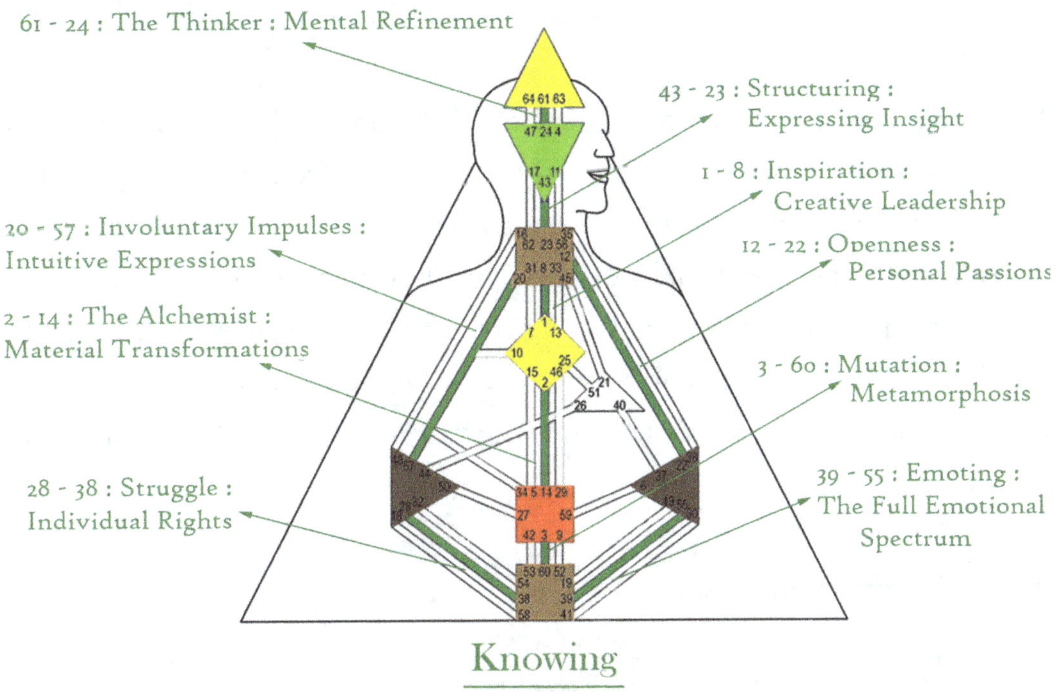

The Integration Circuit involves four Gates that can make connections with each other to form several different Channels between four Centers. This part of the Individual Circuit is associated with the spine or backbone, which connects different areas of the body, energetically. The Channels each indicate strengths within the spinal column.

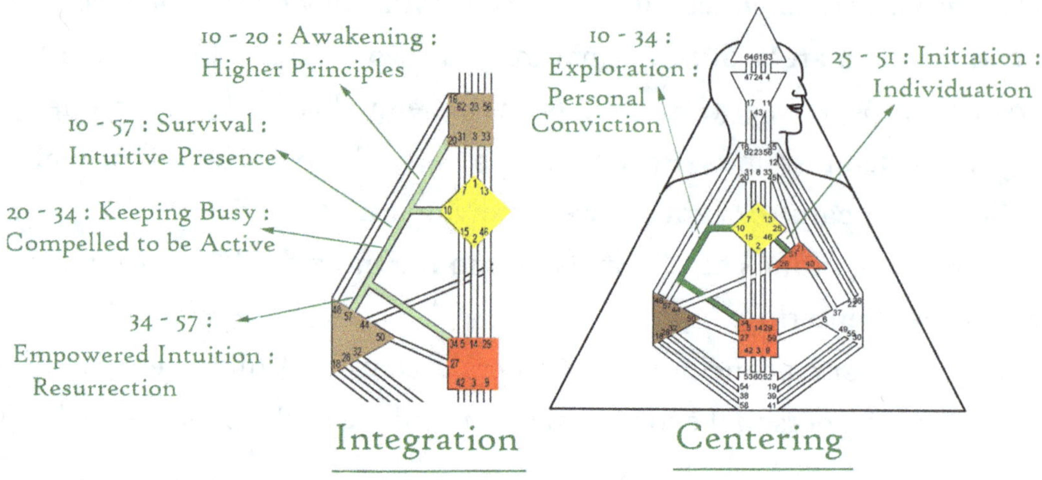

The Centering Circuit has two Channels that connect between the Sacral, Self, and Willpower Centers. Here is the only connection from the Willpower Center into a circuit other than the Tribal Circuitry. This Channel called *Initiation*, 25–51, is often referred to as *The Shaman* Channel, in that it employs willpower to potentially move energy from a material to a spiritual realm. Tribes are known to have Shamans, or Medicine men and women, who empower tribal members to step outside of mundane support rituals and into the search for individuality and spiritual growth.

Knowing Circuitry Channels

The Channel 61–24, The Thinker, Mental Refinement is pressured to comprehend and relay truth. It is the Channel of deep thought that cycles concepts, thoughts, and ideals, refining them over and over, looking for a pure conclusion. Such a Channel can make someone a one-person think tank, or else someone who has the greatest difficulty getting out of their head. Children with this Channel will insist on being told the truth and have the ability to master profound thought. If they can be guided to trust their Authority to know what merits their attention and what does not, they will live a fulfilling life.

At bedtime, fifteen-year-old Euan keeps circling the same question — how people can grow up in the same place yet believe in completely different religions. Long after the lights go out, he turns possible answers over in his mind, refining them again and again until his thoughts finally go quiet.

The Channel 43–23, Structuring, Expressing Insight has the means to intuit and communicate profound perceptions that go outside previously considered standards and limitations. It can state novel concepts as fact and must incorporate speech skills to know when an audience ready to listen, and what tone of voice is going to be the most effective. Subtitled *Genius to Freak*, it becomes clear when statements cause interested surprise, and when they shock. Children with this Channel can consistently stun their audiences, become silent when criticized, or be guided to be comfortable with the sound of their voice and how to best use it.

In the middle of a class discussion, thirteen-year-old Finn suddenly offers a solution no one else had considered, stating it simply as if it's obvious. When the room goes quiet and a few classmates laugh, he shuts down at once, unsure whether he's said something brilliant or strange. The teacher pauses, asks Finn to explain a little more, and the idea begins to make sense — the surprise shifting from awkwardness to interest.

The Channel 20–57, Involuntary Impulses, Intuitive Expressions has the knack of being able to change subjects from dull conversation to alternative interests. Sometimes an intuition is so strong it demands to be expressed, and using a clear tone of voice assists in its delivery to clear stuffy and stilted situations. Children with this Channel can startle their company by expressing profound insights that instantly change an environment, bringing everyone into the present.

As her older sister pulls a chair back to sit down late to the dinner table, nine-year-old Ava suddenly blurts out, "Don't sit there – that chair's going to break." The moment freezes, and within seconds, everyone is checking the legs, surprised she noticed the problem first.

The Channel 28–38, Struggle, Individual Rights has standards that relates to an individual's sovereignty and has issues with rules and beliefs that promote unfairness. Acoustic and intuitive in nature, it easily recognizes where life systems are upheld in preference to individual rights. It is important to attune closely to personal Authority to know which situations to confront, and which to avoid. Children with this Channel can be contrary and obstinate if they feel overlooked, taken for granted, or being bossed around. They can be the first to point out unfairness, and when directed to follow their own Authority, they'll come to know what merits their input, and who and what to avoid.

During a game of soccer at break time, Marcus stops play to point out that Delilah has been picked last again and shouldn't be stuck in goal every time. Even when others groan and tell him to let it go, he stands his ground, unwilling to play along with something that feels unfair to him.

The Channel 12–22, Openness, Personal Passions has a direct Manifestor connection between Emotions and Throat and does whatever it feels to do, whether that fits within rules, beliefs, or arbitrary moral codes. It is passionate in its purpose, romantic in its nature and empowered with elements of Grace, and the potential fortune or misfortune that accompanies Her. Children with this Channel are encouraged to be safe and considerate, but will often transgress what they deem to be unnecessary restrictions, for their way is to open themselves to life in all its majestic and mysterious ways.

At a school concert rehearsal, Lily ignores the instruction to stay in chorus formation and steps out, singing her lines with full emotion and changing the mood of the room in an instant. Some frown at her rule-breaking, while others are quietly moved, sensing that her expression comes from a place too alive to be neatly contained.

The Channel 39–55, Emoting, The Full Emotional Spectrum feels its way through all the highs and lows of life, sometime soaring high and then diving deep, shifting in the blink of an eye without rhyme or reason. It is unreasonable in nature, defies logic and beliefs, and challenges its holder to embrace a million facets of feelings. In its alignment with an abundant spirited nature, it offers the creative potential to mine diamonds from the deep, and pluck stars from the sky. However, it also has the potential for melancholy. A child with this Channel is encouraged to find a creative outlet that withstands all the ups and downs of life and be appreciated and be given and take time for when they are just "not in the mood."

In the space of an afternoon, Arthur moves from laughing uncontrollably while painting in his room to shutting the door and pulling the covers over his head, unable to explain what changed. Later, he returns to the canvas, layering bold color over dark strokes, his feelings finding their way out through something he can shape, even when his mood refuses to make sense.

The Channel 3–60, Mutation, Metamorphosis brings about radical and unexpected transformations. It launches its holder, and everyone close to them, from an old appreciation of life to a new one, and anyone who has a reluctance to any changes involved is left behind. It is unreasonable in nature and can become melancholic while waiting for a new state becomes apparent. Children with this Channel will need to learn how to get over disappointments and embrace a transformational lifetime that brings them new and different friends, pastimes, and ways of living on an irregular (Cosmic) timing basis.

For years, everyone knows Alex as the sporty one — early mornings at the pool, weekends at competitions, shelves lined with medals. Then, almost without warning, the swim bag is abandoned and replaced with notebooks, a guitar, and evenings spent writing songs with a completely new circle of friends. The shift makes little sense to those watching from the outside, but for Alex it feels natural, as if life has quietly moved her onto an entirely different track.

The Channel 2–14, The Alchemist, Material Transformations has the ability to transform our appreciation for the material realms. Without following logical pathways, it has a knack to reorder material and financial arenas, literally transforming the mundane into something that sparkles. Children with this Channel will surprise everyone with original ways of engaging with their world and expanding resources for themselves and the people in it.

What starts as a pile of discarded boxes and old fabric becomes, in Ivy's hands, a pop-up shop in the living room, complete with shelves, prices written on scraps of paper, and a steady stream of family members invited to browse. By the end of the afternoon, she's turned what was lying around into something valuable.

The Channel 1–8, Inspiration, Creative Leadership provides novel ways of guidance and inclusion to maximize potentials for innovative people and endeavors. Acoustic in nature, this Channel provides original leadership that often defies "normal" and traditional ways. It relies on personal trust from those it leads and can outline results, without offering specific pathways to achieve them, instead promising an interesting ride. Children with this Channel can be inspired and often need encouragement to go their own, different way. They will often find themselves providing guidance to the disenchanted and merit guidance in how to embrace their own Authority.

When the class is asked to create a group mural, Jonah doesn't explain how it should be done — he simply describes how it could feel when it's finished and invites others to add what excites them. The group follows, not because he's loud or forceful, but because his vision feels different enough to be worth trusting, even if no one is quite sure where it's going at first.

The Integration Circuitry Channels

The Channel 10-20, Awakening, committing to Higher Principles offers leadership to those who have clear interest in living in the present. Mystical leadership defies the commonplace and society's normal ways of doing things and can be misunderstood by those not paying close attention or with alternative, perhaps more reasoned interests. Life brings multiple challenges in multiple forms, and this Channel either engages in the present or tries to sidestep them. Children with this Channel can find it difficult to live in a sleepy world that repeats itself in old ways and might need encouragement to appreciate that this part of their nature and leadership ability is unique.

At the end-of-term assembly, as the familiar speeches roll on, Catherine suddenly raises her hand and asks why no one ever talks about what this year has actually been like for the students sitting there. A ripple moves through the hall – some cringe at the interruption, others feel a quiet jolt of recognition – as she cuts through routine and brings everyone sharply back into the present moment.

The Channel 20–34, Keeping Busy, Compelled to be Active gives its holder an almost unlimited source of energy to get things done ... now, and keep on getting things done ... now! It is important to appreciate that some things are personally worth getting done, and many things are worth avoiding altogether. Hence, a Sacral Response and the MG protocol are essential qualities to be engaged to avoid exhaustion, overindulgence and to enhance a fulfilled life instead. Children with this Channel can exhibit boundless energy and great activity, however, if they are guided to appreciate their own Authority and what holds meaning for them, and who and what does not, they will live a life of greater achievements and fulfilment.

By mid-morning, Dexter has raced through three games, started building a Lego space-ship, abandoned it to help someone else for a minute, then dashed outside to kick a ball against the fence. He's constantly in motion, driven to act on whatever catches him now.

The Channel 10–57, Survival, Intuitive Presence can exhibit some of the most intuitive and alert capabilities available. Those with this Channel have a lifetime of close encounters, narrow escapes, and sheer good luck if they trust in them-selves and follow their own intuitive abilities. Acoustic in nature, this Channel attunes to the present moment, to circumstances, and to any approaching poten-tial challenges. Children with this Channel can encounter close scrapes and appear to "get away with things" that other children cannot. It is said that the next safest seat is the one beside them.

Halfway across the road, Arla suddenly stops and pulls Esme back just as a bike speeds past, close enough to feel the rush of air. Esme is shaken; Arla is already halfway down the pavement.

The Channel 34–57, Empowered Intuition, Resurrection links life-force energy from the Sacral Center to Intuition in the Spleen Center. It has an uncanny way of attuning to where life force is lacking and can quickly reenergize people and projects. Those with this Channel often become counsellors, coaches, emergency medical technicians (EMTs) or trainers. It is essential that children with this Channel learn to use their inherent Authority to know when to be involved in uplifting other people and projects, and when to stand aside.

Just before the school play is due to start, everything begins to unravel – props are missing, voices are raised, and one of the younger students is close to tears. Seventeen-year-old

Felicity steps in without being asked, locating spare costumes, fixing a loose prop, and quietly steadying nerves. Once the room is humming and the curtain finally goes up, she drifts to the back, her energy spent exactly where it was needed.

The Centering Circuit Channels

The Channel 34–10, Exploration, following Personal Convictions energizes an individual directly through a clear gut response that either commits to, or withdraws from, activities and people. The holder of this Channel will find themselves defying common standards and ways that the mainstream takes, often becoming trendsetters. Children with this Channel must learn the power of standing on their own feet and moving in accord with their own inner convictions, whether anyone else approves or not.

When sign-ups open for after-school activities, almost everyone rushes to join soccer, but Arjun pauses, then writes his name under robotics instead, even though none of his friends do. Weeks later, he stays behind after robotics club, patiently coaxing a stubborn robot to follow a taped line on the floor, until others begin stopping by to see what he's working on.

The Channel 25–51, Initiation, Individuation can dramatically cause transformation for people and situations from the mundane into the real. It initiates radical changes from an attachment to set material ways and traditions to more personally empowering attitudes and practices. A child who has this Channel will often surprise by bringing about radical changes to a family's habits and traditions by innovating new ways to which everyone must adjust to be able to live in integrity.

During a rushed family meal, eight-year-old Fiona suddenly asks why everyone eats so fast when they're together. The question lands awkwardly, but it lingers — and over time, meals begin to slow down, with more talking, more noticing, and a different feeling at the table.

If you have one child who wants to host a neighborhood gathering and another who'd rather disappear into the shed with a book and a cookie, their Circuits can often explain why. Some children draw energy from the Collective, others from their Tribe, and others beat an entirely Individual drum. Many have a mix, of course, which is why families can feel like beautifully organized chaos. Before we look at other aspects of Human Design, you'll find a simple overview of the three Circuit groups and the Gates that belong to each.

With this foundation in place, we now turn to the deeper "hidden wiring" of the chart: the planetary influences, the conscious and unconscious layers, the ancestral threads they carry, and the Splits that shape how energy connects. These elements reveal not just how a child relates to others, but how life itself flows through them.

Individual Circuit Gates

Knowing:

1, Creativity, Creative Self-expression
2, Receptivity, Guidance
3, Beginnings, Implementing the New
8, Contribution, Uniting
12, Standstill, Taking Stock
14, Prosperity, Harvesting
20, The "Now," Contemplation, Watching
22, Grace, Adorning, Favor
23, Assimilation, Stabilizing
24, Returning, Rationalizing
28, The Game Player of Life, Persistence
38, Opposition, The Fighter
39, Provocation, Hardship
43, Breakthrough, Insight
55, Abundance, Spirit
57, The Gentle, Intuition
60, Limitation, Restriction/Acceptance
61, Inner Truth, Sincerity, My-stery.

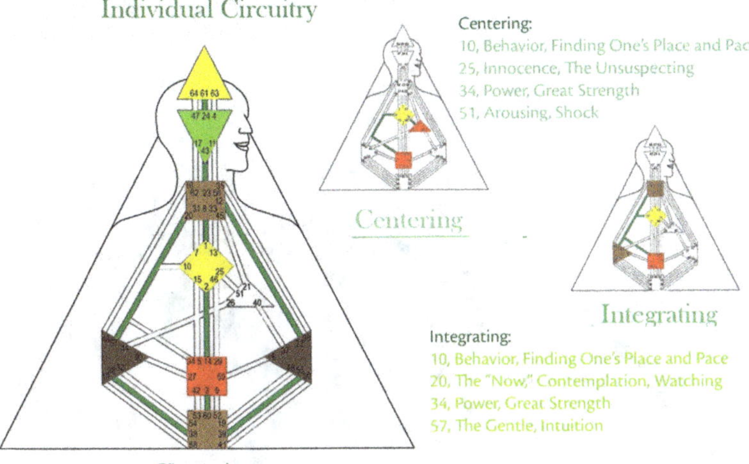

Centering:

10, Behavior, Finding One's Place and Pace
25, Innocence, The Unsuspecting
34, Power, Great Strength
51, Arousing, Shock

Integrating:

10, Behavior, Finding One's Place and Pace
20, The "Now," Contemplation, Watching
34, Power, Great Strength
57, The Gentle, Intuition

Collective Circuitry Gates

Logic:

4, Mental Solutions, Answers
5, Waiting, Universal Timing
7, Uniformity, Common intent
9, Applied Details, Attentiveness
15, Humanity, Extremes
16, Selectivity, Skills
17, Following, Opinions
18, Improving, Finding Remedy
31, Influence, I lead...because...
48, The Well, Freshness and Depth
52, Mountain, Keeping Still
58, Joyous Vitality, The Vital Spark
62, Expressed Details, Clarification
63, Doubts, Critical Perception

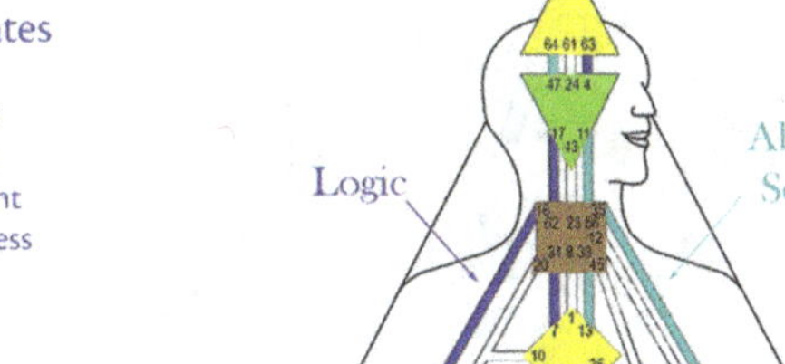

Abstract/Sensing:

11, Harmony, Peace and Ideas
13, The Listener, Fellowship with Mankind
29, Commitment, The Automatic "Yes!"
30, Desires, The "Clinging Fire"
33, Retreat, Withdrawal, Privacy and Secrets
35, Progress, Advancing
36, Crisis Resolution, Darkening of the Light
41, Imagination, Evaluating Potentials
42, Increase, Benefiting
46, Serendipity, Self-determination
47, Realization, Mental Exhaustion, "Aha!"
53, New Beginnings, Development
56, The Wanderer, Stimulation, Traveling
64, Diverse Possibilities, Confusion

Tribal Circuitry Gates

Entrepreneurial:

21, Control, The Hunter
26, Accumulation, Fortitude
32, Duration, Endurance
44, Patterns, Meeting Together
45, Gathering Together, Rulership
54, Ambition, Material and Spiritual

Communal:

19, Approach, Inclusion
37, Family, Community
40, Deliverance, Freedom
49, Revolution, The Rebel

Defense:

6, Conflict Resolution, Emotional Balance
27, Nourishing, Nurturing
50, Values, Stability
59, Intimacy, Dispersion, Genetic Strategy

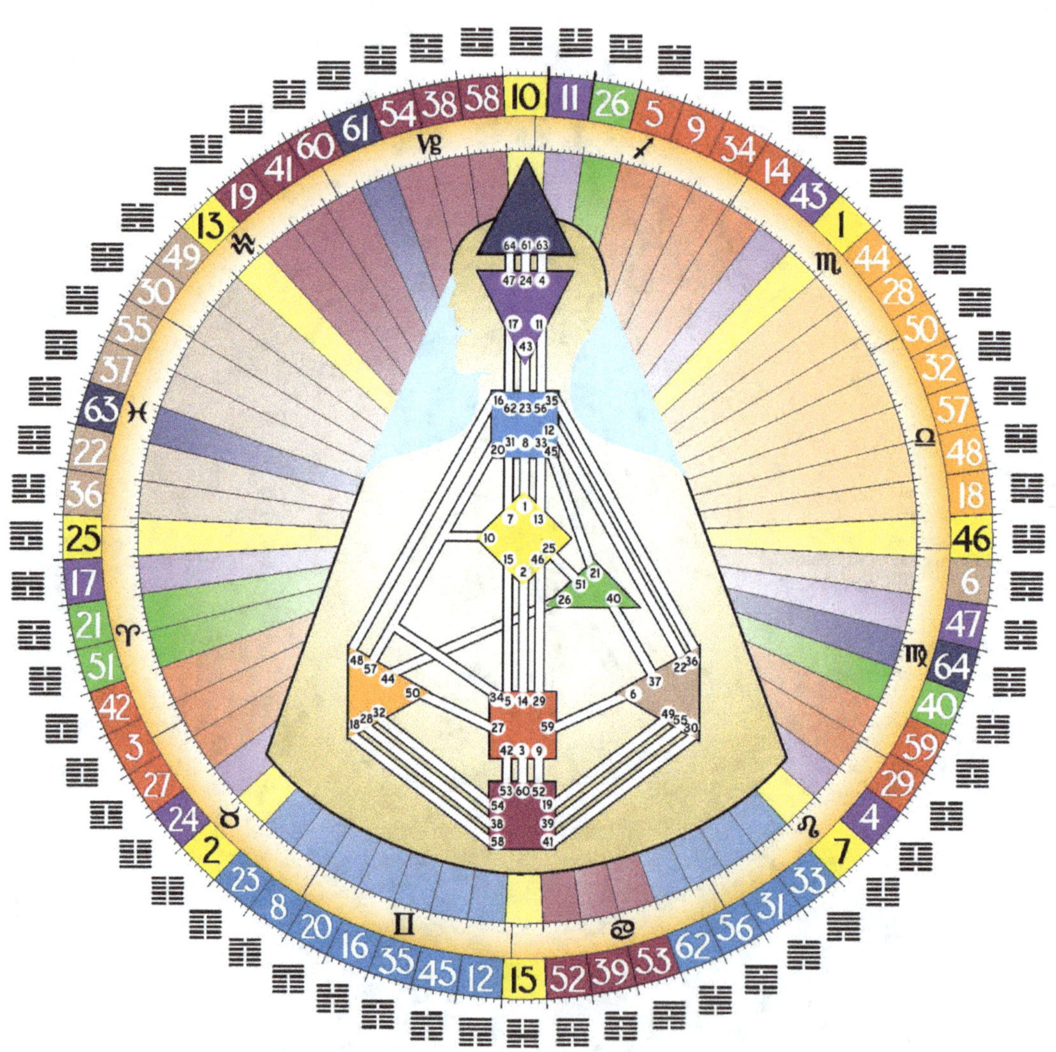

CHAPTER 13

THE HIDDEN WIRING: DEEPER INFLUENCES

"Listen to your being. It is continuously giving you hints; it is a still, small voice. It does not shout at you, that is true. And if you are a little silent you will start feeling your way."

— OSHO

If a Human Design chart were a building, you'd notice the structure first, the solid walls and rooms that are always there. These are the Centers, determining your Type and Decision-Making Authority: the fixed, reliable parts of who you are when they're colored in and consistently active. Yet every building has more going on than meets the eye. There's wiring, plumbing, the heating system – all those invisible influences that determine how the place functions. Human Design has its own version of these hidden systems, and we explored the Circuits in the previous chapter. Here, we turn to the deeper influences: which planet activates a given Gate, the conscious and unconscious layers of a design, and the presence of any splits. Each of these subtler elements can make a profound difference to our understanding.

PLANETARY INFLUENCE

The way each individual Gate is expressed is also shaped by the planet (or planets) that activate it. The strongest of these influences is the Sun, which gives us our sense of identity and purpose. It represents dynamic life-force energy and is tradiitionally seen as a masculine energy (with a lower-case "m"). This is the quality you shine most clearly into the world.

For Martin, this is Gate 54, Ambition. In his teenage years, some people perceived this as arrogance, until he learned to demonstrate that this drive was not merely personal but an ambition directed toward the transformation and progress of the whole group.

By contrast, the Earth is a grounding, supportive, receptive, feminine energy (again, small "f"). The Earth's placement is like the canvas upon which we paint our life.

For Rachel, this is Gate 52, The Mountain, and indeed she seemed unusually calm as a child being described by one teacher as serene at the tender age of thirteen years old.

The Moon mediates between the Sun and Earth, facilitating our movement through experiences. It is a reflection and gives us a sense of the past and our feeling memory.

On learning that his Moon activated Gate 39, Provocation, Mateo roared with laughter – it explained so much of his childhood teasing his brothers, sometimes relentlessly so.

The nodes aren't planets but calculated points in space. The South Node points to the familiar territory – the strengths and patterns we've already developed and are learning to integrate. The North Node points ahead, toward the new direction our soul wants to explore in this lifetime. We naturally move from a

South Node focus to a North Node focus around the age of forty. So while your children are still navigating their South Node themes, you may find yourself drawn toward change, fresh purpose, or a new sense of direction. For some, this shift feels like a gentle turning of the tide. For others, it can feel like standing in the doorway of a midlife crisis. Both experiences are normal and part of the journey.

Mercury is often known as the planet of communication. It describes how we connect with the world around us and how we find our place within it. In Human Design terms, it is linked to all forms of communication and transport, with cyberspace, and with the conscious mind and nervous system.

In Caitlin's family, it became a running joke that she questioned the timing of absolutely everything – very fitting, since her Gate 5, Waiting, was activated by Mercury.

Uranus is considered a higher octave of Mercury, connecting us through intuition to a "higher" mind. It represents the process of awakening, often through shocks, the unusual, or sudden changes.

As Caitlin moved into more senior roles in her career, her gift for sensing the right timing increasingly found its place in service to her leadership.

Venus represents magnetic attraction – who and what we draw toward us. It speaks to our desire for relationship and the places where we seek fulfilment through love, beauty, art, and pleasure.

With her Gate 8, Contribution, activated by Venus, Sofia had a natural gift for creating harmony around herself, even as a very young child.

Neptune is considered the higher expression of Venus. It describes our attunement to unconditional love, spirituality, and the more mysterious or sublime aspects of life. It can open us to mystical insight, but also highlight moments of confusion or illusion.

For Evan, Neptune activated his Gate 43, Breakthrough, which explained why his insights so often came from a more spiritual angle than anyone might have expected.

Mars has long been associated with drive, courage, and the instinct to push outward into life. It fuels our urge to survive, to work, to act, and to express our sexual and creative energy.

Orla was known for diffusing friendship conflicts from a young age, a perfect reflection of her Gate 10, Behavior, activated by Mars.

Pluto is considered the higher octave of Mars, drawing our attention to the parts of life that will transform us. It speaks to deep change, death and rebirth, and the evolution toward a more conscious, purposeful way of acting.

Harper's Gate 26, Accumulation, activated by Pluto, is especially poignant given that she inherited a measure of wealth from her father, who passed away when she was seven.

Jupiter represents the principle of expansion and our reach toward new experiences. The Gates it activates can offer clues about your personal philosophy and how you discover meaning in life.

Naomi's early experience of being sheltered by a Native American community led her to adopt a more shamanic way of living, a beautiful expression of her Jupiter placement in Gate 18, Improving.

By contrast, Saturn (perhaps aptly remembered as "sat-on") represents contraction, limits, rules, and laws. It governs time, space, gravity, cause and effect, the realms of responsibility, consequence, and the less visible work of maturation.

Gareth often struggled to hold on to plenty in any form — toys and teddy bears as a child, then cars, jobs, and girlfriends later on — a pattern neatly reflected in his Saturn placement in Gate 55, Abundance.

If a Gate on your chart doesn't seem to fit you, take a look at which planet activates it because therein may lie insight that resolves the dilemma.

CONSCIOUS AND UNCONSCIOUS AND THE ANCESTRAL LINKS

The most important thing about your Human Design is to accept it. It is a personality blueprint, a genetic portrait, and a karmic map describing what is to be played out for life to be complete, fulfilled and for the individual to be at peace within. A unique feature about Human Design is our ability to recognize and acknowledge the ancestral input we receive in our DNA. Everyone is born into a certain genetic stream, and arriving in a particular family gives us a direct inheritance from the ancestors who preceded us. Questioning why we chose a particular genetic makeup, we sense that it follows directly from our previous incarnations and indicates what needs our attention and what needs completion in this lifetime.

Human Design gives us two calculations: The first for our moment of birth, and the Second from 88 degrees of Solar Arc (approximately three months) before birth. The calculation from birth gives us access to our conscious life experience. The second calculation indicates our genetic inheritance that is hidden in our unconscious. It is our "autopilot" in that it takes us through life without much need for conscious input. It is like driving a car while fiddling with the music system, and yet you stay on the road. It's like eating your lunch while scrolling on your phone. The autopilot keeps us going, *automatically*.

And yet, within the unconscious, genetic traits are various features that, once recognized and appreciated, make our lives much smoother. Many parents and grandparents will recognize physical features or mannerisms in their children and grandchildren that they can associate easily with their ancestors. In fact, with Human Design, we've traced layers of genetic inheritance to at least four generations back.

<table>
<tr><td>21³</td><td>☉</td><td>Sun</td></tr>
<tr><td>48³</td><td>⊕</td><td>Earth</td></tr>
<tr><td>57²</td><td>☽</td><td>Moon</td></tr>
<tr><td>40¹</td><td>☊</td><td>N Node</td></tr>
<tr><td>37¹</td><td>☋</td><td>S Node</td></tr>
<tr><td>63⁶</td><td>☿</td><td>Mercury</td></tr>
<tr><td>42⁶</td><td>♀</td><td>Venus</td></tr>
<tr><td>39⁵</td><td>♂</td><td>Mars</td></tr>
<tr><td>41¹</td><td>♃</td><td>Jupiter</td></tr>
<tr><td>60³</td><td>♄</td><td>Saturn</td></tr>
<tr><td>4⁴</td><td>♅</td><td>Uranus</td></tr>
<tr><td>44⁴</td><td>♆</td><td>Neptune</td></tr>
<tr><td>40¹</td><td>♇</td><td>Pluto</td></tr>
</table>

Inevitably, children are living in very different life circumstances than their forebears, but it is important that they play out any inherited features clearly and comfortably in their own lives. Remember always that there are no "good" or "bad" charts! Everything balances out. Just because great-grandma was a disempowered individual does not mean her great-granddaughter cannot live a very empowered lifetime.

In the left-hand column of numbers, colored red or pink, the Hexagram/Gates opposite the Sun and Earth glyphs, is the inheritance, or the parental input from the father and mother. Then:

- The Unconscious Moon represents feeling memories, perhaps gifts or unfinished business from past incarnations that carry forward to this lifetime.

- Further down, the Unconscious Venus can usually be associated with the genetic input from the maternal grandmother. This echoes the role of the feminine attitude toward love and the use of feminine power and wisdom.

- The Unconscious Mars mostly represents the input from the paternal grandfather. An ability that comes naturally to the child that can be implemented in associations or careers.

- The Unconscious Jupiter indicates the general attitude inherited unconsciously of the family line toward wealth, and the appropriateness of being wealthy.
- The Unconscious Saturn, the family's "karmic" deeds that are for the child to be aware of and be clear about at a time in their life when it is appropriate. All of us are clearing things for ourselves, our ancestors, and our children in one way or another. Again, nothing is "good," and nothing is "bad" here. It is all a part of life as a human in the third and other dimensions.
- The Unconscious Uranus, Neptune, and Pluto go into a more distant past of the family's fates and fortunes. Recognized and acknowledged, these features are more generational, yet contribute greatly to living a life in clarity in current times.

As we follow the planetary story from the personal to the ancestral, a picture emerges of how many layers contribute to a child's experience of themselves. Some influences are immediate and intimate; others sit deep in the family line, shaping patterns that unfold across generations.

SPLITS

Alongside these planetary themes is another feature of Human Design that powerfully affects how a person moves through the world – *splits*. Not planetary, not psychological, but structural, splits describe whether the Centers in a chart function as one unified system or in separate "islands" of energy that rely on others for connection.

Splits are common in Human Design charts; in fact, most people have them. A split occurs when Centers are divided into two or more separate groups without any connecting Channel between the groups of Centers. Any split can have a profound influence on someone's life, as therein often lies an unrecognized drive to join separate parts of a Design by connecting with other people who make an energetic bridge. There can be single, triple, or quadruple splits in a chart.

Any split gives the chart more than one way of relating to any situation. For example, there might be a defined Mind Center, and then a gap in the Design to where there are defined Centers, including the Emotions Center in the lower part of the chart. Such a division can be distracting, offering contrasting and even conflicting ways of experiencing highs and lows emotionally, while trying to work everything out mentally at the same time.

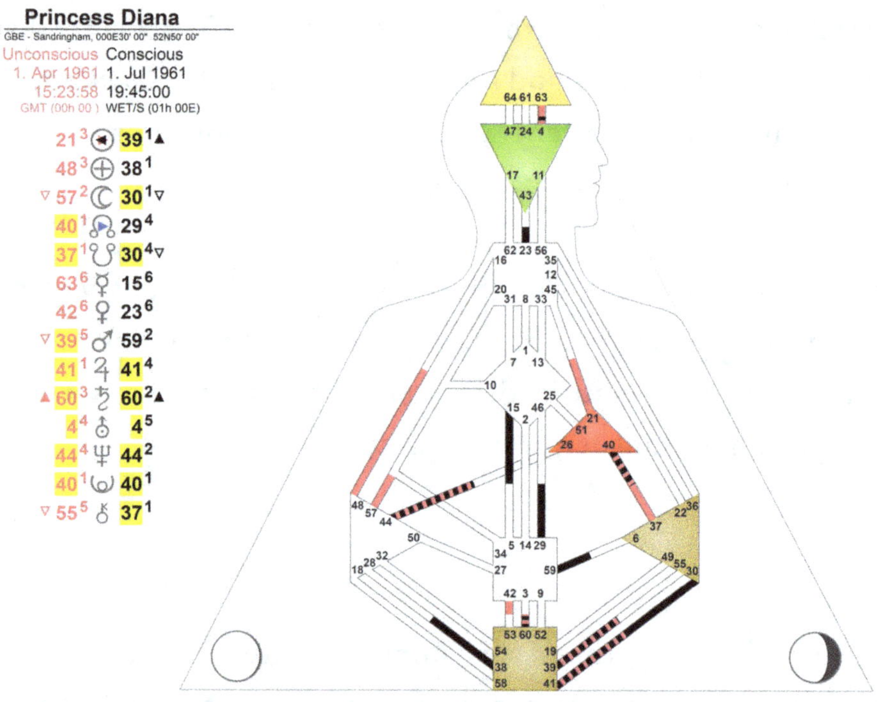

This can produce an unsettling need to seek external opinions or rely on others to make decisions for you. All splits can bring about an urge for collaboration, and any individual with one needs to recognize how easy it is to give away personal responsibility because someone "completes" you energetically by "bridging" your split(s).

Much like the example of Princess Diana above, Joyce was born with a split in her chart, and she found that it was easy, almost essential, to be around her mother, and would literally cling to her mother's clothes or limbs whenever she could. Come the day to go to school, after a very tearful goodbye at the school door, Joyce finds her way to her classroom, still in tears. Once there, she moves around the room and suddenly sits down, contented once again. Quickly, she makes friends with the girl sitting on one side of her, who, as it turns out, has a Design that, like that of Joyce's mother, bridges her split Design.

Splits can be something of a trial until you appreciate that various people around you make different connections for you, potentially influencing you in varying ways. Ultimately, it is essential that you know how to make decisions on your own behalf, and so learning to be patient while allowing differing perspectives within you to come together.

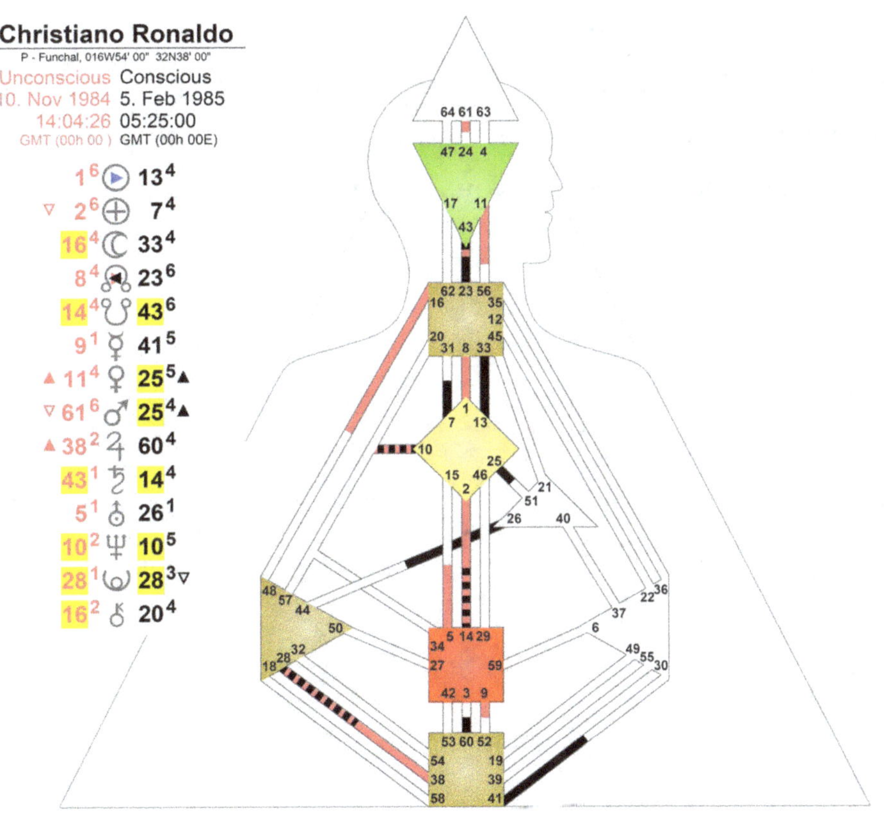

To find cohesive decisions when you have splits, and therefore more than one way to consider what is confronting you, separate yourself from others. By all means, get other people's input, but then leave any environment where people have a vested interest in your decisions and be around other people who have nothing to do with your situation. These people will bridge the splits you have quietly and without any particular interest in you or your decisions. In this way, you can balance any differing perspectives you might have and come to your own clear conclusions.

For children with splits in their Designs, it is great if they can drop the burdens of school to spend time around friends, or people who are outside the school scenario, so they can digest whatever demands are being made on them, in their own way. Cafés, malls, public transport, playgrounds, parks, and phone conversations with disinterested parties are all ways to receive energetic input to bridge any splits to find your own decisions. It requires a little patience and awareness, but sure enough, the clarity comes.

In the next chapter, we step away from the inner wiring of the chart and look outward – to the animals, creatures, and companions who so often mirror children's energies and soothe their nervous systems.

CHAPTER 14

PETS AND OTHER FRIENDS OF NATURE

"One of the first conditions of happiness is that the link between Man and Nature shall not be broken."

— LEO TOLSTOY

Everything has consciousness on one level or another; thus, everything has access to a Design. The Human Design we've been describing for people has the widest range of potentials. Yet, every creature – from the family dog to the horses in a nearby field – expresses a particular essence and purpose through its own type of Design.

Children often sense these Designs long before adults do. They recognize which animals calm them, which ones spark curiosity, and which seem to "get" them without needing words. Paying attention to these natural affinities can offer insight into a child's energy, temperament, and way of connecting with the world. Pets become companions, teachers, mirrors, and sometimes quiet healers, part of the wider ecology that supports a child's growth just as surely as their Human Design does.

The domestication of animals has given us one of the most amazing connections imaginable. However, through Human Design, we find there are also connections to plants, birds, reptiles, fish, insects, and even inanimate objects, such as toys, machines, rocks, and stars.

In this brief chapter, we explore the various Designs, indicating where there are natural overlaps with humans. It is important to remember that everything in nature is ... well, natural. Whenever we, and particularly children, find ourselves in crisis, overwhelmed, or ignored, nature is always ready to lend a comforting lick, purr, neigh, branch to lean on, path in the woods or by the water, toy, rainbow, sunset or stars to gaze at to help us reconnect.

THE MAMMALIAN WORLD

Animals spend most of their time on four legs, and unlike humans, except when we are asleep and lying down, they are mostly horizontal, as is their chart.

It is a *Lunar* chart, in that the timing between Conscious and Unconscious activations is according to 88 degrees of Lunar Arc, a much shorter time span than for humans, so an animal's birth time must be very accurate. (Curiously, humans also have this Lunar chart while sleeping, and thus calculations are also dependent on accurate birth times.)

Instead of being able to access nine Centers and sixty-four Gates, animals have access, by themselves, to five Centers and fifteen Gates.

For animals, their awareness of their life and the world around them comes through the Spleen Center. This Center works in present tense and it is mostly survival-oriented, though it can also be more protection-oriented, too. Animals sense, see, hear, and smell things that humans don't, and therefore, they can heighten our own alertness if we are paying attention to them.

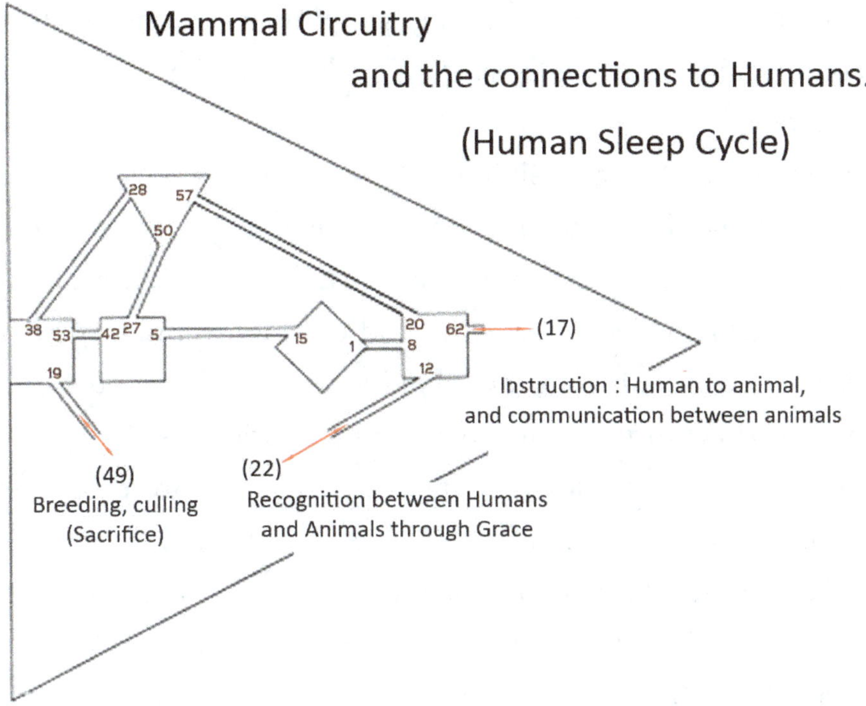

There are three *Transpecial* Gates through which animals and humans can connect: Gate 49 Revolution (The Rebel), Gate 22 Grace (Openness to Spirit), and Gate 17 Following (Recognizing a logical Pathway). A quick glance at the Mammalian chart indicates no Crown, Mind, Willpower, or Emotions Centers. All Mammals have access to five centers – the Root, Sacral, Spleen, Self, and Throat – and only six potential Channels:

- *The Channel 28–38, Struggle,* as part of the Individual Circuit, animals have the means to use "intuition" and their sensitivity to sounds to take alternative routes and paths through life, to push through tough circumstances.
- *The Channel 53–42, Cycles,* is part of the Abstract/Sensing Circuit, which as a Generator Channel provides tremendous staying power, as well as the commencing, continuity and closing of all activities from

waking to action, snoozing, resting, sleeping, to waking again, and seasons of migrations and also from birth, through maturity to old age and death.

- *The Channel 50–27,* Care-Giving/Taking is part of the Tribal, Defense Circuitry, providing nurturing, nourishment and caring of pack members, and for whoever is taken into the "family." It is a Generator Channel that can give its owner boundless energy and staying power.
- *The Channel 57–20, Involuntary Impulses,* as part of the Individual Circuit, furthers intuitive alertness and acoustic sensitivity, and also gives instantaneous voice to changes of any kind. Any animal with this Channel is likely to have inbuilt ESP (Extra-Sensory Perception).
- *The Channel 5–15, Being in the Flow of Life,* is part of the Logic Circuitry, is common to all living things and any animal with this Channel naturally has a Generator Design, with their own timings, habits and seasonal attunement, and great staying power.
- *The Channel 1–8, The Creative Role Model,* is part of the Individual Circuitry, and gives empowering leadership that often defies logic, habits, or particular repetitive patterns. This Channel also gives voice in warning or delight, or when a change of course is sensed as necessary.

Since the sky contains sixty-four Hexagrams/Gates, and animals only have access to fifteen of them, it indicates (statistically) that most animals are going to have a Reflector chart and are going to pick up on the energy of the people and circumstances around them. A few will have Generator or Projector charts, and a very rare few will have Manifestor or MG charts on their own. In the wild or in domesticated farm situations, many animals can live together, and by being in each other's company, share all five Centers, fifteen Gates, six Channels.

Any person who shares any of the fifteen Gates that pets have automatically shares a commonality with them. Anyone who has any of the three Transpecial

Gates, where there are particular connections into the human realms of Mind and Emotions, will have a heightened connection into the mammalian world. Some people will have none of the three Transpecial Gates, and yet, form strong ties to animals, often through the animal's Design as a Reflector, Generator, Projector, an MG, or a Manifestor.

Most animals love children as they love their own young, and if a child can be fearless, calm, and sensitive to make a bond, then their pet can become a treasured companion as they grow up. Animals know perfectly well who is ready to trust a connection with them, and who is not. Mutual trust is essential.

Along with everything in nature, animals live in the present. They can recognize patterns, have a high alertness, especially to the sounds and smells of food, and with training, be ready at a moment's notice to change whatever they are doing to accompany their human.

Children with Gate 49, Revolution (or The Rebel), can be very particular about who they take on as friends, and often, pets can open a whole new area of connection for them. These children can quickly weigh up the characteristics and abilities of their pets and form a strong emotional bond with their pet, offering each other a quality of support that defies logic.

Children with Gate 22, Grace, (Openness to Spirit) had better like animals, even if they have allergies, because pets are going to like them! There is an extraordinary connection that takes place through Gate 22, and it has a magnetic pull for almost all animals. One might say the connection can go beyond emotional appreciation and open up into unearthly realms of recognition and engagement.

Children with Gate 17, Following, (Recognizing a Logical Pathway), will find a particular connection with animals, which may include giving direction and helping pets to comprehend the difference between good and bad behaviors. With this connection, animals can "get" their human very easily, and often their humans have to adjust themselves out of any habitual patterns.

All animals typically have a shorter lifespan than humans, and just as their arrival can bring great joy and delight, so can their passing cause sadness, grief, and pain. For all children, when a beloved pet dies, it heralds a lifelong reminder for us all, that life is precious and fleeting, and that celebrating our time together is so important.

BIRDS, REPTILES, AND FISH

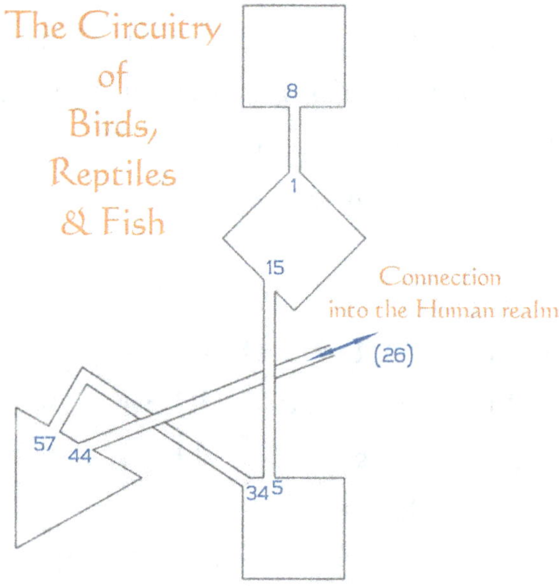

Birds, reptiles, and fish all probably descended from dinosaurs, and have their own Circuitry involving four Centers, seven Gates, and one *transpecial* connection. Anyone sharing a Gate or Channel is going to recognize a particular commonality. Those who have Gate 26 might experience a particular interest or instinctual connection with birds, reptiles, or fish.

In olden times and in many old texts, birds are recorded as messengers who fly or make a call into a scene at a particularly significant moment. In most temples, priestesses had snakes to keep them abreast of changing circumstances. Fish have their own sensitivity to weather and prevailing conditions and have often been essential cohabitants in courtly gardens and familiars to fishermen.

The Channel 34–57 empowers intuitive gifts but also has a potentially massive input of life-force, Sacral energy into the Splenic Center of health and well-being. Many societies have strong connections with birds, reptiles, and fish for their presence and powerful healing qualities. A henhouse of laying chickens, a pet lizard, or a brightly lit aquarium or outdoor fishpond can completely transform any living environment.

Children with Gate 26, Accumulation, can attune to what holds value for the bird, reptile and fish kingdoms and thereby recognize instantaneous, subtle signals and values in their own lives.

INSECTS

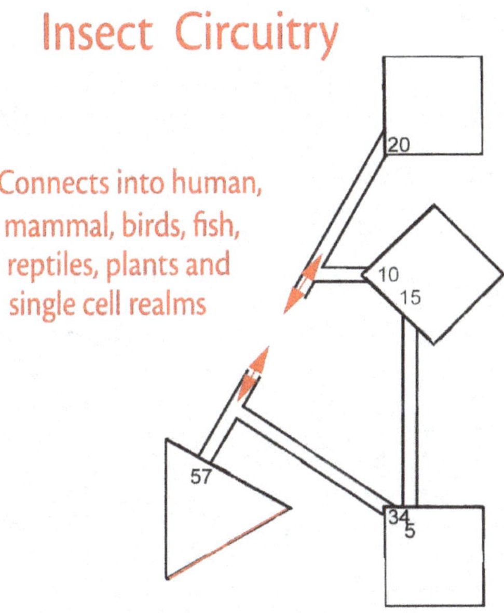

Insects have no backbone or skeletal structure, however, they have access to four Centers – the Sacral, Spleen, Self, and Throat – and six Gates, 34 Power, 10 Behaviors, 57, Intuition, 20 The Now, all part of the Integration Circuitry, and 15 Fellowship (Humanity) and 5 Timing in the Logic Circuitry, and as with all life forms, they access Channel 5–15, Rhythm, and Being in the Flow of Life.

Insects live in the present and have the means to make us present too! They have access through the Leadership Channel 10–20, Awakening, to remind us constantly of their strict adherence to the present moment. Life happens in the present moment, and through their commitment to the present, they take charge of immediate needs without hesitation. Without bees and butterflies, who expand our sense of mystical wonder, life would be so depleted.

Insects interact with all life forms by doing clean-up work, as well as providing a food source, pollination, silks, honey, and other essential and particular additions to life. Humans are believed to be outnumbered by insects in a ratio of 200 million to 1.

Children are either fascinated or repelled by insects. However, they can come to appreciate their essential connection to all of life. We could not live without them, and even though reaching for a fly swat or insecticide spray might be an immediate reaction to their presence, relocating them to an environment where they are more at home is another choice.

Perhaps an entomologist can link their Human Design attributes and qualities together because we get the gist of it but are not informed enough to join all the dots together?

PLANTS

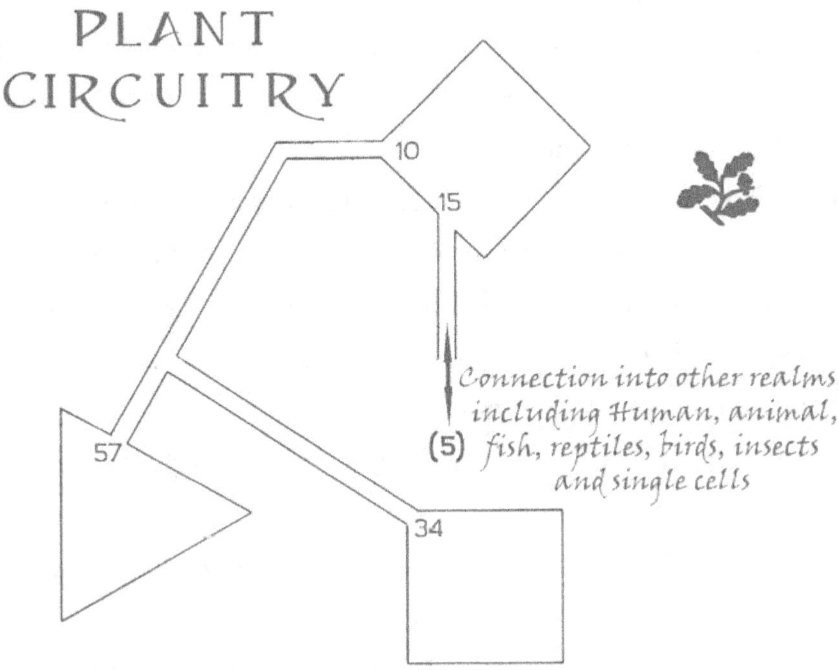

Plants, including everything from mosses to trees, have their own connection to life and consciousness through three Centers – the Sacral, Spleen, and Self – three Channels, and four Gates.

Their transpecial connection is through Gate 5, Waiting, and being ready for the right timing of the "gardener" or wandering animal, who, in tune with prevailing and changing lunar, weather, and seasonal patterns, harvests, eats, gathers seeds, and plants again. Those children with Gate 5 in their Design will find they can develop green fingers or thumbs and a natural attunement to plants and their needs and properties.

Plants can be great educators through their extraordinary osmosis process, and how they grow in their own way of sprouting, growing, flowering, shedding and, eventually, passing away, providing seeds and shoots for the next generation, all in their own seasons and time frames. Herbalists have found that plants can provide a vast resource for healing, through Gate 57; administer a profound source of power, wellness, and growth, through Gate 34; and give behavior-altering and boosting characteristics through Gate 10. Gate 15 provides a remarkable tolerance to changing circumstances and climates, so much so that it is said that a single seed can turn the whole world green. All of nature relies on the plant world for food, shelter, medicines, and material.

Children can be encouraged to pay attention to the seasons of their own lives through the changes in the plant world around them. Planting trees at an early age can bring great pleasure and fulfillment in later years as both child and tree grow together. Horticulturists are well advised to propagate their "Mother" plants when planetary transits, or their own Designs "activate" the Plant Circuitry.

Compared to minerals, liquids, and gases, surprisingly, wood is perhaps the rarest of all materials in the Universe. The plant world has been constantly watching. It has been affected by the stars and our Universe since the very dawning of creation, and many plants hold secrets of wisdom, healing, and vision that are often recognized in the human world. Plant medicine can reveal much through reconnecting us with our own nature and providing healing for us on many levels.

THE WORLD OF VIRUS, BACTERIA AND SINGLE-CELL LIFE FORMS

A single cell is often a complete living unit in itself, such as bacteria or yeast. When single cells are combined with other cells, they become the building blocks for larger and larger components of all organisms, in everything up to animals, humans, and all of Nature.

They involve two Centers – the Sacral and the Self – and three Gates, and have the interactive opening through Gate 60, Limitation. The Channel 5–15, Being in the Rhythm of Life, is common to all living things. Gate 3 is where innovation or new forms take place. And Gate 60, The Old, is the trigger for mutations.

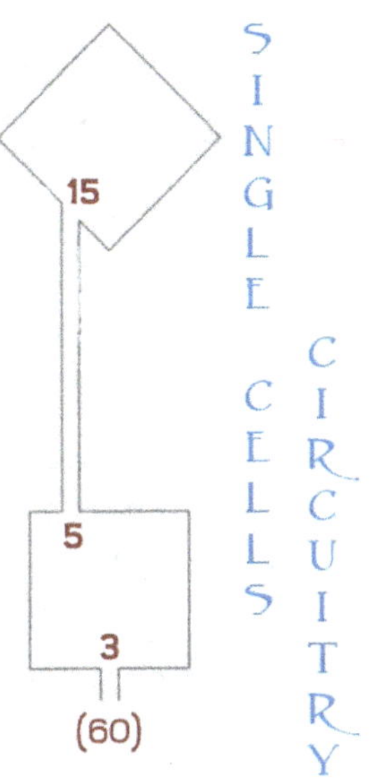

Virus mutation has changed the course of life in many ages for humans and other species, and in most cases has driven an uptick in consciousness evolution. Plagues have led to increased hygiene awareness and medical breakthroughs, making travel safer, and allowing disease to be both treatable and containable. Sometimes the biggest changes in life are caused by mutations in the smallest portions of our beings.

In one way or another, the recent Covid infections caused a significant change in the world, particularly to humans whose immune systems were challenged by an unfamiliar virus, and who used experimental vaccines to counter Covid through specific gene targeting and remodeling. The virus responsible for the Covid-19 pandemic was able to mutate into multiple variations and has rearranged many parts of the genetic makeup in human and other bodies. Its long-term effects are yet to be evaluated.

INANIMATE OBJECTS

Inanimate objects also have their place in our lives. *The Hobbit, Harry Potter*, and *Toy Story* – books and movies – showed the whole world that sometimes our imagination transports us into realms that we've probably all believed, or wanted to believe, as children. Within these tales, it first became apparent, and then obvious, that certain objects held an extraordinary mystique. Whether we are always aware of it or not, inanimate objects also have consciousness.

Have we not urged (or cussed) a car or device to work when we felt desperate, or when it was having a tough time operating properly? Have we ever "wished upon a star," or prayed to an object, or for what the object represents to us, to give us luck, or intercede on our behalf? Whether our entreaties have been acknowl-edged, proved successful or not, there is always the possibility that inanimate objects hold a key to our own interactions with life. And yes, all inanimate objects have their own Design, albeit a very innocent one.

There are ceremonies for empowering various objects, events, and shared experi-ences. For example, a wedding ring can be imbued with intention for the marriage, just as communal bread and wine can be blessed with prayer. Laying the cornerstone of a new building sets the foundation for the purpose of the building. Ceremonies are also performed for ship launches, first 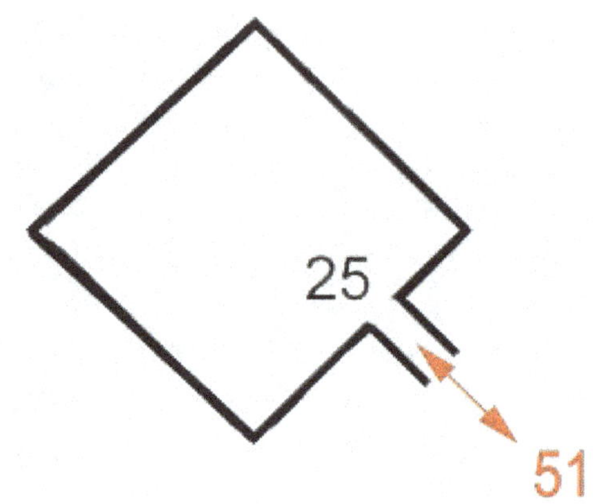
flights, creating "magic" wands, empowering malas, jewels, and other crystals, in which each object is imbued with intention through the Channel of Initiation (25–51). Some ceremonies have a more profound effect than others. However, if Gate 51, The Arousing, and the application of conscious willpower are involved, the object in question is more likely to hold the quality of initiation and the power of intention.

All inanimate objects are innocent in nature (Gate 25), and yet, through simple ceremony, can hold an energy or frequency that withstands external challenges. Auction houses all over the world sell artworks and memorabilia that hold signifi-cance and, therefore, perceived value from other times.

Perhaps this offers a way of understanding the acute distress a child can feel if their most beloved teddy bear or similar is lost or damaged in some way? In writing together, we found we each had stories of a cherished teddy bear being torn apart or lost only to be found in very different condition some weeks later. The fact that these tales were vivid to each of us many decades later is a testament to the potential power of inanimate objects.

There is no reason a child cannot sanctify and enjoy their doll's tea party attendees, toy, bike, irreplaceable teddy bear, tree house, or pet rock as something of great significance in their life ... and as they grow older, remember to appreciate the wonder of empowering and being empowered by so many things in their material world.

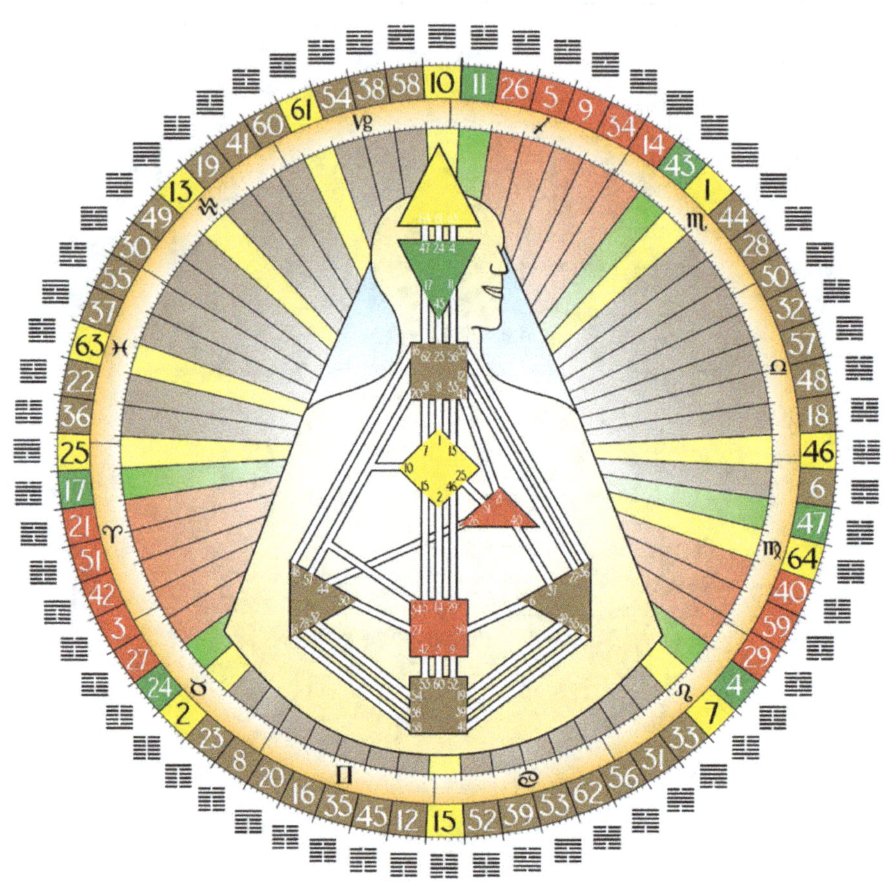

CHAPTER 15

WHAT DO I DO WITH ALL THIS?

"The greatest gifts we can give our children are the roots of responsibility and the wings of independence."

— MARIA MONTESSORI

Our concerns as parents and carers evolve as our children grow up. We start with our most precious baby and worry about sleep schedules (ours as well as theirs!) and eating habits. Then come the toddler years – how do we keep them safe as they climb the furniture? And how do we endure the meltdowns of their frustration, as seemingly we keep thwarting them? Just when we feel we might have a handle on things, they are off to school, and we hope they behave well and make friends. A blink later, we're worrying about their involvement in social media, which of their enthusiasms to encourage (and pay for), and how to set them up for success with the "right" qualifications. Meanwhile, they throw us curved balls, sometimes a playground spat, other times a potentially dangerous lurch toward anorexia or self-harm, the devastation of the loss of their first love, or a great desire to go skydiving with new friends. As you will have realized through these pages, while Human Design cannot answer all these conundrums, it can offer you some clues to help you navigate the joys and challenges of raising your children.

HEALTHY HABITS

Education systems worldwide promote reliance on brainpower. True, our minds are the most amazing biocomputers. But it is also true that we are so much more than that. There is a skill in learning to live in our bodies that goes beyond the physical exercise that may be encouraged in school. To that end, you may want to teach your children some specific skills:

- **Journaling.** One of the most potent ways of releasing the mind from overthinking is to put your thoughts on paper, or screen. This might be with words or pictures, written in linear form or as a mind map, spider diagram. Your child may be happy to share these thoughts with you or prefer to keep them private. Either way the process will benefit them. Respecting their choice of privacy will build trust, especially during the teenage years when trust can be tested.
- **Breathing.** Sounds simple, we all know how to breathe, right? One of the best ways of diffusing strong emotions for *any* Type and Authority is to focus on our breath, especially lengthening the exhale. It calms our nervous system and helps take us out of the automatic "flight of fight" mode that strong emotions can evoke. With little ones you can make a game of counting the in and out breath. Square breathing (in, hold, out, hold for a count of x) can also help prepare the body for sleep.
- **Meditation.** Another great tool for stilling an overactive mind, the benefits of meditation have been known for thousands of years and have become better understood in the Western world over the last few

decades. There are many different styles that will appeal to different people. If in doubt, start with guided meditation – there are plenty of freely available sources – and encourage your child to choose what works for them.

- **Creativity.** We are all creative beings, and yet somewhere along the line we seem to forget and put the paints and crayons of our childhood away. Encourage your child to explore many forms of creativity, be it dance, making music, gardening, cooking, pottery ... find something that will "stick" with them. Encouraging creativity is a great way of helping people out of the doldrums at any age.

- **Movement.** Distinct from physical training or education, it is important for us to use our bodies. And yet school sports can be a competitive minefield, especially for those without a defined Sacral. Encouraging your child to find ways of using their bodies – be it through walking or yoga, using the gym or finding a less usual sport they enjoy – will serve them well through their adult years.

Each Human Design chart offers some clues as to specific challenges and opportunities. The following is by no means exhaustive, but may give you a starting point for supporting your child.

SLEEPING

Those with a defined Sacral Center need to burn off energy every day to have good quality sleep. In young children, this can often be seen in the very active child who appears to be full on and then simply stops and falls asleep wherever they are. For those with Format Channels (42–53, 3–60, 9–52), the need for daily exercise can be most pronounced as they have the pressure of the Root adding to the power of the Sacral. It can be so hard for a child with lots of physical energy to sit still in class until they have burnt off some of the excess – if this is your child, you can help them by building in exercise to their morning routine, whether it's a run around the garden or walking to school, for example.

For all Types (including those with a defined Sacral Center), a busy mind can mitigate against falling asleep easily. Those with a defined Crown and/or Mind have these Centers of inspiration and processing running 24/7, so they need to be encouraged to observe their thoughts, rather than engage with them, once they've gone to bed. These people sometimes find it helpful to have pencil and paper beside the bed so if something important pops into their mind they can "park it" for morning. Those "Eureka" moments often hit as the Mind relaxes!

EATING

Those with a defined Emotional Solar Plexus are more prone than others to eating disorders as they attempt to assuage their emotions with food, alcohol, or other substances. So, while all children need help to understand and work with their emotions, these children also benefit in particular from carving a distinction between what they need nutritionally and what they may crave emotionally. Learning to distinguish between being hungry for good-quality food and feeling upset or bored and then eating to alleviate these feelings will set them up for a healthier life. Similarly, rewarding these children with chocolate, chips, or their favorite cereal may encourage an unhealthy relationship with less nutritious fare.

By contrast, clues to fussy eating may be found in a defined Splenic Center, the seat of our intuition and instinct. Those with Gate 57 can have a fear of the future and be especially wary of "new" foods. Those with Gate 44 associated with a fear of the past may not want to try something a second time if it didn't taste good the first time around. Those with Gate 32 can fear change, and this might show itself in a reluctance to move to solid food, eat at school, or try new dishes, for example. Gates 18 and 48 are often found balancing between saltiness and sweet, bitter, sour, and savory. Gate 28 might also be associated with under- or overeating and drinking.

Similarly, those with lots of Tribal Circuitry may be especially sensitive to whether something smells or tastes "right" or has a "pleasing" texture. Does this belong in their diet? There is balance to be had in encouraging children to try different foods and encouraging them to recognize what suits their digestive system and what maybe doesn't.

If eating becomes a battleground, then I would look to see if either you or your child has defined Willpower, most especially Gate 21, the Gate of Control. Toddlers can seek to take control of at least something in their lives by refusing some foods. Offering choice amongst good alternatives may go some way toward helping, for example, carrots *or* beans, chicken *or* fish, apple *or* orange. Teenagers can feel similarly adrift, and food becomes something they can control, so encouraging them to cook for the family from time to time can broaden their understanding, share the burden, and give them responsibility for some meals.

NO! SHAN'T! WON'T!

Children often seek to assert themselves notably in the toddler and teenage years, the former as they establish themselves as separate beings and the latter as they individuate from their family of origin. Both are often also caused by frustration. Toddlers can see what they want to do but don't yet have the capacity to do it – that toy just out of reach on the shelf, the older children they can't catch up with, the step that's too big to climb, and so on. Healthy teenagers test limits, and a wise parent offers "safe" arenas for such exploration – be it in sport, travel, or other ways of forging their independence.

An understanding of their Human Design chart can offer some insight into where the apparent contrariness might be coming from or what is exaggerating it. As we've seen in Chapter 9, Manifestor Types are the initiators and, as such, can be intolerant of anyone getting in their way at any age. As children, they need firm boundaries – just as few and unrestrictive as their parents and carers are comfortable with.

Children with defined Willpower can be encouraged to harness that determination to succeed, finish that project, run faster, jump higher, go the extra mile. There is no point in butting heads, any more than with a Manifestor, if they are going after something, rather than a flat "no," you'll get further by explaining the conditions under which they'd get a "yes". Then hold that line. Boundaries and clear consequences will make for a happier home.

Those with Gate 49 come with a tendency to say "no," as a natural drive toward revolution or renewal. What's behind the "no"? It is an emotional response to a feeling that's off, an unwanted behavior, or a sense that they're being ridden over roughshod. Inquiry may lead to surprising insight into their world.

Gates 38 (Opposition) and 39 (Provocation) are both in the root and, consequently, children with these Gates can exhibit pressure to challenge authority and poke life respectively. Those with Gate 38 can benefit from learning when and how best to challenge to get the result they are hoping for – and within the family can be a great training ground! Those with Gate 39 (and those around them) need to understand that their energy alone can be provocative without them having to do anything at all, so growing something of a thick skin can be an advantage. Gate 39 is attention-seeking and naturally flirtatious, which may give pause to parents of teenagers, especially – again helping youngsters to understand the impact of their ways without squashing their fun is a gift.

EMOTIONAL OVERLOAD

Count to ten and breathe.... We can all feel overwhelmed with emotions at times, and children lack the regulation that adults have developed, at least in theory. The Emotional Solar Plexus is both a Center of Awareness and a Motor. Those with a defined Emotions Center have that motor running 24/7 with a wave pattern that may be gentle or quite extreme, depending on which channels are activated. Life is a drama, to a greater or lesser extent. Those with an undefined or open Emotions

Center ride the emotional waves of people around them and have no easy way to dissipate the feelings they pick up, which can lead to overwhelm. You may like to refer to Chapters 7 and 10 for more on the Emotional Solar Plexus.

Whatever the Design, we all have feelings; when they are too much to bear, we may need permission to express them. Yes, it really is okay for a boy to cry and a girl to get angry! A meltdown may not be pretty, but it is preferable to having stuck emotions that can trigger you again later. Then breathe, slowly, to calm down the body's nervous system. It can often help to breathe with someone in a synchronized way – not only can this help to slow breathing, but it is a tangible way of knowing someone is with you and has got you.

FRIENDSHIP GROUPS

Most children have trouble with friendship groups at some stage, be it a playground squabble, falling out over a real or imagined love, a "dare" that goes wrong, and so on. Some children dive back into the fray, seemingly not much flustered, while others are in deep pain for quite a while. Parents can help normalize such upsets as part of the rough-and-tumble of life. If your child has the 19–49 Channel of Sensitivity, they are likely to sense everyone's feelings acutely. If they have a lot of Tribal Circuitry, any sense of being "left out" may be more concerning for them than for those with more Collective or Individual Circuitry. Profiles with a Line 1 may find friendship upsets can rock their foundations, and those with a Line 4 may take any sense of rejection really hard. As above, those with defined Emotions may be better equipped to handle drama than those without ... but there are always sensible limits to how emotions are expressed.

Children benefit from having their experiences validated – it is part of their truth – and Human Design provides a framework for understanding that their peers will not share all their foibles and have different ways of operating. As they grow up, it will help them to understand themselves, other family members, and their friends, to share their Design and your own.

LEARNING STYLES

Attributed to many, and probably originally from Aristotle, is the quote: "Tell them what you're going to tell them, tell them, and then tell them what you've told them." This works well for those who learn by listening, maybe not so well for those who are visual or kinesthetic (learning by doing, literally using touch) unless you adopt all three modes in the hope that at least one will stick. There are clues in Circuitry, as we've seen, to how the different Channels are associated with different senses. Collective Channels are visual, Tribal are kinesthetic, and Individual are auditory. If your child's Human Design chart shows strong activation in one Circuit above the others, it might be worth exploring whether they learn most readily in the way that Circuit indicates.

You might look for further clues in the Gates activated in the Mind Center – how does your child's biocomputer best process ideas and information? Gates 4 and 17 are future-focused, logical, and experimental, while Gates 47 and 11 are experiential, seeing what worked best in the past. All four Gates are in the Collective Circuit, so visual. The two Gates in the Individual Circuit, 24 and 43, are auditory, and those with these Gates will be listening to whether what's said "rings true" or "sounds right."

Difficulty learning may not be attributable to any one aspect, of course.

Chetan was approached by a family whose son Francis was seemingly very unhappy in his life, highly energized and constantly bouncing off the walls wherever he was, to the point that his school principals insisted he was either put on drugs or expelled. Needless to say, the boy's parents were dead set against drugging their child but had seemingly run out of options.

Again, Francis's parents' and brother's charts were considered along with the "errant" son's, and the situation became immediately apparent: Francis had a 2/4 Profile with a Projector Design in a very open chart, indicating that he was happy in his own company and easily influenced and even overwhelmed by people around him with Generator, Manifestor or MG Designs.... as his parents and sibling had.

The recommendation put forth was that Francis be given his own room, and be invited to take part in family activities, with the understanding that if he was not clear to join in, he be left alone. What transpired within two weeks was a calm household and no more eruptions at school because Francis was given space and time to process energy in his own way, without being overcome by it. The need for drugs was eliminated.

NEURODIVERSITY

To date, no studies have been undertaken to explore whether there is any correlation between neurological differences and Human Design. We all attune to the world differently, and this may be more obvious in children who relate from a place on the autistic spectrum, or struggle with dyslexia, dyspraxia, ADHD, ADD, or other challenges. For example, while we all have some irregularity in our sensory and emotional processing that can compromise self-regulation, this can be seen to a higher degree in those on the autistic spectrum.

Everyone has a unique sensory blueprint and builds (or conditions) their mind in a variety of ways to manage their uncomfortable internal state. Looking at a Human Design chart can offer areas where particular help can benefit a child, neurodiverse or so-called neurotypical alike. The undefined and open Centers of someone's Design is a way into the kind of wisdom that brings development and potential transformation. Youngsters who don't connect to others in traditional ways are often hypersensitive or under-reactive (or both, varying by system – for example, being hypersensitive to touch and under-reactive to sound), so the world can seem especially harsh and confusing. Chapter 7 on understanding fear and feelings and Chapter 8 on drive, willpower, and pressure would be good places to start reviewing what might be most helpful to your child.

LIFE DECISIONS

We've reviewed Decision-Making Authority in detail in Chapter 10, so suffice it to say that your best way of making decisions may be very different from your child's. Clearly, when they are little, we make every decision for them – what they eat, where they sleep, who they play with, and so on. As they grow up, these decisions and many more are gradually transferred to them as they develop their own agency. The current tendency to encourage decision-making in the Mind is flawed, so teaching our children to use their own Authority gives them a huge advantage in life. This can start early – "What do you feel like wearing today?" or "Do you want to wear your blue top?" for example. Once children are adept at making the smaller day-to-day decisions, you and they can start trusting them to make the bigger decisions of what classes to take, which friendships to develop, etc.

However good their decision-making, young people are especially prone to the influence of others, and if they take longer to tune into their own Authority, the time-lag can add complexity. Rather than sitting with an "I don't know," it can be helpful to force a provisional decision along the lines of "If you did know now, what would you decide?" without *any* pressure to live with that provisional decision. It can give a yardstick against which to measure their feelings, gut response, intuition, values, sense of identity, or what further information to explore. Another way in which parents can add great value is in providing context, which they have simply by virtue of having been around longer and knowing more; for example, maybe your young adult desperately wants to go to the local college, and this would change if they had visited others and seen a wider range of options.

SELF-IDENTITY

Clearly, Human Design is an important way of understanding ourselves and how we differ from others. Knowing their Type can save upset and false expectations, especially for the non-Sacral children who are in the minority. Witness the Manifestor who is forced into team activities, the Projector who feels left out, and the Reflector who is simply overwhelmed. Normalizing these things for them can help enormously, as it makes them okay ... as they are ... no "fixing" needed.

Chapter 5 delves into the Self Center in detail and shows how a defined Self has a clearer sense of identity than an undefined or open Center, which has something of the quality of a chameleon. This too is okay, and encouraging a sense of exploration and play can help children feel good about themselves as they "try on" different roles and ways of being.

SEX, DRUGS, ROCK AND ROLL

Parenting teenagers can be alarming, as they have a propensity to experiment without any sense of the potential dangers of which adults are all too aware. This can be exaggerated if you are, for example, an Emotional Generator and your child is a Willful Manifestor, off forging their way you know not where nor with whom! Similarly, anyone with a Line 3 in their Profile is naturally an explorer and more likely to experiment than other Profiles, left to their own devices. Navigating the teenage years is a lot about communication and boundaries – yours as well as theirs. So, how does your teenager process information? Check out their learning style (see above) and try communicating accordingly. Teenagers can tune out "no" if it's said too often, so how can you say "yes with conditions" that keeps everyone safe ... and you sane?

Each of the Gates on the Sacral Center is related to sex, except for Gate 34, which is pure power. Chapter 4 takes a detailed look at each of these Gates. Looking at your own chart and that of your child will give you a clue about how you might each approach intimate relationships, your similarities, and differences. Depending on your own family culture, it can be an interesting conversation to look at how your charts differ in this regard and how that has played out for you in practice. In so doing, you are giving your child a broader context and greater understanding, from within which they will make their own decisions.

Many teenagers experiment with drugs and alcohol as "forbidden fruit" or as a way of seeming more grown-up in front of their peers. You will have your own sense of acceptable boundaries and the consequences of infringement. It is worth noting that those with an undefined or open Self Center will have more trouble metabolizing alcohol than those with a defined Self Center. The teenage years often come complete with a lot of drama, and your teenager may not simply be rebelling, but rather may need help to find healthy ways of dissipating overwhelming emotional angst, without resorting to drugs, alcohol, over- or under-eating, vaping, or other unhealthy approaches.

"WHATEVER"

Teenagers can be masters of apathy, apparently preferring to sleep away their mornings, then dragging themselves in front of a screen, maybe with a large bowl of cereal. Dare to say anything and, if they respond at all, you get the ubiquitous: "Whatever!" You may have a teenager who is simply recharging, perhaps a Projector who has run out of juice, or a Generator that's a bit burnt out with uninspiring schoolwork. Alternatively, you may be seeing the effect of Gate 41, Imagination, which is being expressed as an unwillingness to engage – a preference for living in a dreamy, spacey state, at least for now. Those with Gate 58, Joyous Vitality, may not be perceiving the joy and be wallowing in self-judgment until something sparks them back into life. Gates 19, Approach, and 54, Ambition, may be waiting for approval and support before they can truly connect. Whether you're appreciated at the time or not, your teenager will value you being alongside them rather than appearing to judge them. Frustrating as it may be, "catching them doing something right" will pay greater dividends in the long run than venting your own angst.

MENTAL WELL-BEING

Of course, if you or your child is mentally unwell or in distress, the advice of an appropriate medical professional is needed. A Human Design chart cannot be used as a diagnostic tool. It can highlight areas for which it might be worth teaching resilience and coping mechanisms. For example, those with an open Root Center can pick up and magnify the stresses of other people around them and tend not to do so well with a lot of pressure – it overloads their adrenal system. Sadly, we all pick up these pressures from time to time, so teaching your child to slow their breathing, walk off stress, and shake themselves out (we can learn so much from other mammals that literally shake off tension and upset) can help them avoid potential pitfalls. The other pressure Center is the Crown; an undefined or open Crown may lend itself to picking up too many thoughts, ideas, and inspirations, which may make it hard to switch off and sleep. Learning to observe thoughts without getting hooked and letting them go, much like credits rolling at the end of a film, can be a hugely helpful as can keeping a notepad so inspiration can be parked.

The other most obvious place to look for clues for training resilience is the Emotional Solar Plexus. Those with open Emotions pick up the emotions of others and magnify them. Channel 39–55 is the Channel of Emoting, and those who have this Channel will experience the highest highs and the lowest lows without (necessarily) any obvious rhyme or reason. Those with Channel 19–49 are highly sensitive, and for them, it can feel as if the rest of the world stomps around in clodhopper boots. Emotional understanding is one of the most valuable things you can teach your child, and looking at their chart (and your own!), you have a great starting point and can meet them where they are.

The person with undefined or open Emotions will benefit enormously from being around others with Emotional Definition to help process difficult feelings. If they have a defined Sacral, they may want to run, use a punch bag, or kickbox them out of their system, for example. Without a defined Sacral, they may prefer to write out their feelings and then transmute the energy by burning them. The folk with Channel 39–55 can process these emotions and are helped by music (as an Individual Channel, it's acoustic) and getting creative, whether that's drawing, cooking, wood turning, or whatever engages them. Those with Channel 19–49 also process their emotions and may want a hug or to be held (as a Tribal Channel, it's kinesthetic related to touch). Pets and trees are open to being hugged if no person is available!

You may want to reread the relevant chapter, depending on the chart you are looking at, to get a sense of what might be most important for your own well-being first. Then, perhaps look at those nearest and dearest to you. What habits might be most helpful for each of you to develop to maintain and strengthen your own mental well-being?

COMBINING CHARTS

You will have noticed that throughout this chapter, there are references to both your chart and your child's. When we are present with another, our charts combine, which is why your child may appear to behave very differently when alone or with their other parent, grandparents, or different siblings. If all nine Centers are defined when you put your charts together, other people may sense that they are not needed in some way, or you are complete without them. There is a degree of certainty in the relationship, and it may seem a bit stuck sometimes.

With one or more Centers left undefined between you, there are obvious places to "play" together:

- An undefined Crown gives the opportunity to find out what is inspiring.
- An undefined Mind gives an opportunity to explore thoughts and ideas.

- An undefined Throat lends itself to unlimited ways of expressing things.
- An undefined Self gives an opportunity to play different roles without attachment.
- An undefined Heart to discover what holds value for each of you.
- An undefined Spleen to explore matters of health and well-being, along with potential fears.
- An undefined Sacral to understand energy (and the mystery of sex, with a partner).
- An undefined Emotional Solar Plexus to observe the dramas playing out around you.
- An undefined Root to avoid the stresses of others and ground yourselves.

You might also want to look at the charts of each family member so you can leverage your individual strengths between you. For example, who has the defined Root and handles stress well? Or has a logical Mind (Gates 4 and 17) for planning? Or who is more likely to be detail-conscious (Gates 9 and 62)? None of these are fool-proof. After all, the expression of our Human Design isn't always perfect, but it can give a useful place to start in exploring family dynamics.

We'll close this exploration of Human Design with another case study.

Speaking to your children in a way they can readily process makes such a difference. Ariel always loved Tuesday afternoons when she and her brother, Jake, went to their granny's home after school. When the time for tea came, Granny would open the fridge and, looking at the contents, would throw out all sorts of ideas about what they could cook, usually together. "Hmm, we can make cottage pie, spaghetti bolognese, even a mild chili — what do you fancy?" and Ariel would ponder for a few moments before making her choice, "Spaghetti bolognese, please." By contrast, Jake would usually remain silent until Ariel spoke and then promptly veto it. "No, I don't want spaghetti" ... and a row would ensue.

Ariel's mom, Lucy, stumbled over Human Design and became intrigued about her own MG Design and, as often happens, then wanted to explore the rest of her family's charts with Pippa. Dad, Jim, was also an MG, Ariel a Projector, and Jake a Generator. On a whim, Lucy asked about her mother too — and hearing that she was also a Projector, realized that was probably at the heart of the similarity between her daughter and her mother. Ariel and Granny liked to look at options, mull over them, and then tune into what resonated. Jake was better with yes-or-no questions, hence being able to respond to the implied "do you want spaghetti bolognese?" rather than being overwhelmed with options.

Lucy dived deeply into Human Design as Ariel was on the cusp of becoming a teenager, and she was concerned that her usually accommodating daughter was begin-ning to show signs of rebellion. Lucy liked to be busy (having the Channel 20–34) and drove her family to keep up — the weekends would start with a 5K run now both the chil-dren were old enough, usually followed by brunch with friends, home to get chores and homework completed so they could be out again later for a walk or exploring a nearby museum or gallery. Sunday was usually social, visiting family or having guests over after Church, before completing chores and homework before bed, or if they were done a quick trip out again. Ariel was old enough to progress to the 10K run but was resisting it, and once home, on a Saturday, was becoming reluctant to go out again. Understanding that Ariel was "wired differently" and didn't have her mother's energy was a huge revelation to each of them. Ariel wasn't being lazy — she simply didn't have the energy to be on the go and with others all the time.

Lucy shifted her expectations and allowed Ariel more space, relishing that her son, Jake, did have the energy to keep up. Ariel started spending some of her weekends with her granny, enjoying the peace that came from being away from the overwhelming energy of the rest of her family. Jake liked having some time alone with his parents, especially when they played family soccer and then had hot chocolate together.

Pippa and Lucy had another conversation when the family seemed to be pulling in different directions a few months later. Jim's bachelor brother had died unexpectedly, leaving him with a significant inheritance. Figuring the children were old enough to have input into what to do with the money, Jim had opened the conversation with them all. Jim was a reserved man, slow to make decisions by comparison with his wife and son. Lucy promptly suggested they move to a bigger house, causing outrage from both children, horrified at the thought of leaving the only home they'd known. Ariel wanted to make a significant donation to the local cat shelter since Uncle Bob had always kept cats, at least until the last one got run over. Jim had wondered about a modest extension to their current house so he could have a home office, and Jake asked if he could, at last, have trombone lessons.

Lucy had an open Emotions Center and had come to realize that she picked up her husband's emotions, often expressing them for him. She recognized that Jim's suggested office extension was also something of a memorial to his workaholic brother. In a similar vein, Ariel's desire to contribute to a cat's shelter was also something of a memorial that was meaningful to her. Ariel's Self Authority meant that her best decisions were those that resonated with her sense of self – hmm, was it time to introduce a pet to their home? Jake relied on his Sacral energy, as did Lucy herself, and she explained that she found decision-making for herself so much easier than waiting for the family to align. Lucy and Pippa talked about how each family member could honor their Authority and the memory of Bob, and get away from the endless discussions about the pros and cons of each suggestion.

Pippa bumped into Lucy about a year later. She told her that shortly after their conversation Jim had declared it was too soon to make decisions, other than they could now afford for Jake to have trombone lessons. She'd quietly explored the property market and found something nearby that had space for Jim's home office and a craft room for her and the children. Taking them all there on a surprise visit one Saturday, they'd all agreed it was a good idea – especially as it was in the same quiet cul-de-sac that Granny lived on. They'd moved in three months ago, shortly followed by Shilling and Copper, two kittens that they'd rehomed from the local animal shelter.

What needs to change, if anything, in your own family to accommodate and celebrate your different Designs? Sometimes it's something quite practical adjusting bedtimes, creating quiet spaces, recognizing when comfort might come more easily from a pet or a tree, or simply accepting that not everyone processes things at the same pace. Sometimes it's just shifting your expectations, recognizing that your child's way of being in the world isn't wrong, it's just different from yours.

You won't get this right all the time, none of us do. You'll forget. You'll default to old patterns. You'll project your own fears and hopes onto them despite your best intentions. That's not failure, that's being human. The gift of Human Design isn't perfection; it's awareness and awareness creates space. Space for your child to be exactly who they came here to be.

After all, they're not your children to mold. They came through you with their own design intact, ready to thrive in ways you might never have imagined. Now you know how to help them do exactly that.

*"Your children are not your children. They are the sons and daughters of
Life's longing for itself. They come through you but not from you,
and though they are with you, yet they belong not to you."*

— KHALIL GIBRAN

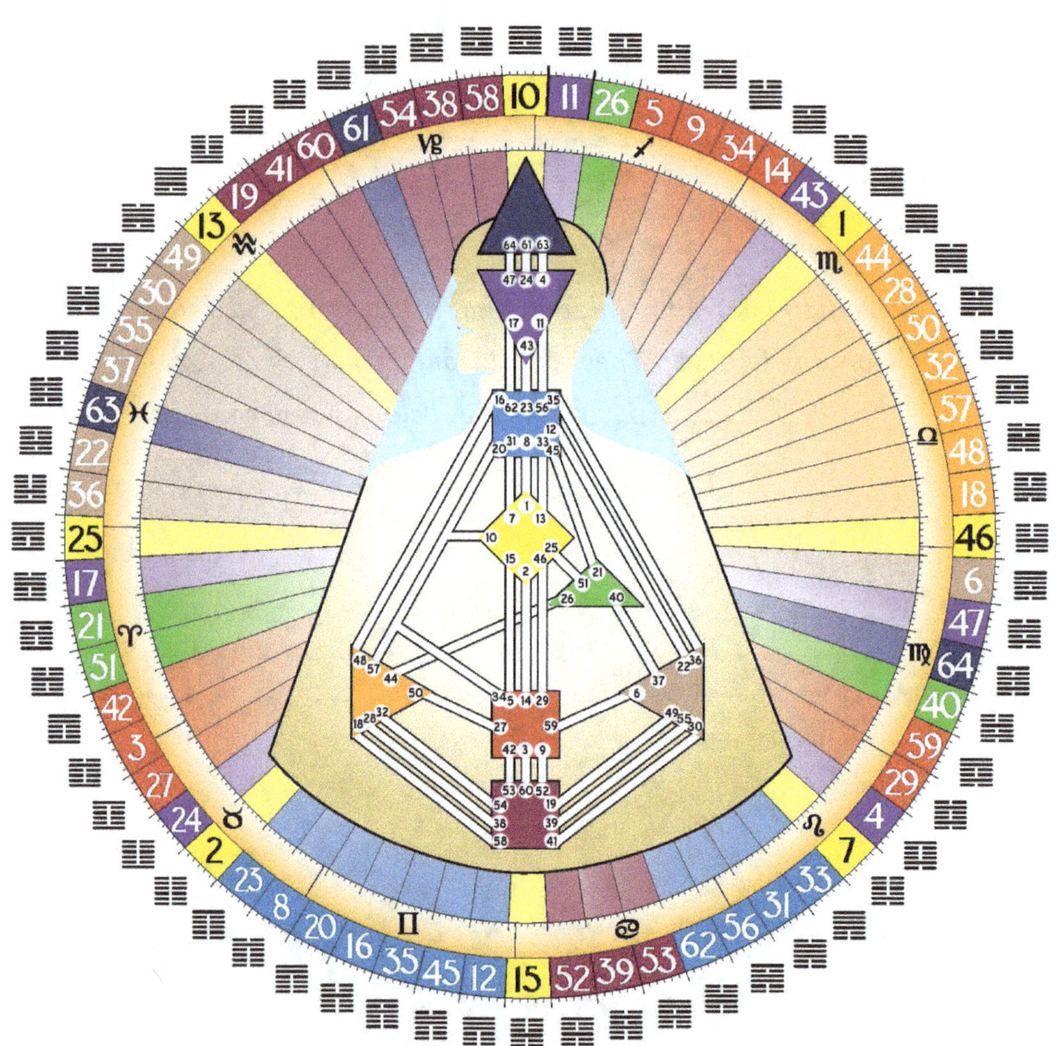

CONTINUE THE CONVERSATION

By now you will have begun to see your child through a different lens. Human Design does not ask us to shape children into who we think they should become. Instead, it invites us to recognise who they already are and to support the unfolding of their natural design.

For many parents this understanding opens the door to further exploration. Some become curious about their own design and how it influences the way they guide their children. Others want help interpreting a child's chart and translating the insights of Human Design into everyday family life.

If you would like to continue exploring these ideas, there are several ways to do so.

FOR DEEPER STUDY OF HUMAN DESIGN

Chetan Parkyn teaches and speaks internationally on Human Design and its practical application in modern life. He is also engaged in accessing and clearing adverse ancestral patterns and imprints. You can learn more about his work, courses and speaking engagements at

www.EvolutionaryHumanDesign.com

FOR PERSONAL GUIDANCE IN APPLYING HUMAN DESIGN WITHIN FAMILY LIFE

Pippa Wilford offers personal Human Design readings and mentoring for parents who want to understand their children more deeply and apply these insights thoughtfully in everyday family life.

Further information and enquiries

www.dagaz.me/humandesign

psw@dagaz.me

A personal reading can often help illuminate both your own design and your child's chart with greater clarity. Readers of *Designed to Thrive* are welcome to mention the code **THRIVE** when booking.

Whatever path you choose from here, the invitation of this work remains the same. To meet children with curiosity rather than expectation, to trust their natural intelligence, and to support them as they grow into the people they were born to be.

With best wishes,

Chetan & Pippa

P.S. If this book has been helpful to you, a short review on Amazon helps other parents discover it. Your reflections make a real difference.

Acknowledgments

CHETAN WRITES:

Life is a Mystery to be lived ... Mystery becomes My-Story when we attune ourselves to the wonders around us as a reflection of our inner selves.

I am so grateful for the presence and guidance from Osho, so bravely describing and encouraging the "New Man" who opens the whole world to the Aquarian Age of peace and prosperity.

Ra brought the Human Design System to life after a harrowing experience of receiving it and then having the great courage to introduce it as a modern-day guidance device. We spent a lot of time together in the early days, sometimes laughing at our unique perceptions of Human Design, and eventually found our paths had to diverge to introduce Human Design in our own unique ways.

My beloved partner, Carola Eastwood, a genius spiritual astrologer, healer and business coach, quickly recognized the power of Human Design and held the space and encouraged me to go deeply into it. Learning and attuning to the Designs of her five children and now grandchildren opened levels of communication and interactions that have been wonderful to behold.

Pippa trusted me to guide her into a deeper appreciation of herself and Human Design. When we started talking about the impact Human Design has on parents and children, it became clear we would write this book together. It becomes our way to introduce families to the enormous potentials in which Human Design expands our connections through love, mutual growth, and conscious communications.

Pippa's writings, extraordinary wisdom, and the team she has assembled to publish this book have my heartfelt appreciation.

My sincere thanks to the many thousands of people for whom I've read, taught and who have taught me about themselves and myself through Human Design.

PIPPA WRITES:

This book exists because Chetan Parkyn invited me to write it with him, building on the foundation Ra Uru Hu created. As my Human Design teacher, mentor, and co-author, Chetan has guided me both in understanding myself and in finding the courage to share this work. His wisdom, alongside that of his wife, Carola Eastwood, has shaped these pages in countless ways. I am deeply grateful to you both.

To Natasa Smirnov, our editor, whose clarity and focus transformed a sprawling manuscript into something coherent and useful. Your ability to see what a book wants to be – and to help it become that – is a rare gift. Thank you for making this work stronger than it could ever have been without you.

To Madeline Kosten, whose thoughtful layout and design gave this book its visual form. Your care, attention to detail, and steady guidance helped bring the finished work into being.

The stories and examples throughout these pages come from friends, family, and clients who generously shared their experiences of raising children. Though anonymized, each has contributed something essential to understanding how Human Design shows up in real family life.

To my children, Mark and Rachel, now adults navigating their own paths with grace and courage: being your mum has been my greatest teacher. To Magnus, their loyal dog, who reminds us daily that unconditional love is both a design and a lived reality.

Finally, to the Universe, for its mysterious and mischievous ways of bringing the right people and moments together. I am honored to play a part in bringing this work into the world.

About Chetan Parkyn

Trained originally as a mechanical engineer, Chetan's life was transformed by a Shadow Reading in Mumbai, India, in 1979 while living in Osho's commune in Pune. The Shadow Reader, asked Chetan to come work with him "because you know how to do this work…" and when Chetan declined – and the Shadow Reader had finished laughing – said "… you'll be doing this work anyway … because there is a new system coming, and you are going to introduce it to the whole world through books, teaching and giving Readings…" Chetan was shown by a psychic Palm Reader how to read hands, found he had the knack, and practiced it, and other esoteric systems everywhere. When the foretold "new system" arrived in his life in 1993, Chetan recognized his Human Design chart immediately and has spent the past thirty-three years mastering this new system. As the author of the first major book on the subject, *Human Design: Discover the Person You Were Born to Be* (2009), now available in fifteen languages, he brings Human Design to the whole world. Chetan leads professional trainings at all levels of Human Design worldwide.

Chetan has this to say about his discovery of Human Design: "Leaving a career as a deep-sea dive engineer, my overland travels took me to India, where with the encouragement of Osho, I was finally awakened to my true purpose – helping people develop self-knowledge and self-empowerment so they experience success in the way that brings them fulfilment."

Chetan lives with his partner, Carola Eastwood, and two golden retrievers, Rajah and Reine, near San Diego, California.

ALSO BY CHETAN PARKYN

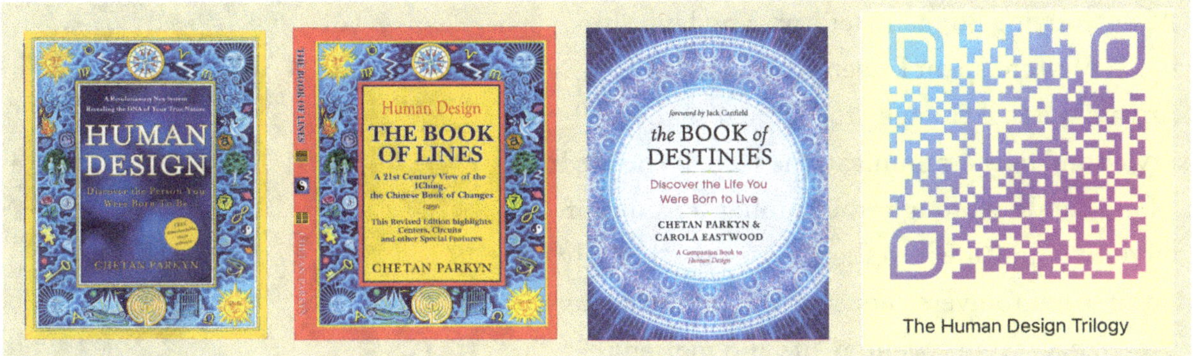

Human Design: Discover the Person You Were Born to Be

The Book of Lines: A 21st Century View of the IChing, the Chinese Book of Changes

The Book of Destinies: Discover the Life You Were Born to Live (with Carola Eastwood)

About Pippa Wilford

After studying English literature and law, Pippa Wilford spent fifteen years leading organizational change projects across the civil service and telecommunications sector. The birth of her children brought the familiar tensions of modern family life into sharp focus, particularly within a neurodiverse household, prompting her to step back from corporate life and reorient her work toward human development.

Pippa trained as a coach with Henley Business School and as a transactional analysis complementary counsellor, before discovering Human Design – a system that brought coherence and clarity to the parenting challenges she had lived through and long sought to understand. She studied with Chetan Parkyn and qualified as a Human Design consultant, also training as a Color Mirrors teacher, and working with families through a charity supporting end-of-life conversations.

She is the author of *The Nurtured Nest* (2023) and co-author of *Unfold Now* (with Heidi Tyler).

Pippa brings a grounded, compassionate approach to helping individuals and families understand themselves and one another more deeply. In her own words, she "seeks understanding with curiosity and humor, sharing wisdom that supports integrity, trust, and harmony."

Pippa lives on the south coast of England with her adult children, Mark and Rachel.

ALSO BY PIPPA WILFORD

The Nurtured Nest: Creating Time for Yourself and Fostering Harmony in Your Home

Unfold Now (with Heidi Tyler)

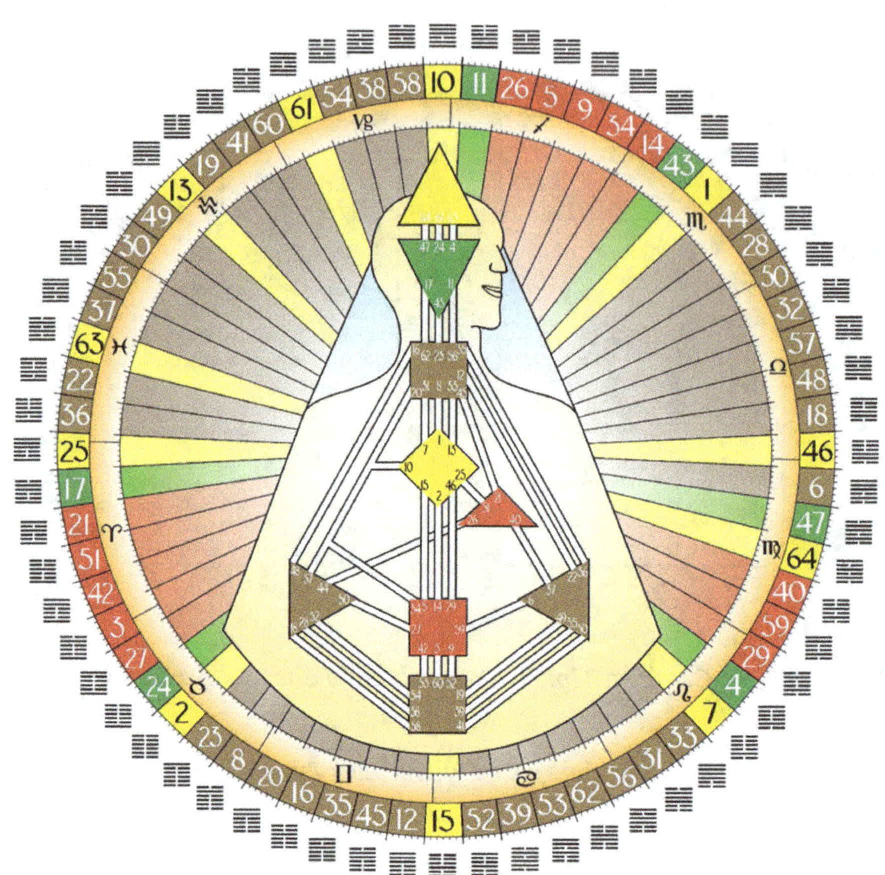

PRAISE FOR DESIGNED TO THRIVE

"We've each gotten to see ourselves so much more clearly through our human design, including our strengths, super powers, and life path potential. We've also gotten to understand the ways our designs are similar and different, which makes a big difference with pace of life, how we structure time together and how we communicate. Human Design and our readings with Chetan have been such an enhancement to our lives individually and to our relationship. It supports us in having the highest connection we possibly can."

— SLOANE (CHIEF INSPIRATION OFFICER) AND COLETTE

"This book is not simply read, it is recognized. It speaks to something we already know but may have forgotten in the current noise of expectations, roles and the quiet pressure to get it right even while the world is in a warp speed of change.

As a Generator and 6/2, and as a mother and grandmother, I have lived the arc of family across time. I've seen how easily we misunderstand one another and how profoundly everything changes when we begin to see clearly. This work offers that clarity.

It gently reveals that each child arrives with a design intact. That identity is not something to construct, but something to honor. This book will be a handbook for me with my expanding family as they grow into teens and adulthood, and additionally my children who are now parents and help through decision-making, emotions and the struggles that are inherent but more easily solveable.

This book invites us to recognize that the very differences that create tension, are also the blueprint for harmony. This is the kind of work that changes not just relationships...but the stories a family carries forward."

— BECKY ROBBINS, PAINTER, ARTIST, CO-FOUNDER OF ROBBINS RESEARCH INTERNATIONAL, HOST OF AGELESS FREEDOM PODCAST

"On my journey into motherhood, this book, *Designed to Thrive,* reminds me that every child arrives with their own inner compass. My role is to simply hold the space for them to grow into the person they were always meant to be."

— AGGIE HSIEH, SINGER, ACTOR, AND MOTHER-TO-BE

"*Designed to Thrive* offers a wiser and more compassionate vision of parenting—one that begins not with shaping a child, but with truly seeing and honoring who that child already is."

— PEIXIA LAI, PH.D., BESTSELLING AUTHOR AND FOUNDER OF
COLLABORATIVE COMMUNICATIONS ACADEMY TAIWAN

"If anyone in my life had helped me understand I was a direct Manifestor as a child so much more would have made sense to me. Living in a sacral world that wants everyone to be able to generate all day every day, I could have made better decisions and recognized what was more in alignment with my true energy levels. We often see how we are different from others and that comparison can lead to confusion in many areas of our lives. Discovering our own unique flavor is a gift to a child. Human Design is such a clarifying tool to a deeper and powerful way of loving myself more for who I am and I've witnessed this for everyone in my life for over 30 years. It is my wish and I believe every parent's wish to experience the authentic unique voice in each child and have them see it, feel it and be it too!

Thriving in a world of immense change is truly available by preparing your child to make their best decisions for themselves can be the most empowering thing we can assist them with. I believe this book will create change from the inside to keep our families thriving together."

— ANGEL EVANS, CEO AND FOUNDER OF BIOMETECH.COM

"Pippa's insight into our family's design has been a game changer for the way I parent. Through her work — and now through this book — I understand myself and my children so much better. We are all different, move at different paces, and see life in our own ways, and that no longer feels like a problem to fix, but something to understand. Thank you, Pippa, for the guidance and mentorship."

— ANDREA REINDL, FOUNDER OF LEGACY CREATIVE